Professional Wrestli[n]
in the Pacific Northw[est]

T0041051

Professional Wrestling in the Pacific Northwest

A History, 1883 to the Present

STEVEN VERRIER

McFarland & Company, Inc., Publishers
Jefferson, North Carolina

Photographs courtesy of Matt Merz.

Library of Congress Cataloguing-in-Publication Data

Names: Verrier, Steven, author.
Title: Professional wrestling in the Pacific Northwest : a history, 1883 to the present / Steven Verrier.
Description: Jefferson, North Carolina : McFarland & Company, Inc., Publishers, 2017. | Includes bibliographical references and index.
Identifiers: LCCN 2017040419 | ISBN 9781476670027 (softcover : acid free paper) ∞
Subjects: LCSH: Wrestling—Northwest, Pacific—History.
Classification: LCC GV1198.13.N67 V47 2017 | DDC 796.81209795—dc23
LC record available at https://lccn.loc.gov/2017040419

British Library cataloguing data are available

ISBN (print) 978-1-4766-7002-7
ISBN (ebook) 978-1-4766-2967-4

Front cover: Oregon native Jake Pappenheim, who wrestled under the name "Kurt von Poppenheim" (Matt Merz)

Printed in the United States of America

McFarland & Company, Inc., Publishers
  Box 611, Jefferson, North Carolina 28640
  www.mcfarlandpub.com

To the promoters, the wrestlers, and the fans—
together, architects of pro wrestling's
rich Northwest tradition

Table of Contents

Preface

While growing up in small-town Ontario, Canada, I seldom missed a wrestling show on television, and I was an ardent fan of one of the programs I discuss at some length in the pages that follow—*All-Star Wrestling*, from Greater Vancouver, British Columbia, which for years was syndicated across Canada.

Long after leaving that small Ontario town, I continued to keep a finger on the pulse of the wrestling industry even while pursuing graduate studies in the United States and engaging in jobs and travel in distant parts of the world. In some of those distant corners I came across professional wrestling companies reflecting the nature and distinct character of their settings, and it soon became apparent that the spectacle of professional wrestling was in many ways a microcosm of the setting and society in which it existed—and of the world at large. While much of what takes place in a wrestling ring may be staged, it is abundantly clear that wrestling itself is a player on a larger stage. As a result, wrestling, when given a chance to shine—as it often did during the "territorial" days of wrestling when there were dozens of thriving regional wrestling companies across the United States and around the world—has done much to reflect and help define what is special about region after region.

After settling in the Pacific Northwest in early 2014, I set out to research the history of the wrestling industry during its entire lifespan in the region, from 1883 to the present. In pursuit of that goal, I viewed much of the surviving video footage, read widely, and contacted numerous people involved in the wrestling industry as I began working on a narrative chronicling key events and players over a 13-decade period and drawing connections between some of the events that took place in Northwest wrestling rings—and behind the scenes—and other facets of life and history in the Pacific Northwest and beyond. The account that follows aims to provide a meaningful historical perspective on wrestling in Oregon, Washington State, and British Columbia from 1883 to the present, over 134 years after the sport appeared in the region.

Many years of closely following historical events and observing the wrestling industry played heavily in my decision to write this book, but a project of this sort would have been far more difficult without the assistance of some key people who were willing to share their expertise when I brought my undertaking to their attention. While numerous writers, historians, and wrestling specialists helped in some way to lay the groundwork for this book, special mention has to be made of a few: Vance Nevada, who generously offered information, contacts, corrections, and suggestions to support and strengthen this project; Dean Silverstone, who kindly offered support, information, and reminders of what makes the wrestling industry so special; the late J Michael Kenyon, who after reading my manuscript with a critical eye took the time to point out areas where I needed to do more research; Matt Farmer, who was always quick to answer questions and share his broad knowledge of wrestling personalities and events in the Northwest; Mike Rodgers, who read my manuscript, answered questions, and made important suggestions; and Matt Merz, who provided key information on wrestling, past and present, in Oregon and Washington and generously shared many outstanding photographs that would have been difficult to find elsewhere. All of these people have done much over the years to preserve wrestling history in the Northwest, and I am thankful for their support.

Meanwhile, of the wrestlers and promoters, past and present, that I interviewed for this book—some of whom are quoted in the pages that follow— nearly all were extremely gracious in sharing their time and thoughts, and I am grateful for their input.

Besides being so generous in supporting my effort, Vance Nevada and Dean Silverstone are authors of outstanding books—cited numerous times in the pages that follow—that are vital to an understanding of wrestling history in the Northwest. Nevada's *Wrestling in the Canadian West* and Silverstone's *"I Ain't No Pig Farmer!"* (with Scott Teal)—both published by Scott Teal's Crowbar Press, which has done much to preserve wrestling history which otherwise might have been lost—focus on important aspects of wrestling history in British Columbia and Washington. This book, meanwhile, is intended to provide a solid historical backdrop for such works—as well as for any future books that may be written about any aspect or period of professional wrestling in the Northwest.

And finally, I hope this book will meet the approval of people with a keen interest in wrestling … and others who may not care much about wrestling but are simply interested in viewing the Pacific Northwest over a 134-year period from a new perspective.

Introduction

The 2003 version of WrestleMania—almost universally considered pro wrestling's premier annual event since its inception in 1985—drew a full house of over 54,000 to Seattle's Safeco Field. That was far and away the largest crowd ever to attend a professional wrestling event in the Pacific Northwest.

The 54,000 fans drawn to March 2003's WrestleMania 19 did not hail entirely from the Seattle area, Washington State, the Pacific Northwest, or even the United States and Canada. WrestleMania, established by Vincent K. McMahon in his World Wrestling Federation's march to national and international dominance in the pro wrestling industry during the 1980s, had evolved into a major sporting or quasi-sporting event attracting thousands of fans from around the world to a series of events held over several days and culminating in a wrestling spectacular that typically sold out major venues long before WrestleMania Sunday in late March or early April of each year.

WrestleMania 19 was no different. Headlined by a series of matches including former Olympic gold medalist Kurt Angle vs. Brock Lesnar, Stone Cold Steve Austin vs. Dwayne "The Rock" Johnson, and Hulk Hogan vs. 57-year-old Vince McMahon, WrestleMania 19 drew a gate estimated at nearly $3 million and is believed to have contributed millions more to the Seattle economy.

While WrestleMania 19 numbers may pale in comparison to a Super Bowl's, cities and major sporting facilities vie annually for the opportunity to host a WrestleMania event guaranteed to attract a large number of visitors to local hotels, restaurants, and other hospitality businesses. Wrestling fans have often been regarded as a rowdy bunch not noted for having a particularly high disposable income, but this perception has largely been forgotten when it comes to fans willing and able to travel hundreds or thousands of miles to attend the world's preeminent annual wrestling event, for which tickets can run into hundreds of dollars—and higher for ringside.

It seems almost certain that the majority of WrestleMania 19 attendees coming from outside the Pacific Northwest would have regarded that event as the most significant wrestling show ever held in Washington, Oregon, or British Columbia. And since McMahon's wrestling organization—renamed World Wrestling Entertainment (WWE) after McMahon, following a lawsuit by the World Wide Fund for Nature (WWF, known as the World Wildlife Fund in the U.S. and Canada), agreed in 2002 to stop calling his promotion the WWF—towered over every other wrestling company in the world, it goes without saying that many Northwest natives, especially younger ones, in the stands at Safeco on March 30, 2003, had the same view. After all, crowds of over 50,000 in wrestling—with hundreds of thousands more watching on pay-per-view television around the United States and Canada and many more viewing the event on television around the world—aren't at all the norm. Even among WrestleMania events, WrestleMania 19 was considered a big success.

The financial success of WrestleMania 19 speaks for itself. But whether this event was the most significant professional wrestling show ever held in the Northwest is open to debate.

Some fans will point out that Safeco's WrestleMania was a one-time event having no particular roots in the Northwest and leaving no legacy of note. While it may have contributed millions of dollars to Seattle businesses, the perception of many is that Seattle, as a WrestleMania host, was essentially just a brief stop for an East Coast–based traveling show. WWE, after all, is based in Connecticut—in the Northeast, not the Northwest—and many financial benefits from WrestleMania 19 would go back to the Northeast as well. True, WWE would return to the Northwest from time to time—typically, for a few brief tours each year hitting major cities and some smaller centers—but, the reasoning goes, how can one stop on an East Coast–based traveling show's itinerary be considered the most significant event in the history of professional wrestling in the Pacific Northwest?

Many old-timers and historians of professional wrestling would simply argue that it can't. They would point out, rightly, that pro wrestling had a long and storied history in the Northwest dating back well over a century before WrestleMania 19—and centuries of history elsewhere, in some form or another, before that.

According to Scott M. Beekman in his book *Ringside*, a survey of wrestling spanning many centuries and styles, "professional wrestlers" existed in the eastern Mediterranean area before the age of Christianity (Beekman, 1). While there was likely little in common between the early "professionals" and the wrestlers headlining WrestleMania 19, it seems clear that "professional wrestler" is a job title that came into existence over 2,000 years ago.

Wrestling, of course, was a popular physical activity or means of settling scores in ancient cultures spanning much of the world. It can be presumed that in many of those cultures—including the Egyptian, Roman, and Greek—

there was a ready audience for skilled grapplers engaging in hand-to-hand combat. And it may be reasonable to presume that some wrestlers learned to play to the crowds they attracted, perhaps injecting into their wrestling a bit of the showbiz their WrestleMania counterparts would one day become so noted for.

Roughhousing and grappling existed in various forms throughout the Dark Ages, Middle Ages, and Renaissance, but it was in the British Isles that wrestling in a form that would be recognizable to most current-day North Americans took shape. In the 1600s and 1700s, as emigrants from the British Isles poured into what are now the United States and Canada, they brought their grappling traditions with them.

The earliest recorded wrestling events staged in the United States took place around the time of Lincoln's death. Already popular in much of Europe, wrestling became a carnival attraction in the United States in the 1860s, as carnival wrestlers—often, skilled amateurs—would challenge "all comers" to step forward and engage in wrestling matches for a chance to win prize money.

While the most prominent wrestling style in the United States and Europe was based on the Greco-Roman tradition (permitting moves applied only from the waist up), the new carnival circuit brought on the advent of "hooking," which featured what today are characterized as "submission holds." "Hooking" allowed an experienced grappler to have the upper hand in a match because a less experienced wrestler would be unlikely to get out of a "submission hold" without giving up or suffering injury. As wrestlers traveled the circuit—primarily along the U.S. East Coast—wrestling grew in popularity and drew from an increasing variety of sources.

The mix of styles—mainly Greco-Roman, the Irish collar-and-elbow style, and the style brought by early settlers from England—became known as "catch-as-catch-can" (a term still used). Catch-as-catch-can wrestling was a popular attraction following the Civil War, even getting some coverage as a legitimate sport in newspapers along the Eastern Seaboard. The truth, however, was that many carnival wrestling matches were not legitimate at all. "Local" challengers were often not locals but wrestlers themselves more intent on putting on entertaining shows than engaging in legitimate contests. As legitimate wrestling contests often turned into what David Shoemaker, in his book *The Squared Circle: Life, Death, and Professional Wrestling*, calls "multihour slogs" (10), wrestlers and carnival promoters—as their boxing brethren were sometimes prone to do in the mid to late 1800s—often took the precaution of helping things along by emphasizing the showbiz aspect of wrestling over true competition. As a result, Beekman reports, "the effects of carnivals on the development of modern professional wrestling are immense" (39).

Based largely on carnival wrestling's popularity in the eastern United

States, wrestling events spilled over into sporting venues in the East and in other areas of the country with significant population bases. As far as the West Coast was concerned, professional wrestling arrived in California—particularly, the San Francisco area—by the late 1860s and established itself there over the course of the 1870s. From that time, although the Pacific Northwest was slower to develop a significant population base, it would not be long until pro wrestling traveled up the coast to Oregon.

1

Early Decades of Wrestling
in the Northwest

John Terry reports, at OregonEncyclopedia.org, that the Portland *Oregonian* announced in July of 1883 that Portland would host its first-ever professional wrestling event at Mechanics Arena the following month. The show would feature Scottish grappler Donald Dinnie facing Duncan (D.A.) McMillan, who would go on to enjoy a long, successful career across the U.S. and Canada and further prominence as a wrestler in the Northwest.

McMillan won the match, but little else seems to be known about that first wrestling event held in the Pacific Northwest. Even so, it is clear that interest in professional wrestling had migrated to the Northwest to stay. Yet, with its limited population—Portland, Seattle, and Vancouver, BC, all having populations under 100,000 until the early 20th century—the Pacific Northwest remained largely on the sidelines as the wrestling business gained steam in larger population centers of North America.

Numerous wrestlers were recognized as champions in those early days—much as almost every wrestling center or "territory" had its own set of champions before the McMahon-WWF expansion in the 1980s. During the closing decades of the 1800s, the focus at wrestling events clearly was on entertaining the crowd. Matches were held in boxing-style rings, and wrestling in those days was a worthy competitor to boxing. In an effort to one-up its competitor by introducing something boxing didn't attempt until much later, wrestling made room for women competitors by the 1890s. And then, in 1901, wrestling rolled out an innovation that seemed an easy ticket to double the action and mayhem it could offer. According to the *Pro Wrestling Illustrated* website at www.pwi-online.com, tag team wrestling made its United States debut that year in San Francisco.

Prominent wrestlers around the turn of the 20th century included Farmer Burns, Tom Jenkins, and the original Strangler Lewis, but the biggest attraction in American professional wrestling in the early 20th century was a pair of bouts between Frank Gotch, a son of German immigrants who settled in Iowa, and George Hackenschmidt, a powerful and well-traveled wrestler from Estonia.

Hackenschmidt, already recognized as a wrestling champion in Europe, earned recognition as a world champion in the United States after defeating American champion Tom Jenkins in 1905. Known for playing to the crowd and showing disdain for American wrestlers, Hackenschmidt, billed as the Russian Lion, proved to be the perfect opponent for Gotch, who was one year Hackenschmidt's junior and had already traded victories with Jenkins and earned recognition as the American Heavyweight champion. The second Gotch–Jenkins meeting, won by Gotch, was a major early milestone in the history of wrestling in the Northwest. That match—a surefire attraction that could have headlined shows at many major venues nationwide—took place on January 27, 1904, in Bellingham, Washington.

During that period, Bellingham—with a population of only about 20,000—was often hosting several wrestling events per month at the Beck Theater, considered the city's leading entertainment venue with seating for over 2,000. Major wrestlers including Gotch, Jenkins, and Farmer Burns made multiple appearances at the Beck during the early part of the 20th century and especially in 1903–1904, a period in which Bellingham could be viewed as one of the more prominent—and unlikely—centers of North American professional wrestling.

Bellingham for that brief time was the hub of a wrestling circuit that included other stops in the northwestern part of Washington. But the major population center on the circuit was Vancouver, BC—although one of the regular performers in Bellingham, Duncan McMillan, who had headlined the 1883 show in Portland, had some history of promoting wrestling matches at a bar he owned in Seattle.

Another prominent wrestler who appeared in Bellingham and Vancouver was John Berg, an attraction in the Northwest who also headlined shows across North America—often participating in lengthy matches—over the course of about two decades beginning near the start of the 20th century. Berg, sometimes known as Young Hackenschmidt, demonstrated his remarkable endurance in a 1913 match in Seattle, where—recognized, according to the May 24, 1913, Sausalito [CA] News, as the national light heavyweight champion—he wrestled to a two-hour draw with Huber "Polly" Grimm.

At the time of the 1913 encounter, Grimm, who had been a standout amateur athlete at the University of Washington, excelling in baseball and football while becoming a national Amateur Athletic Union (AAU) heavyweight wrestling champion, was in the early stages of a promising professional wrestling career that saw him appear—sometimes billed as the Northwest or Pacific Coast champion—mainly in the Northwest and the Midwest before returning, in 1917, to his childhood home of Centralia, Washington, to focus on practicing law.

According to Canadian wrestling historian, former West Coast wrestler, and author Vance Nevada, it was during Bellingham's heyday in the early 1900s that pro wrestling made its Vancouver debut. As far as Canada is concerned, wrestling had already made a big splash in the larger Canadian cities of Toronto and Montreal. In fact, Nevada reports in his book *Wrestling in the Canadian West* that Toronto may well be the North American city in which pro wrestling was first introduced. While an August 20, 1868, match between Homer Lane and Lew Thompson in Harrisburg, Pennsylvania—or another Homer Lane match that appears to have taken place before a small crowd in New York City more than two months earlier—is often regarded as the first professional wrestling match on the continent, Nevada reports that "Toronto was hosting wrestling at the Royal Opera House almost a full year before" (10). Wrestling also made a few appearances in the Canadian province of Saskatchewan one year before debuting, under the promotional leadership of Duncan McMillan, in Vancouver (Nevada, 10).

According to Nevada, often biweekly wrestling exhibitions held at the Vancouver City Hall Auditorium and the Opera House in Vancouver regularly drew crowds exceeding 1,000 for single-match events as early as 1903, and an October 5, 1904, Frank Gotch American Heavyweight title defense at the British Columbia Provincial Fair in the Vancouver suburb of New Westminster drew a strong crowd of 7,000. Gotch's opponent was a British Columbia grappler named Dan McLeod, who had also held the American championship before becoming a prominent wrestler in the Bellingham circuit. According to www.wrestlingclassics.com, 800 Gotch supporters accompanied Gotch to Vancouver on a special train, presumably to offer support in the face of home-province support for the challenger. Wrestlingclassics.com also reports that the Gotch American title defense in New Westminster saw $10,000 change hands in betting.

Gotch was a dominant wrestler, however, winning his New Westminster defense against McLeod in two straight falls. After leaving his Bellingham base in late 1904, Gotch continued his dominance in the eastern United States, also making appearances in other parts of the country and in Montreal, Canada's largest city at the time and a major wrestling market.

Gotch's success was building to the match the public most wanted to see: Iowa's Frank Gotch vs. the foul-mouthed Russian Lion, George Hackenschmidt. The public got its wish when it was announced that Hackenschmidt would defend his World Heavyweight title against Gotch at Chicago's Dexter Park Pavilion on April 3, 1908.

The Gotch–Hackenschmidt encounter was a scheduled two-out-of-three-falls match, as were most title matches of that era and many world title matches all the way into the early 1980s. Before a crowd the *New York Times* estimated at 8,000, Gotch took the first fall by submission with a toe hold after a grueling two hours. As was the case during most of the first six decades of the 20th century, the wrestlers returned to their dressing rooms between falls. When it came time to resume the match, Hackenschmidt did not return to the ring for the second fall.

Although there are reports of Hackenschmidt conceding after the match that Gotch had been the better man, the Estonian soon changed his tune, complaining that Gotch had oiled up his body and fought unfairly. In modern-day terms, this was the first step toward building to a rematch.

Gotch's celebrity soared following his victory over Hackenschmidt. Touring as the most recognized and respected wrestling champion in North America, Gotch further cemented his reputation in the Northwest with a July 1, 1908, victory in Seattle over Dr. Benjamin Franklin Roller, who headlined shows in British Columbia and Washington during the early years of a career that saw him become a three-time United States Heavyweight champion and a nationally known wrestler in the U.S. as well as a main eventer in Montreal, Toronto, and Vancouver. Gotch's reputation rose further with a 1910 victory in Chicago over European standout and fellow world title claimant Stanislaus Zbyszko, who had wrestled Gotch to an hour-long draw the previous year in Buffalo. Gotch dominated their second match, winning in two straight falls— the first in just six or seven seconds as Gotch reportedly "surprised" Zbyszko as the latter came over to shake his hand. Though Gotch usually did not wrestle more than once or twice a month, he was a tremendous attraction whose popularity extended far beyond wrestling circles.

Gotch–Hackenschmidt II was the most ballyhooed wrestling match of its era, attracting 30,000 spectators to the new Comiskey Park in Chicago on Sept. 4, 1911. Once again, Gotch was a decisive winner, although it was widely reported that Hackenschmidt was injured going into the match and stories emerged that one of Hackenschmidt's training partners had been paid to injure Hackenschmidt's knee in advance of the rematch with Gotch. Other reports indicate Hackenschmidt had suffered an accidental knee injury at the hands of Roller, another of his training partners, prior to the bout. Whatever the full truth may have been, serious questions were raised about the nature of Hackenschmidt's injury and the nature—that is, the legitimacy— of the match itself.

Of course, observers had been asking questions about the nature and legitimacy of professional wrestling long before this, and the in-ring theatrics, often made-up identities and overblown characters, and at least some elements of buffoonery contributed to an overall decline in wrestling's popularity in the 1910s. While Gotch was a popular world champion and a legitimate celebrity, he retired just a few years after his Comiskey Park rematch with

Hackenschmidt and died in 1917 at the young age of age 39 as a result of a kidney ailment.

As for Gotch's historical impact on wrestling in the Northwest and Washington State in particular, Matt Farmer, an ex-wrestler widely recognized within the Northwest wrestling community as a leading historian of mat action in the region, acknowledges that "for a few years, Bellingham was a strong small town market for wrestling." But Farmer adds that Gotch and his partners had a habit of "going into regions and running them dry." Bellingham was no different, Farmer says. "In hindsight, Frank Gotch didn't leave the business in better shape than when he entered it. Much like the Midwest after the second Gotch–Hacken-schmidt match, after Frank left the Northwest it suffered a few years of bad business. I guess you can say they hot-shotted the territory"—setting their sights on short-term profit rather than long-term suc-cess—before leaving northwest Washington in search of new moneymaking opportunities elsewhere.

While wrestling shows were occasionally held in Wash-ington and Oregon in the 1910s, British Columbia—and espe-cially Vancouver—was the lead-ing market in the Northwest for wrestling during that decade. Yet Nevada reports that "Canadian audiences in the west did not initially respond well to the emerging culture [of showmanship in] profes-sional wrestling" (11).

Following an Oct. 11, 1912, match in Vancouver between local wrestler George Walker and his Greek opponent, Pete Bazukos, who, Nevada writes, displayed "the bravado that [became] typical of mat villains

Dr. Benjamin Franklin Roller was a professional football player, University of Washington phys-iology professor, and practicing physician before becoming a full-time wrestler in 1906. After holding the United States Heavyweight championship three times and headlining shows in the Northwest and throughout much of North America, Roller retired as a wrestler in 1919 and spent his remaining years practicing medicine and surgery.

in the twentieth century" and even took a swing at the referee, the *Vancouver Daily World* declared the next day, "Wrestling in Vancouver has been conducted on a high level of cleanliness up to this time, and the fans don't propose to have their pleasure spoiled by any such proceedings as were in evidence last night" (Nevada, 11).

Key wrestling personalities during the years following Gotch's departure from the ring included Joe Stecher and (the second) Strangler Lewis. Stecher was a skilled grappler and three-time world champion described by Beekman as "probably the last champion to engage in a scheduled shooting [legitimate wrestling] match to defend the title" (52). Lewis, meanwhile, proved an excellent challenger to Stecher, taking him to the limit in a five-hour-plus contest that the referee eventually ruled a draw. Stanislaus Zbyszko—who wrestled on a January 1913 show in Pendleton, Oregon—remained a prominent name despite his one-sided loss to Gotch in 1910. Meanwhile, a "Masked Marvel"— an early prototype for thousands of masked wrestlers appearing over the following century in the United States, Canada, especially Mexico, and numerous other countries—appeared on the East Coast, wrestling Lewis to a two-hour-plus draw in New York in early January of 1916 before losing later that month, in a world title challenge at the original Madison Square Garden, to Stecher in two straight falls.

Wrestling seemed to hit its stride again in the 1920s, partly due to the influence of promoter Jack Curley. Based in New York, Curley was a strong proponent of entertainment-oriented wrestling, although wrestling "entertainment" in the 1920s was more likely represented by a long, punishing headlock than a "chairshot" or a dive off the top of a cage, as one might see today. Curley had a background in carnival wrestling, and his priorities lay more in stirring up fans and selling tickets than in promoting true athletic competition. Earlier in his career, Curley had promoted shows in the Pacific Northwest, and, according to longtime wrestling historian and former *Seattle Post-Intelligencer* sportswriter J Michael Kenyon, "Curley had a huge impact on the history of wrestling in the Northwest amid all the wild and wacky events of his ... promotions in Seattle and Portland" in 1909.

Even more influential than Curley on a national scale was the "Gold Dust Trio" of promoter "Toots" Mondt, Billy Sandow, and Ed "Strangler" Lewis—the second Strangler Lewis, who took the ring name of earlier wrestling champion Evan "Strangler" Lewis. The Gold Dust Trio, in association with powerful Boston promoter Paul Bowser, moved pro wrestling closer to its current configuration by establishing a troupe of wrestlers who went from city to city to perform a traveling wrestling show. Although Lewis, normally the touring champion of this group, was hardly a showman by today's standards, the emphasis was clearly on entertainment, sometimes evidenced by newly invented—or, at least, previously unseen—submission holds.

While Lewis was a skilled grappler with experience in legitimate contests—including his five-hour draw with Stecher—as a member of the Gold Dust Trio, he was both an athletic performer and one whose athletic ability overshadowed his ability as a showman. Lewis was usually the preferred champion of his troupe largely because he had the ability to avert a double-cross in the event an opponent ever tried to surprise him with an unscheduled victory or had designs on making the champion look weak in the ring. While Lewis did trade victories from time to time, he exemplified the sort of champion many wrestling promoters favored all the way until the 1960s or 1970s: a legitimately skilled grappler who could defend himself in the event another wrestler or a rival promoter cooked up a plan to make the champion look weak or even to "steal" his championship.

But despite the concentration of power in the hands of the Gold Dust Trio, the 1920s also saw some measure of wrestling decentralization with the emergence of new circuits similar to the one based in Bellingham two decades earlier. And as it turned out, one key wrestling promotion established in the 1920s would be based in Oregon and would go on to defy all odds by surviving and often thriving over a period of well over six decades.

2

Beginning of
the Owen Dynasty

Following its Portland debut in August of 1883, wrestling did not gain a strong foothold in Oregon until four decades later. While Joe Acton—a 140-pound British native who wrestled across the United States and held an early version of a world championship in the 1880s—settled in Oregon in the late 1890s and trained grapplers into the early 20th century at Portland's Multnomah Athletic Club, and while Jack Routledge, Jack Curley, and a few other promoters staged wrestling events in Oregon prior to the 1920s, wrestling did not become more than an occasional attraction in the Portland area until Virgil Hamlin, who had worked as a timekeeper on Routledge's shows, began promoting regular events in 1920. In 1922 Hamlin's shows found a home at the Heilig Theatre in Portland.

Ted Thye was an assistant to Hamlin and had already made a name in Portland as a successful light heavyweight and middleweight wrestler. Claiming a version of the World Middleweight championship and, later, a version of the World Light Heavyweight title, Thye headlined many of Hamlin's cards in Portland and proved a popular local attraction. Thye also became a part-time headliner and multi-time titleholder in Australia after debuting there in the early 1920s.

Meanwhile, Herb Owen, an ambitious farmer from Cove, Oregon, moved to Eugene in 1925 with his wife Bertha and their three children. Although Owen initially worked as a furniture salesman in Eugene, it seems safe to assume he was intent on establishing a family business later to be taken up by sons Don and Elton.

In 1927 Herb Owen began promoting boxing events in Eugene. Seeing opportunity in the wrestling game, he began promoting wrestling events in small and midsized cities such as Medford and Salem, using wrestlers booked out of Hamlin's office in Portland. Terry reports, at OregonEncyclopedia.org, that "the first of [Herb Owen's wrestling] cards to gain attention was an

April 1929 match between George 'Wildcat' Pete of Eugene, the junior middleweight wrestling champion of the world, and Gus Kallio, the middleweight champion." According to the *Oregonian*, as Terry reports at OregonEncyclopedia.org, Kallio won that match with a head scissors and a hammerlock.

While the Hamlin-Thye promotion in Portland was clearly the dominant wrestling organization in Oregon and the Northwest in the late 1920s and early 1930s—dispatching wrestlers to events at locations throughout much of Oregon, Washington, and British Columbia—it did not control all aspects of wrestling in Oregon. Although Hamlin ran regular events at the Portland Auditorium, rival promoter Roy Starbard carved a small niche and ran shows in the Portland area from 1930–1932.

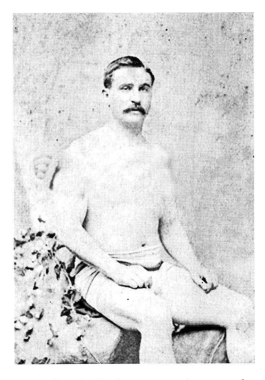

During Starbard's run in Portland, the Hamlin office was hit by allegations of staging fixed matches—hardly a break-through observation by that time. Author Dean Silverstone, in his memoir *"I Ain't No Pig Farmer!,"* reports that Abe Kubey, a partner of Starbard's, charged that Hamlin had presented illegitimate matches in Seattle, where, Silverstone says, "[Hamlin's] company had single-handedly revived pro wrestling after it had been moribund there for nearly 20 years" (104).

In the wake of this "allegation," a bill requiring wrestling promoters running events in Washington to have lived in the state for at least a year—a bill obviously aimed at keeping Hamlin and Thye out of Washington—was passed by the state legislature but, Silverstone reports, vetoed by Governor Roland Hartley (104).

Back in Oregon, Starbard

British native Joe Acton, a prominent wrestler in Europe and the United States, was billed as the World Catch-as-Catch-Can champion, 1881–1887. An attraction in much of the United States in the 1880s, Acton trained wrestlers and continued to do some wrestling himself after moving to the West Coast in about 1889. For several years beginning in the late 1890s, Acton was a trainer in Portland, where he lived until his death in 1917.

and Hamlin remained fierce competitors, but ultimately it was Herb Owen, the small-time promoter in Eugene, who during the Depression became the preeminent promoter of professional wrestling in his state.

There are varying accounts of how Owen maneuvered his way to becoming the top wrestling promoter in Oregon. Silverstone reports that in March of 1932, "Starbard's home in Gresham [OR] mysteriously burned," and four months later, Starbard stopped promoting, with Herb Owen "coming up from Eugene to scoop up the [promoter's] license" (104).

Owen, considered an associate of Hamlin and Thye's since he booked wrestlers out of their office, cashed in while Thye was on a visit to Australia, according to Oregon wrestling historian Mike Rodgers at www.kayfabememories.com. According to Rodgers and other sources, while Thye was in Australia, Herb Owen somehow succeeded in putting the Portland-based wrestling promotion and booking company in his own name—and since only one company was legally allowed to promote professional boxing and wrestling in all of Oregon, Owen was given the green light to become the wrestling czar of Oregon.

Barry Owen, a grandson of Herb's who was later active in the Owen family promotion for many years, disagrees, seeing it simply as a case of his grandfather's choosing to expand the family business. "There was no monopoly," says Barry Owen. "Anybody could put in and get a license."

Despite the turn of events, Hamlin and Thye continued to promote shows around Portland during much of the Depression and also booked wrestlers for tours of Oceania. After Hamlin got out of the wrestling business in the late 1930s, Thye continued promoting mainly in Oregon and maintained his connection to the wrestling business in Oceania. Owen, meanwhile, supplied wrestlers for shows in cities such as Eugene, Salem, and Klamath Falls and ran weekly events at the Portland Labor Temple—featuring performers including future Northwest wrestling promoters Harry Elliott, Rod Fenton, and Franklin "Tex" Porter—until sons Don and Elton, both of whom had assisted their father, took over the promotion in 1942.

3

British Columbia, 1930–1949

The Depression era saw plenty of wrestling activity in British Columbia, and Vance Nevada's *Wrestling in the Canadian West* provides an excellent view of this period of BC wrestling.

Emil Klank was a former carnival wrestling promoter from Chicago who later traveled the world as a manager of champion wrestlers including Frank Gotch, Stanislaus Zbyszko, and Joe Stecher. Klank also wrestled mainly in the Midwest in the early 1900s, although the *Tacoma Daily Ledger* reports he lost a September 1907 match to Dr. Benjamin Franklin Roller in a West Seattle saloon, reputedly with a $1,000 side bet between the participants at stake. Nevada reports that after Klank's wrestling, managing, and carnival promoting days were over, he settled in British Columbia and began promoting wrestling events there on Feb. 13, 1930 (Nevada, 12).

According to Nevada, Klank promoted in Vancouver in association with the Hamlin-Thye office in Portland, with Thye himself appearing on many of the Vancouver shows (12). Also appearing in Vancouver for Klank's promotion were several wrestlers who were prominent throughout much of the United States and Canada, including Stecher, whose three world title reigns had totaled over five years; the "Golden Greek" Jim Londos, one of the most popular wrestlers in the eastern U.S. during the 1930s, who, according to J Michael Kenyon, had participated as a teenager in small, mid–1910s wrestling shows in a variety of Oregon towns under the name of Jim Wilson; Gus Sonnenberg, a former NFL player originally booked by Boston promoter Bowser and known for introducing the "flying tackle" to wrestling; Earl McCready, a former three-time NCAA heavyweight wrestling champion and Canadian Olympic wrestler as well as a standout in the pro ranks in the 1930s and 1940s; and Ed "Strangler" Lewis, who after wrestling Stecher to a five-hour draw in Omaha in 1916 went on to win multiple world championships and earn an enduring reputation as one of the greatest wrestlers ever.

Though Vancouver had hosted successful wrestling events prior to 1930, Klank is credited with being the first promoter based in the city. Klank promoted weekly shows using both prominent names and local wrestlers and, according to Nevada, booked over 350 wrestlers for Vancouver shows from 1930 to 1934—a period in which many wrestling events featured only three matches (12).

The most successful match promoted by Klank was a January 1932 encounter between Strangler Lewis and Tiger Daula, a well-traveled wrestler often cast as the "mighty Hindu." Over 7,000 spectators attended the Jan. 22 show at the Vancouver Arena, which roughly matched the Oct. 5, 1904, attendance for the Frank Gotch title match in nearby New Westminster. Introducing fans to a broad selection of both local and traveling wrestlers, Klank had success as Vancouver's inaugural wrestling promoter before giving up the promotion in late 1934 and returning to the United States, reportedly for health reasons.

While Klank was the preeminent Vancouver wrestling promoter in the early 1930s, he was not the only one, as anywhere from about a dozen to upwards of 25 shows were held around the city and surrounding communities most months during the early 1930s. Although competing events—often held at athletic clubs or cultural centers—were decidedly of a more small-time nature than Klank's events, Klank, says Nevada, was known to recruit some of the opposition wrestlers to fill out his cards (12).

Vancouver was not the only city in British Columbia to establish a wrestling promotion in 1930. According to Nevada, cigar shop owner Fred Richardson began promoting wrestling events in the provincial capital, Victoria, at the Tillicum Athletic Club on Valentine's Day of 1930, just one day after Klank's first show in Vancouver (13). Richardson's association with the Klank promotion helped ensure a steady flow of wrestlers to the Tillicum. Among notable wrestlers who appeared at the Tillicum in the 1930s were Baptiste Paul, a First Nations wrestler from Saanich, BC, who would later achieve success across North America and internationally as Chief Thunderbird, one of the earliest native North American characters in wrestling; Frank Stojack, a British Columbia native who grew up in Tacoma, played pro football, and had significant success with his airplane spin finisher over a 20-year period in British Columbia, Washington, and Oregon before settling into a position as the sheriff of Pierce County, Washington; Leo Numa, a Washington State native who was a big name across much of the continent as well as an attraction throughout the Pacific Northwest from the 1930s to the 1950s and, during periods when he wrestled as the Red Shadow, what J Michael Kenyon described as "the region's most notorious masked man ever"; and Robin Reed, an amateur wrestling great still remembered by some wrestling historians as, pound for pound, one of the greatest grapplers who ever lived.

Reed, an Arkansas native, attended school in Oregon, where he took up wrestling before attending Oregon Agricultural College (later Oregon State University). In college he won three AAU titles and did some high school coaching before winning a gold medal as a featherweight in freestyle wrestling at the 1924 Paris Olympics. Following his undefeated amateur wrestling career, Reed coached Oregon Agricultural College's wrestling team to an AAU national championship before debuting, at about 140 pounds, as a professional wrestler in the Midwest en route to getting some recognition as the World Welterweight champion and returning to the Northwest, where he made some main event appearances in British Columbia and Oregon before retiring after about a decade as a pro to pursue a career in real estate.

British Columbia native Frank Stojack graduated from Washington State University and went on to play pro football in the United States and Canada while putting together a wrestling career that took him to stardom in the Northwest and across much of the United States. Late in his career, Stojack was recognized as the NWA World Light Heavyweight champion. For nearly a decade from the early 1950s to the early 1960s, Stojack held elective political offices in the Tacoma area.

Also appearing at the Tillicum were two wrestlers who would become notable promoters: August Sepp, an Estonian native who promoted in Seattle mainly in the 1930s and organized carnival wrestling shows around the Northwest long after that; and Al Karasick, apparently a native of Belarus who, over the course of a quarter-century promoting in Hawaii, would feature numerous wrestlers with connections to the Pacific Northwest.

The Tillicum promotion in Victoria had to withstand what Nevada describes as "the first territorial war in western Canadian wrestling" (16) when A.E. Chilton, who had worked as a referee for the Tillicum promotion in 1930, began promoting rival cards in August of 1932. Though Chilton managed to lure Tillicum headliner Rocky Brooks to his promotion, he was unable to compete successfully with Richardson's Tillicum promotion. The two promotions engaged in a heated struggle, often presenting opposing wrestling shows in Victoria—then with a population of about 40,000—on the same night. With the city not large enough to support two wrestling promotions running head-to-head, Chilton's promotion closed its doors in May of 1933, just nine months into the game.

Klank's successor in Vancouver was George Fitch, a World War I veteran who received Klank's endorsement after having assisted Klank in running his promotion. Fitch had also gained some recognition locally through his day job as secretary to the city's mayors from 1922 to 1934.

Holding his first show at the Vancouver Auditorium on Dec. 13, 1934, just two weeks after Klank ran his last event there, Fitch retained many of the wrestlers Klank had used and, Nevada says, continued the pattern of bringing in name wrestlers from the U.S., including mid–1930s world champion Danno O'Mahoney (18). Also appearing on many of Fitch's shows was Paul Boesch, a popular young wrestler from New York who was also appearing in Oregon and Washington and would go on to become a prominent wrestling figure in the Pacific Northwest and elsewhere.

While Fitch continued Klank's practice of mixing local wrestlers with name attractions on his shows, Nevada reports that Fitch faced criticism from local wrestlers "upset about the lack of opportunities to work on his cards" (18). According to Nevada, local wrestlers discussed starting a wrestlers' union—a proposal that has surfaced from time to time throughout the history of pro wrestling. While Fitch had employed over 50 local wrestlers in 1935 alone, Nevada points out that some of Vancouver's wrestling clubs shut down during the height of the Depression, leaving local wrestlers fewer opportunities to perform (19).

Nevada also reports that the Vancouver Athletic Commission began to take an increasing interest in professional wrestling during Fitch's tenure as a promoter. In 1936 the VAC ruled that professional wrestling shows in Vancouver had to be advertised as "exhibitions" and not legitimate sport—a ruling that stood until the 1970s, even though, Nevada says, the VAC "did not release the industry from the required fees owing to the Commission under the classification of sport" until 2002 (19).

Fitch drew healthy crowds by highlighting local wrestlers, touring champions, women wrestlers, and some wacky characters—most notably, perhaps, the white man-hating native, Chief Chewacki. Unlike Chief Thunderbird, Chewacki—in real life, George Mitchell from Oklahoma—was not a bona fide Native American, as would be the case with many "Indian" wrestling characters that followed him. Though not widely remembered, Chewacki can be considered an innovator of his time, not only for helping pave the way for wrestlers of any ethnicity to play native North American characters but also for introducing "foreign" objects to the wrestling ring in a big way. Calling Chewacki "the father of illegal foreign objects," Greg Oliver and Steven Johnson, coauthors of several books on wrestling, write, in *The Pro Wrestling Hall of Fame: The Heels* ["heel" meaning "villain"], "Carpet tacks, steel wool, coat hangers, stove lids, Mercurochrome, pepper, ether-soaked cloths, horse prods ... you name it and chances are Chewacki tried to [smite] his opponents with it in the 1930s and 1940s." Oliver and Johnson continue, "Chewacki was suspended by just about every athletic authority that ever sanctioned a match" (125). It should come as little surprise, then, that Nevada reports "Chief Chewacki also drew the first known suspension from Vancouver rings" (19).

Fitch stepped down as a promoter in mid–1937, handing the company over to Percy Hicks. Under Hicks, the Vancouver promotion became known as Big Time Wrestling, but only for a brief period did the promotion show signs of living up to its new name. Hicks held weekly cards in Vancouver for about a year—sometimes featuring megastars such as Londos and NFL great-turned-wrestler Bronko Nagurski—but as Vancouverites' interest in wrestling seemed to wane in 1938, Big Time Wrestling was scaled back to become a seasonal promotion that essentially coincided with the middle of hockey season, while very limited wrestling activity took place in the city during the remaining six or seven months of the year.

The downturn in wrestling interest did not hit only the promotion in Vancouver. In 1938 the Kamloops, BC, Athletic Association closed its doors after three years and 80 events featuring mainly Canadian wrestlers and American grapplers based in the Northwest. According to Nevada, before running out of gas in 1938, this small promotion based in Kamloops, 220 miles northeast of Vancouver and featuring primarily middleweight wrestlers, "had a good run in the mid–1930s at the height of the Great Depression" (20).

Wrestling had also been shut down in Victoria by this time. Entertainment dollars were in short supply during the Depression, and it was hard for smaller promotions to stay afloat. While the Hicks promotion did face some minor competition in the 1940s, during the latter part of the 1930s Big Time Wrestling's only competitor of note was a depressed economy. Unemployment ran high in Vancouver, partly because the city, noted for its access to natural resources and its mild climate by Canadian standards, attracted thousands of job seekers from other parts of the country, resulting in a shortage of jobs for locals. Wrestling, meanwhile—like most other forms of entertainment—faced the challenge of trying to earn dollars that just weren't there.

Hicks' competitors in the 1940s included the Vancouver Sports Club/Vancouver Wrestling Club and the Pender Wrestling Club, two organizations that revived and built on the wrestling club culture that had established itself in British Columbia before bottoming out during the Depression.

The Vancouver Sports Club, headed by Harry Miller, was established in

1941 shortly before the attack on Pearl Harbor and the United States' entry on the Canadian/Allied side into World War II. Vancouver's Orange Hall, which had hosted many wrestling club events a decade earlier, was the site of the Vancouver Sports Club's debut card in November of 1941.

When Miller's assistant and regular referee Jack Whelan—formerly an assistant to Percy Hicks—took over the promotion in 1943, the Vancouver Sports Club became known as the Vancouver Wrestling Club. By 1943 the Vancouver Wrestling Club held events every Wednesday and Saturday night at Orange Hall, attracting what Nevada describes as a "steady following" (24), and in 1944 the Vancouver Wrestling Club moved its events to the Vancouver Athletic Club gym.

The Pender Wrestling Club, which began operation in 1944, was headed by Sam Nolan, who had wrestled for Miller's Vancouver Sports Club, Hicks' Big Time Wrestling, and small club promotions in Vancouver.

Nevada reports that Nolan's entrée to promoting was the result of another wrestling club's encounter with the Vancouver Athletic Commission over its wrestlers apparently inciting fans to riot. While the VAC discussed the possibility of suspending wrestling events until the war was over, as the dust settled, Nolan emerged with the rights to promote wrestling cards at Seaman's Hall in Vancouver (Nevada, 26).

Nolan was noted for using a variety of lesser-known wrestlers, and on one of his shows he used a wrestling "gimmick" polished off by Vince McMahon decades later: The owner of the promotion wrestles on his own card with the ownership of the promotion at stake. In Nolan's case, the owner won. (In McMahon's case, he lost, although he managed to win the company back a few weeks later.)

Even with limited competition in Vancouver, Percy Hicks' Big Time Wrestling faced a series of ups and downs in the years during and immediately after World War II. Three years after cutting costs by scaling back to a winter–spring promotion, Big Time Wrestling managed to draw only 700 fans to a November 1942 show. This, according to Nevada, led to Hicks' decision to take a lengthy hiatus from promoting in order to regroup (21). Although Hicks' return in July of 1943—featuring a wrestler called the French Angel— attracted 4,500 spectators, Nevada reports that Big Time Wrestling's schedule after that was erratic and not conducive to maintaining good crowds (21).

With Vancouver's wrestling clubs having some success in the interim, Hicks sat out for another year before staging a return event on June 30, 1944, featuring Jim Londos and Wladek Zbyszko (Stanislaus' younger brother), two of the most prominent wrestlers in the world. Beginning in 1944, Big Time Wrestling cards were held at the Vancouver Athletic Club gym, where one of its competitors—the Vancouver Wrestling Club—was still holding events twice a week. According to Nevada, the Vancouver Wrestling Club scaled back to running shows once a week and, "featuring a local talent roster and a much lower payroll, continued to draw competitively with Percy Hicks" (22).

However, with three competing promotions running weekly shows in Vancouver—and two in the same building—the Vancouver Athletic Commission stepped in, ruling that Vancouver was not a large enough market to support three wrestling promotions running weekly shows. When the commission ruled that Hicks could continue running weekly shows on Fridays while the Vancouver Wrestling Club and the Pender Wrestling Club would trade off on Tuesdays, Nevada reports, the commission chairman declared, "One of our duties is to protect the fans and that's what we're going to do" (25).

The ruling clearly favored Hicks' Big Time Wrestling promotion, which could continue holding events every week with the big advantage of a reduction in its weekly competition. The Pender Wrestling Club, meanwhile, while required to scale back to a biweekly schedule, could at least continue to present shows on Tuesday nights as it had been doing. As far as the commission's ruling was concerned, the big loser seemed to be Jack Whelan's Vancouver Wrestling Club.

Whelan's fierce objection to the commission's ruling seemed to center on a few key points. First, he had already scaled down his operation—from holding semiweekly events to running once-a-week shows—in an apparent effort to accommodate the competition and better serve wrestling fans. Second, the venue in which he was promoting events—the Vancouver Athletic Club gym—was unavailable on Tuesday nights, the night he was assigned for alternating events with the Pender club. Determined to stand his ground, Whelan continued to run weekly shows in the Vancouver Athletic Club gym. When the commission considered taking action, Whelan took his case to the public, arguing that his weekly shows provided a necessary outlet to local wrestlers, and pointed out that his shows had contributed a generous amount in city and provincial taxes.

The commission backed off, and Whelan continued his schedule of running weekly shows on Saturday nights. According to Nevada, attendance was normally around 1,000 (25)—not great, perhaps, but enough to persuade Hicks to put Big Time Wrestling back on the shelf for another nine months in order to regroup.

Although the Pender Wrestling Club was still attracting interest at Seaman's Hall, Whelan's Vancouver Wrestling Club had become the dominant wrestling organization in Vancouver and British Columbia by late 1944 and into early 1945—until the curtain dropped when his lease to hold events in the Athletic Club gym expired in February of 1945.

Big Time Wrestling continued to have its ups and downs after Hicks dusted it off again in mid–1945. The Pender Wrestling Club, meanwhile, showed some resiliency in continuing weekly events through early 1947. But then Sam Nolan ceded ownership of the club to Jack Keeley, who shut down the Pender Wrestling Club—host of 144 events over a three-year period—after less than three months at the helm.

And then, just two months after the demise of the Pender club, Jack Whelan, ex-promoter of the upstart Vancouver Wrestling Club, reemerged as the head of Big Time Wrestling. Featuring a cast of wrestlers including future Northwest wrestling promoters Neal "Tex" Hager, Tex Porter, and Cliff Parker and appearances by Oregon native Jake "Jack Poppenheimer" Pappenheim—future Northwest headliner Kurt von Poppenheim—and Raymond "Gorgeous George" Wagner—one North America's leading wrestlers and ring personalities of the 1940s and 1950s—Whelan enjoyed two moderately successful years at the helm of Big Time Wrestling before stepping away from wrestling in 1949.

4

Major Developments, Early 1930s–Early 1950s

While wrestling in Washington State during the Depression and into the 1940s is often believed to have taken a backseat to the action that was taking place in Oregon and British Columbia, Washington was also hosting successful shows in a variety of small and large cities during that period. Some cities—among them Tacoma, Spokane, Bremerton, Walla Walla, and Olympia—were home to weekly shows, and as Matt Farmer reports at www.wrestlingclassics.com, "some of the larger cities [even hosted] more than one show a week." Seattle, Farmer writes in his www.wrestlingclassics.com post, sometimes hosted multiple wrestling shows on the same day during the Depression years.

Geographically isolated from the major population markets of the East and denied easy access to most of the nation's top wrestling stars, Washington State in the early 1930s depended largely on the Hamlin-Thye office in Portland for wrestlers needed to supply shows in the Evergreen State. Despite facing allegations of "fixed matches," some Seattle-based promotional competition, establishment of the Washington Athletic Commission in 1933 complete with the adoption of a handbook outlining "Rules and Regulations of Professional Wrestling," and a political effort to require wrestling promoters in Washington to be bona fide residents of the state, Hamlin and Thye weathered the storm and continued to promote or co-promote events in Washington as a sideline to their promotional activities in Oregon.

From a historical perspective, the Depression-era promotion of note in Washington was headed by Paul Boesch, who had wrestled for George Fitch in Vancouver and Hamlin-Thye in Washington and Oregon. While remembered today primarily for what he later achieved in wrestling outside the Pacific Northwest—particularly for his decades-long career as a successful promoter in Houston—Boesch, at the time a popular wrestler in his mid-twenties, kicked off his promotional career with a brief run in Seattle, initially in partnership with Floyd "Musty" Musgrave, in association with the Hamlin-Thye office in Portland.

The *Pro Wrestling Illustrated* website credits Boesch with inventing mud wrestling "by mistake" during his promotional run in Seattle. PWI reports that Boesch promoted a "Hindu match" between a wrestler named Prince Bhu Pinder and nationally known Gus Sonnenberg in 1937. The match was supposed to be held on dirt, which, PWI reports, simply got watered so much before the match that the wrestlers ended up going at it in a pool of mud. Word and photos got around, and the concept traveled, with the first women's mud match reportedly taking place a year later.

Another notable event that took place at a wrestling event in Washington State during the 1930s/early–1940s era was the in-ring death of referee John Stevens at a show promoted by August Sepp at Seattle's Civic Auditorium. What made Stevens' death especially notable was that it did not take place during a match but after a post-match "beating" by one of the wrestlers, LaVerne Baxter, who, according to the March 7, 1940, *Seattle Times*, testified at the coroner's inquest that "Stevens wanted to be 'roughed up' … so that the crowd would get the idea that Stevens was a 'hero being beaten up by the villain.'" Though Stevens' death was ruled accidental, it fueled a serious political discussion about whether pro wrestling should be outlawed in Washington. While a ban was never imposed at the state level due to the determination that wrestling was mainly for show, wrestling in Seattle, according to Nevada, "was essentially banned by official city edict between 1940 and 1945" (21), as no wrestling events were allowed in publicly owned buildings in the city during that period. While a ban of any sort around Seattle certainly did the wrestling business in the Northwest no favors, Matt Farmer says, overall, damage directly attributable to the ban in public facilities was minimal. "Really, it had very little effect on the business," Farmer reports via email. "It was just a political hiccup, which happened during a period of time when wrestling as a whole across the country was in a down cycle. It really had very little long-term effect on wrestling."

Promotions based in the Pacific Northwest were only a few of a growing number of wrestling circuits to operate during the 1930s and 1940s. During all or part of those decades, promotions regularly ran events from offices in such cities as New York, Chicago, Boston, Detroit, Montreal, Los Angeles, St. Louis, Minneapolis, Toronto, Kansas City, Houston, Omaha, Columbus, and Atlanta. Other regional or local promotions were based in smaller cities across the continent. Although competition was fierce with each promoter determined to defend his turf, promoters often traded talent in order to freshen up their events and win over new fans.

During the 1930s/1940s era, wrestling became noted for the "gimmicks" employed by promoters to play up the theatrical aspects of their shows.

Stereotyped characters such as Native Americans, ethnic heroes, foreign menaces, hillbillies, and classic "good guys" and "bad guys" filled spots on wrestling cards throughout North America. Tag team wrestling became a staple on many shows, and women wrestlers were a popular attraction in some areas—though outlawed in others. "Midget" wrestlers were introduced in the 1940s and remained in many promoters' repertoires for decades afterward. In many ways, the 1930s and 1940s set the tone for what wrestling would be for several decades to come.

The most impactful North American wrestler of that era on a national scale was a name likely unfamiliar to most wrestling fans in the Pacific Northwest—or even across the United States and Canada. Wrestling was coming into its own in Mexico during that period after a piecemeal presence dating back to the 1860s, and a wrestler named Rodolpho Guzmán Huerta began appearing under various names in the Mexico City area in the mid–1930s. Appearing with Empresa Mexicana de Lucha Libre (EMLL; now called Consejo Mundial de Lucha Libre, or CMLL, and recognized in 2017 as the oldest wrestling promotion in the world), Guzmán donned a silver mask and became El Santo, a character that evolved into a movie and comic book hero and a national icon far beyond any other North American wrestler of his day.

Meanwhile, prominent wrestlers of the 1930s/1940s era in English-speaking North America and Québec included Strangler Lewis, Jim Londos, Dick Shikat, Gus Sonnenberg, Ed Don George, Danno O'Mahoney, Bronko Nagurski, Ray Steele, Bill Longson, and Lou Thesz—all popular attractions almost everywhere they wrestled, and most of whom made appearances in the Northwest. Standing out among that illustrious pack were two men. Lewis, one-third of the powerful Gold Dust Trio in the 1920s, remained a hugely popular attraction in the 1930s and continued to draw crowds in the 1940s. Wrestling occasionally in Oregon, Washington, and British Columbia over the course of his long career, Lewis is widely credited with creating the sleeper hold, mimicked by hundreds of wrestlers worldwide ever since. He was a noted "shooter"—a legitimate grappler—selling out events in many arenas, and his September 1934 match at Chicago's Wrigley Field against Londos drew over 35,000 fans, easily eclipsing the city's attendance record for wrestling set 23 years earlier by the fabled Gotch–Hackenschmidt rematch.

Thesz, trained by Lewis and other veterans in "hooking"—or applying painful submission holds—was noted as a no-nonsense grappler in an era of often outlandish gimmicks. While freely admitting years later that his matches throughout his career were not legitimate contests, Thesz took pride in trying to make his matches look as athletic and legitimate as possible. Never hesitant to show contempt for fellow wrestlers who were too indifferent or inept to apply the same approach to their performances, Thesz was complimentary of wrestlers he saw as capable of mixing it up and committed to putting on athletic and believable matches. At the top of his list was fellow multi-time world champion Strangler Lewis, who along with Thesz would be near the top of any legitimate list of the greatest pro wrestlers ever.

Though suffering a decline for obvious reasons while the nation was focused on war, wrestling was a big-time attraction in many cities and territories throughout North America when Don Owen, assisted by younger brother Elton, took over father Herb Owen's Portland-based wrestling territory in 1942. With a limited, though often receptive, market for wrestling in Oregon, the Owens promoted shows that were relatively small by East Coast or Midwest standards but further established pro wrestling as a fixture that would remain popular in Oregon over the long haul.

While 1941 saw the start of commercial television broadcasting in the United States, wrestling would have no airtime for several years. Television was only taking its first steps as an entertainment medium, and for wrestling, the early 1940s were a time of large and small "house shows" or events held in venues all the way from packed arenas to dingy bars. In these familiar settings, promoters continued to roll out every innovation, outlandish character, and compelling storyline they could think of in an effort to attract fans and draw "heat," or a rabid reaction from audiences.

Don Owen was no different. Although he had graduated from the University of Oregon, much of his education was in the form of what he had learned during 15 years of assisting in his father's promotional ventures. Elton had been similarly well prepared for promotion and filled a dual role by stepping into the ring on occasion. Elton, who had wrestled in college, had moderate success in the pro ring, with his biggest victory taking place in a July 15, 1944, main event in Eugene against Gorgeous George Wagner, who later would shorten his name and ascend to the wrestling stratosphere as Gorgeous George.

Presenting a mix of characters, situations, and matchups not unlike what many successful promoters were offering in other areas of the United States and Canada, Don Owen, minus a large population base, depended primarily on local wrestlers and others drawn to the Northwest for reasons including the opportunity to wrestle for an up-and-coming promotion. National names appearing in Portland during the 1940s were few, and the biggest-name attraction to wrestle for Owen—other than Gorgeous George Wagner—was the nationally recognized women's champion Mildred Burke, who appeared on a Portland show shortly before a 30-year ban on women's wrestling in Oregon took effect in 1945.

Following a wartime lull, Washington State stepped forward in 1945 to join Oregon as a rising wrestling market in the American Northwest. This was largely due to the presence of one man: Lou Thesz. Thesz, a decade into one of the most brilliant wrestling careers on record, was stationed for part of his World War II Army enlistment period at Ft. Lewis, near Tacoma. Assigned by the Army to serve as an instructor in hand-to-hand combat techniques, Thesz managed to maintain an impressive schedule of ring appearances during the waning months of the war, meeting a variety of opponents in Washington cities including Tacoma, Seattle, and Vancouver—as well as across the Columbia River in Portland, Oregon—on shows promoted by or held in association with Ted Thye's Western Athletic Club. Perhaps the most notable of Thesz's matches in Washington in 1945 was a victory, shortly after the end of the war, in Bremerton, against his old teacher—and his future manager—Strangler Lewis. That match came three weeks after another Thesz victory over Lewis, in Portland, 10 days before the war ended.

The second half of the 1940s was a time of recovery and transition as the United States and Canada set out on a path of relative prosperity, procreation, civil rights, and consumerism. Wrestling was in transition too, drawing healthy crowds in many cities and bracing for major changes to come.

A bellwether of change was the first weekly wrestling television show in the United States, produced in 1945 by KTLA-TV in Los Angeles. Though there were relatively few televisions in homes at that time, TV was starting to take off as an entertainment medium, and wrestling—action-packed, easy to produce, and inexpensive to broadcast—had found its perfect partner in television.

KTLA's success in broadcasting wrestling quickly spurred other channels to produce their own wrestling shows. Meanwhile, attendance nationwide reached an all-time high, with women comprising much of the wrestling audience. Promoters, looking to take full advantage of the increase in wrestling's popularity, responded by doing what they had always done: engaging in fierce battles to one-up the competition and draw as many fans as possible to *their* promotions' version of the wrestling product.

In hope of establishing order in the wrestling industry, Des Moines, Iowa, promoter Pinkie George invited a few fellow Midwest promoters to join him at a July 1948 meeting in Waterloo, Iowa, aimed at reducing promotional rivalries, fostering cooperation among wrestling promotions, and unifying championships. While the vast majority of wrestling promoters in the United States sat on the sidelines, those in attendance—representing promotions in Des Moines, Omaha, Minneapolis, St. Louis, and Kansas City—reached agreement on some key issues concerning consolidation of power in the wrestling industry. In short, they saw the benefit of having a strong, centralized wrestling body looking out for their interests. In exchange for recognizing the authority of the new National Wrestling Alliance (NWA), each member promoter would be granted the exclusive right to promote wrestling events within his recognized promotional area or "territory." Any rival promotion encroaching on an NWA member's territory would be targeted by the Alliance, whose members would come to the aid of their fellow NWA promoter by loaning key wrestlers and blacklisting those appearing on cards promoted by opposition promoters running shows in NWA territories.

The NWA Heavyweight champion—Lou Thesz for seven of the Alliance's first eight years—would regularly travel from territory to territory to defend his title against the various territorial champions and top contenders. The NWA champion, like the Alliance's member promoters, was required to follow directives of the NWA Board of Directors, and to ensure he did—as Thesz outlines in his autobiography, *Hooker*—the champion was required to post a bond in the thousands of dollars, to be forfeited in the event he ever decided to disregard the Board of Directors' instruction to lose the championship.

Tim Hornbaker, in his book *National Wrestling Alliance: The Untold Story of the Monopoly That Strangled Pro Wrestling*, points out that there has been "a continuous string of falsehoods attached to the organization's fabled conception" (10). One apparent falsehood of unknown origin but widely cited is that Don Owen was a founding member of the NWA. In reality, the NWA already had 30 members across the continent by the time Owen joined the organization in 1951. Incidentally, Hornbaker reports that, at the same NWA annual meeting at which Owen's application for membership was formally accepted, Ted Thye was one of several promoters whose applications were not accepted (23). This meant, essentially, that as of September 1951, Owen was granted an exclusive "right" by the NWA to promote wrestling events in an extensive territory encompassing much of the Pacific Northwest.

5

Golden Age and Connections to the Northwest

While many current-day observers believe the height of wrestling's popularity in North America coincided with the rise in nationally televised wrestling on cable in the 1980s and 1990s, the term *Golden Age of professional wrestling* is generally applied to the period from the late 1940s to the mid–1950s.

As was the wrestling boom in the 1980s and 1990s, wrestling's Golden Age was fueled by television. Following on the heels of KTLA's introduction of the first weekly wrestling program in the United States in 1945, other television channels quickly got on board and started enticing fans to attend their local wrestling events.

The wrestling boom beginning in the late 1940s, however, was not primarily the result of locally televised matches aimed at drawing fans to wrestling events in specific cities. Instead, national television networks—though numbering only four at the time—were coming into their own, and wrestling, which was much easier to televise than stadium or large-arena sports, was seen as a surefire winner.

Wrestling got the majority of its national television exposure on the DuMont Network, the only one of the four U.S. television networks of the 1940s not to survive to the present day.

The DuMont Television Network was an offshoot of DuMont Laboratories, a major developer of early television technology in the United States. When the company began manufacturing television sets in 1938, founder Allen DuMont determined that sales were being hindered by a lack of programming available to the public. DuMont's response was to begin operating a prototype television station in New York City, with Federal Communications Commission (FCC) permission to broadcast programming during a nine-hour block of time beginning at midnight—certainly not a time slot designed to spike television sales.

But within a decade DuMont had over 30 affiliated stations, most within the East-to-Midwest portion of the country wired for live broadcasting. Affiliates in the South and West, meanwhile, received most of their DuMont programming as a result of kinescope recording, a method involving recording content shown on a video monitor, somewhat similar to the more "modern" method of recording bootleg versions of movies before their official video release by aiming a camera at a cinema screen. By 1951, DuMont affiliates in the West—including Seattle's KRSC-TV (later, KING-TV)—were able to broadcast live content.

Growth of the network was steady in the early 1950s, reaching a peak of about 200 station affiliates by the height of DuMont's popularity and viewership in 1953–1954, when DuMont was available to a fast-growing number of television viewers in all 48 states at the time.

In Washington State, KTNT-TV replaced KRSC as the Seattle-area DuMont affiliate, while affiliates in the Spokane area were KXLY and KREM. In Oregon, meanwhile, Medford's KBES and Portland's KPTV—the nation's first commercial UHF station—carried DuMont programming.

But despite all its growth and success within a few short years, the DuMont Television Network met constant challenges.

For one, it faced an uphill climb when it came to signing established talent to its roster. While the other networks—ABC, NBC, and CBS—had existed as radio networks before venturing into television, DuMont had no history in the entertainment industry before the television network was founded. Much like wrestling promotions, the other networks had established talent rosters at their disposal, which put DuMont—the new kid on the block—at a big disadvantage.

Inability to secure the most recognizable talent often made it difficult to secure program sponsors and exclusive affiliates. As a result, the DuMont Network was forced to produce relatively inexpensive programming aimed at a national audience. Part of DuMont's solution to its challenges was to go heavy on sports.

On Dec. 23, 1951, the network offered the first live national broadcast of an NFL game, and by 1953 DuMont was televising NFL games in prime time. The network also began televising NBA games nationally in 1953. Boxing was another favorite sport televised prominently during most of DuMont's run as a national television network.

But the sport that many people credit with putting DuMont on the map was professional wrestling—a staple on DuMont during virtually its entire run as a national television network. For seven years, from 1948–1955, DuMont hosted professional wrestling programs emanating from arenas around New York City and, most prominently, the Marigold Arena in Chicago. *Wrestling from Marigold* aired on DuMont from September 1949 to March 1955 in a format ranging from 90 to 120 minutes, usually on Thursday and Saturday nights.

Chicago promoter Fred Kohler rose to the top of the wrestling industry through his promotion's exposure on the DuMont Network. While it could be challenging to get broadcast time on affiliate channels DuMont shared with other networks, *Wrestling from Marigold* made headway, earning clearance on a broad selection of DuMont affiliates from coast to coast. The result was that Kohler's wrestlers became the most recognizable wrestlers in the country.

Kohler assembled a stable of top wrestlers eager to take advantage of the exposure DuMont could provide and the boost that exposure could give their bank accounts and careers. Earning fees from the wrestlers he booked out to other promoters nationwide, from the promoters themselves, and from the DuMont Network, Kohler in some ways could be considered a blend of the 1920s Gold Dust Trio in the Northeast and late 20th/early 21st-century WWF/WWE mogul Vince McMahon. Like McMahon, Kohler was noted for supplementing his income by marketing wrestling-related products—primarily, calendars and photos—and, according to www.wrestlingclassics.com, had such success at pitching wrestling-related goods that money mailed from DuMont affiliate cities was "delivered to his offices in dozens and dozens of stuffed mail bags daily."

While wrestling promotions around the United States continued to run and sometimes televise local wrestling shows, it was clear, as Shoemaker reports, that "new fans wanted to see the TV stars" (40) with national exposure and national reputations. Though television station executives nationwide were eager to broadcast both locally promoted wrestling and network wrestling, viewers tended to see the nationally televised shows as the "major league" product. Among wrestlers who translated their exposure on national television in the 1950s to success in the Northwest during that decade were Cowboy Carlson, Killer Kowalski, Whipper Billy Watson, and the returning Gorgeous George.

Some of the most memorable wrestlers ever made appearances on *Wrestling from Marigold*. Over-the-top characters were key in ensuring that Kohler's wrestling product captured national interest, and his troupe had many of those. While names such as Bozo Brown, Benny Rooster, Farmer Don Marlin, and other characters including Morris Shapiro, Cuban Pete, Chief Lone Eagle, Swedish Angel, and Canadian Angel may not have stood the test of time, other wrestlers appearing at the Marigold were unforgettable.

Buddy Rogers is the figure on whom Ric Flair—considered by many the greatest professional wrestler ever—modeled much of his career. Rogers, born Herman Rodhe, was a son of German immigrants and an excellent all-around athlete during his youth. He became a police officer at a young age and started wrestling part-time in his home state of New Jersey before serving in the U.S. Navy and then hitting the road as a full-time wrestler in the mid–1940s.

Though Rogers achieved notable success under his own name early in his career, it was after bleaching his hair and adopting the "Nature Boy" persona that he saw his career really take off. Rogers became a huge attraction in the Midwest and was one of the hottest commodities in wrestling even before appearing on *Wrestling from Marigold*, which cemented his national reputation as probably the most charismatic performer in wrestling and one that people, at various times in his career, either loved or loved to hate. From DuMont and the Midwest, Rogers branched out to the East Coast, where he became the biggest attraction for the World Wide Wrestling Federation (WWWF, forerunner of the WWF/WWE), then owned by Vince McMahon Sr., father of WWF/WWE owner Vincent K. McMahon.

Rogers' impact on wrestling was so profound that numerous wrestlers based their characters at least in part on his flamboyant, cocky persona. Flair may have been the most obvious—adopting the "Nature Boy" moniker, Rogers' glib arrogance, and even his "figure-four leglock" finisher—but in the Pacific Northwest, shades of Rogers could be seen in Jesse Ventura, who spent most of four years in the Northwest honing his bleached-blond character under Don Owen before becoming a nationally known wrestling personality in the WWF and, later, a Hollywood actor and governor of Minnesota.

Rogers' influence in the Northwest was probably reflected most by Paul Perschmann, a wrestler from Minnesota who attended a training camp in his home state with Flair. After wrestling mainly in the Midwest under his own name, Perschmann ventured out to Portland, where he became a huge regional draw after taking Rogers' first name and becoming "Playboy" Buddy Rose, one of the most hated and most popular wrestlers on the West Coast. While Rose became a star in other promotions, including the World Wrestling Federation, he achieved his greatest success by far while wrestling for Don Owen, and it is entirely possible that he owed some of that success to Rogers.

Québec's Guy Larose was another wrestler who achieved some success under his own name before having his career take off in the early 1950s after he adopted a new persona that struck a nerve with wrestling audiences. Gone was a young, "scientific" wrestler from Joliette, Québec, and in his place was the nasty, scowling "Teuton Terror" Hans Schmidt, the role Larose would play for over 25 years. While Hans Schmidt refrained from most of the goose-stepping, Nazi-sympathizing, over-the-top theatrics many later "German heel" wrestlers would exhibit, he was without a doubt an arrogant, Americanhating, roughhousing, bald, scary-looking "foreign terror"—and a perfect fit for the DuMont television stage.

Hans Schmidt influenced a long line of mainly bald, fascist-saluting "German heel" wrestlers all the way through the late 1970s and early 1980s, when the expansion of major wrestling promotions started spelling the beginning of the end for the regional wrestling territories. For a 30-year period after Hans Schmidt wreaked terror at the Marigold and in many living rooms nationwide, a whole generation of "German heels"—the majority no more German than Guy Larose—helped keep memories of World War II vivid long after Germany was no longer viewed as an enemy of the United States, except perhaps through East Germany's association with the Soviet Union.

While Hans Schmidt was the first German heel character in wrestling to play to a national audience, he was not the first character of that sort. Beginning in 1939, Milwaukee native Frank Altinger took his Nazi-sympathizing character Frederich von Schacht from territory to territory and on occasion incited fans to riot. But before becoming Frederich von Schacht, Altinger played Hans Schacht, an equally German but a less offensive, perhaps overly proud, Prussian character with some apparent similarity to Oregon's Kurt von Poppenheim, who introduced his heel Prussian aristocrat character to fans in the Pacific Northwest a few years before Hans Schmidt was born and became a regular on *Wrestling from Marigold.*

Prominent wrestlers in the Pacific Northwest following in Hans Schmidt's footsteps included Poppenheim's sometimes-tag team partner Fritz von Goering; the von Steiger brothers, a villainous 1960s/1970s tag team in Oregon and Washington and, occasionally, British Colum-

Oregon native Jake "Kurt von Poppenheim" Pappenheim was one of the first professional wrestlers to achieve prominence as a German villain. The vast majority of Pappenheim's success came in the Northwest, where he was a top performer from World War II until the early 1960s.

bia; Dutch-born Killer Karl "Baron von" Krupp; Kurt von Hess; and Siegfried Stanke, who wrestled in Oregon and headlined in Vancouver in the 1970s.

Another heel making a big impression on the DuMont Network was Fred Blassie, who, like so many wrestlers before him, got his start as a professional wrestler on the carnival circuit.

After serving in the U.S. Navy during World War II, Blassie wrestled as "Sailor" Fred Blassie when he appeared on Marigold cards in the early 1950s. He went on to become one of the most despised heels in wrestling—often appearing as "Vampire" Fred Blassie, with his biting becoming one of the most dreaded "holds" in wrestling and close-up shots of Blassie biting opponents making for impactful television. Blassie was also a capable wrestler who enjoyed runs as an enormously popular babyface—or fan favorite—particularly in Southern California, during the course of his long career. Similar to a Rogers or Flair, Blassie came across as a confident bleached-blond, dapper competitor, and he earned an enviable reputation across the country by taking full advantage of the power of television during the 1950s. He went on to headline shows across the United States and overseas for another three decades before retiring as a wrestler in his early fifties and parlaying his flamboyance and speaking ability into a successful career as a wrestling manager in the WWF. Among the many acts Blassie handled in storyline during his decade of managing were the East–West Connection, a tag team composed of 1970s Northwest wrestling stars Jesse Ventura and Adrian Adonis, and fellow 1970s Northwest alumnus the Iron Sheik.

Another heel coming into national prominence through appearances on the DuMont Network was known for anything *but* his speaking skill. In fact, Michigan native Ed Farhat seldom spoke in anything but gibberish once he donned his wrestling character.

Farhat was a relative newcomer to wrestling when he made his debut on the DuMont Network. The character he introduced, the Sheik of Araby, was a scowling, evil-eyed brute from the Arab Middle East. Although Farhat was by no means a skilled wrestler, his character was probably the most complete embodiment of the foreign menace stereotype that wrestling fans had ever seen. His appearance coming down the aisle toward the ring—with his crazed look, his boots with the toes pointed up, and the camel design on his trunks—would rile any crowd, and television captured the moment perfectly. As the Sheik of Araby knelt and bowed low on his prayer rug in the corner of the ring before each match, audiences in the arena and in their living rooms were eager to see this foreign menace get a beating.

That didn't happen often, however. The Sheik—as he was called during all but the early part of his career—sometimes took a pummeling, but most often, he turned the tables by pulling a foreign object—usually a pencil—out of his trunks and jabbing it into his opponent. He would finish off opponent after opponent with his "camel clutch" submission hold, and during much of his career he was noted for being able to "throw fire" seemingly out of nowhere and cause serious storyline injury to his opponents.

During much of his wrestling career, Farhat doubled as the NWA promoter for the Detroit territory. As many other wrestler-promoters used to do, he kept his promoter role a secret from the public—but in Farhat's case, obviously, any revelation of his behind-the-scenes role would have exposed more of the nature of professional wrestling than any promoter was willing to divulge at that time. Without a doubt, Farhat is more remembered for his character who stared down entire audiences while speaking a form of Arabic nobody in the English-speaking *or* Arabic-speaking world was likely to understand, and exposure early in his career on the DuMont Network played a big part in establishing his status as a headliner in every territory he visited. And while the Sheik never ventured into a Pacific Northwest wrestling ring during the course of his long career, he engaged in many wild matches around the Midwest and elsewhere with a long list of prominent wrestlers associated with the Northwest, including, among many others, Gene Kiniski, Whipper Billy Watson, Lou Thesz, Don Leo Jonathan, Johnny Valentine, Sweet Daddy Siki, Tex McKenzie, Guy Mitchell, Haystack Calhoun, and Abdullah the Butcher.

Another monumental heel during wrestling's Golden Age was a young, Polish Canadian wrestler from Windsor, Ontario, born Edward Spulnik. After training briefly to be a wrestler, Spulnik adopted the ring name of Wladek "Tarzan" Kowalski and headed for St. Louis—for decades, one of the leading wrestling markets in the U.S.—to kick off his career. After squaring off early in his career against accomplished opponents such as NWA champion Orville Brown and Buddy Rogers, Tarzan Kowalski was already a proven commodity when he made his first appearances on Fred Kohler's wrestling cards in Chicago in 1949.

As Tarzan Kowalski, Edward Spulnik—at 6 feet 7 inches and close to 275 pounds—stood out as a larger-than-life performer both in the arena and on the television screen. But it wasn't until a freak accident took place in Montreal on Oct. 15, 1952, that his career rose to an entirely new level and earned him the ring name that he would keep for the rest of his career. As Kowalski recalled in a "What I've Learned" feature in the Aug. 31, 2008, digital edition of *Esquire*, "my name changed in one day—all because of a cauliflower ear."

A cauliflower ear is a brittle mass of what used to be an ear—traditionally, as far as wrestlers are concerned, the result of being on the receiving end of too many headlocks for too many years. As Kowalski continued in *Esquire*, "I was wrestling a guy in Montreal. Yukon Eric. I used to jump off the top rope and put my shinbone across my opponent's chest. So I tied Yukon Eric up in the ropes. Then I climbed to the top turnbuckle and jumped. He saw me coming and tried to turn away. But my shinbone scraped his cheek so tight, it caught his cauliflower ear. The ear flew off and rolled across the ring like a little ball."

A few days later, Kowalski went to visit Yukon Eric at the hospital. As Richard Goldstein quotes Kowalski as telling the *Chicago Tribune* in 1989 in Kowalski's Aug. 31, 2008, obituary in the *New York Times*, "There was this 6-foot-5, 280-pound guy, his head like a mummy, dwarfing his bed. I looked at him and grinned. He grinned back. I laughed, and he laughed back. Then I laughed harder and left."

Fortunately for Kowalski, there were reporters in the hospital who heard him laughing in Eric's room. According to Kowalski in *Esquire*, "The next day, the newspapers were filled with stories of me laughing at the sight of Yukon Eric's missing ear. When I walked to the ring the next week, people were throwing bottles at me. 'You're nothing but a killer!' someone screamed. From that moment on, I was Killer Kowalski."

Kowalski played up his brutality, and his reputation quickly spread throughout Canada and the United States. When he returned to the Marigold Arena as a "Killer," Kowalski was recognized as one of the top heels and attractions in all of wrestling. His ring work could be characterized as a cold, calculated, and highly efficient combination of backbreakers, knee drops, stomach claws, and scowls. Though audiences despised Killer Kowalski—who, like Rogers and Schmidt, agitated fans to the point of getting stabbed—he was a well-traveled wrestler who was always in demand. While he is best remembered, as noted in his *Times* obituary, as "one of professional wrestling's biggest stars and most hated villains when wrestlers offered a nightly menu of mayhem in the early years of television," and for long, successful stays in Montreal and the WWWF/WWF, his travels also took him to British Columbia for a successful run in the Vancouver territory—which spilled into parts of Washington—in the early 1960s. Kowalski also made appearances in Washington State in the 1950s during the height of his national television fame and in July of 1954 challenged Thesz in Seattle for the NWA Heavyweight title.

While Kowalski apparently never ventured into a wrestling ring in Oregon, his presence was certainly known there through the impact of early television and perhaps recalled by longtime wrestling fans over two decades later, following the arrival in Oregon of an up-and-coming wrestling wild man named Killer Brooks.

Yukon Eric, who lost the ear, was born Eric Holmback in Monroe, Washington. After playing college football in Washington, Holmback wrestled under his own name early in his career in a variety of territories, including Don Owen's Pacific Northwest Wrestling. In the late 1940s Holmback became

Alaskan strongman Yukon Eric, a character he introduced to Northwest fans through appearances with Thye's Western Athletic Club and later took to numerous wrestling territories and several titles, although, after Oct. 15, 1952—at least as far as fans were concerned—he would never escape the shadow of his encounter in Montreal with Kowalski. Though he had success as a wrestler—with victories over some big-name grapplers of his era in both singles and tag team encounters—Holmback, suffering personal problems and facing difficulties following a divorce, took his own life in 1965.

Reggie Lisowski was a young man from Milwaukee who started slowly in the wrestling business after leaving the Army following World War II. After training in Milwaukee, he debuted as a wrestler in 1949, appearing mainly in the Chicago area, where he worked at several jobs to supplement the meager income he earned from wrestling early in his career.

Lisowski, a barrel-chested powerhouse, employed a brawling ring style which more than made up for any finesse that was lacking in his wrestling. He was a daunting figure on 1950s DuMont television, a brute of a man who gleefully pummeled opponent after opponent into submission. In 1958 Lisowski appeared briefly in British Columbia.

Another wrestler of similar disposition who had some exposure on the DuMont Network was former Green Bay Packer offensive lineman William "Dick" Afflis, already well known as Dick the Bruiser from his years on the gridiron before becoming a wrestler in 1954.

Dick the Bruiser employed a ring style much like Lisowski's: plenty of brawling; no fear of being in a good fight; and little regard for the rules, his opponents' well-being, or the fans. Both wrestlers had a similar look, and later in their careers—when they formed the legendary tag team of Dick the Bruiser and the Crusher, the ring name Lisowski adopted in 1959 and was known by for the rest of his long career—would be billed as cousins.

That didn't seem to be a far stretch. Both loved to fight, both bleached their hair, both had gravelly voices, and both loved a good cigar and plenty of beer long before Stone Cold Steve Austin came along in the 1990s and took the beer-guzzling working class antihero to a new level in wrestling.

While Bruiser and Crusher did not become a tag team—or even "cousins"—until the mid–1960s, it was during the era of 1950s network television that they established the unforgettable characters that would be blended into a tag team still regarded as among the best of all time. And it was largely through their exposure on 1950s television that the pair cast the mold for countless brawling-style wrestlers who would follow in their footsteps and grace almost every wrestling territory or organization ever since— including 1960s/1970s Northwest brawlers Lonnie Mayne and Bulldog Bob Brown. Gene Kiniski, meanwhile, perhaps the best rugged-style wrestler the Northwest has ever seen, was a prominent player in 1965 in the Indianapolis territory run by Afflis, where he engaged in a series of heated battles with Bruiser and held the promotion's World Heavyweight title for four months almost as a dress rehearsal for capturing the coveted NWA Heavyweight title only two weeks after leaving Bruiser's Indianapolis territory.

DuMont television played a big part in establishing other wrestling heel prototypes and stereotypes that would prove enduring. Japanese characters including Mitsu Arakawa, Great Yamato, and Great Moto helped set the stage for later devious, salt-throwing Japanese characters Haru Sasaki, Kinji Shibuya, Mr. Fuji, and Mr. Saito, who in the 1960s and 1970s would wrestle in the Northwest but do little to dispel stereotypes that had contributed to long-standing discrimination there against people of Japanese descent. Lord James Blears, meanwhile, played a snobbish Brit, a character he brought to Oregon during brief periods in the 1950s and 1960s. But the Golden Age wrestling character whose snobbishness and sheer showmanship best ignited fans via national TV and in arenas across the country—and who became the biggest star in wrestling—was former Oregon-based wrestler George Wagner, who became known from coast to coast as Gorgeous George.

George, while struggling in his early years on the mat to make a decent living as a wrestler, was a seasoned grappler long before making his network television debut on Nov. 11, 1947. After spending part of his childhood in wrestling-rich Iowa, Wagner did some wrestling as a youth in Houston, Texas, before apparently leaving high school at age 14 to help support his family. Like many other wrestlers of his day, Wagner worked for a time as a carnival wrestler before getting booked locally as a professional wrestler and then embarking full-time on a wrestling career while still in his teens.

According to the Gorgeous George page on the Professional Wrestling Hall of Fame and Museum website at www.pwhf.org, early in his career George "wrestled professionally for small sums wherever he could." Though he won titles while in his early twenties, George was far from satisfied with the struggle and level of success he encountered early in his wrestling career. And while he showed some promise as a smallish, good-guy wrestler with some sound amateur moves, George decided that his bland, dark-haired, regular-guy persona wasn't likely to take him to the level of success he wanted to achieve in wrestling.

George and his first wife, Oregonian Betty Hanson—whom Wagner had met and married in a wrestling ring, with Don and Elton Owen serving as ushers, while Wagner was gaining experience as a wrestler in Oregon during his mid-twenties—did some brainstorming and experimenting before hitting on the effeminate, satin-robed, glamor-boy type of character Gorgeous George would soon become. According to www.cagesideseats.com, George Wagner had been following the exploits of a wrestler of similar size, Ohioan Wilbur Finran, who had hit pay dirt as Lord Patrick Lansdowne, a snobbish cheater accompanied by valets and adorned in expensive robes, who, www. cagesideseats.com reports, "would wait for the bell to ring and then begin an intricate series of stretches ... which he would continue until the entire arena was frothing at the mouth." According to multiple reports, Wagner decided to model his new wrestling persona on Lansdowne.

George and Betty Wagner's brainchild Gorgeous George was first unveiled to a wrestling audience in the early 1940s. Reports indicate that a woman in the crowd sarcastically referred to George as "gorgeous" when he was fussing over his new robe and the name simply stuck. University of Tampa journalism professor and Gorgeous George biographer John Capouya sheds further light on the incident, confirming, in his provocatively titled book, *Gorgeous George: The Outrageous Bad-Boy Wrestler Who Created American Pop Culture*, the woman-in-the-audience story but adding that the woman was actually Betty (Capouya, 102). According to Capouya's account, Betty, seated at ringside at the Eugene, Oregon, National Guard Armory while George made his ring entrance and proceeded to twirl and model his blue satin robe, said to her mother, "He's gorgeous!"

Gorgeous George wrestled all over the United States and Canada during the early 1940s—a period in which many fellow wrestlers and athletes took a detour into military service. But Capouya reports, "George reported to Lane County [OR] induction centers many times, took his physicals (at the first one he weighed in at 185 and was measured at just five-foot-eight and a half), and got his serial number. Yet he never served. For five years he was granted one deferment after another, including a mysterious 4-F exemption, meaning he was unfit for military service for 'physical, mental or moral reasons'" (72). No doubt, those deferments helped reinforce the public's negative opinion of Gorgeous George as he performed before home-front audiences—in the Northwest and throughout much of the continent—and continued to hone his bleached-blond, effeminate, cowardly, dastardly, demeaning character in one arena and territory after another.

George made such a splash that he would likely be a well-remembered performer to this day even without the opportunities that awaited him during the early years of network television. But his marriage to early U.S. network television—both on DuMont broadcasts from Chicago and ABC network broadcasts from Southern California—proved a perfect match for both, with each helping raise the other to new heights.

According to Capouya, during the early days of American television following World War II,

> Gorgeous George did as much as any single person to ensure that new device became a fixture. He, along with Milton Berle and the lovable Kukla, Fran, and Ollie, were the first true stars of the medium that would change American life, and in that transformation the transformed George became a national celebrity. Just as

legions perched eagerly near their radios during the 1930s to follow Seabiscuit's epic races, millions of postwar Americans gathered … as families, everyone from grandparents to newborns … in front of their massive TV consoles and tiny screens, laughing, hooting, and shaking their heads in disbelief at the Gorgeous One, entranced by the new technology that brought him and their living rooms so vividly to life.

In the dozen or so years that followed World War II, he was ubiquitous. Everyone knew Gorgeous George. The *Los Angeles Times* reported that many women were having their hair done in a Gorgeous homage. Popular comedians of the day, including Red Skelton, Jack Benny, and Bob Hope, told Gorgeous jokes. Songs were written about him [4–5].

George and Betty Wagner shared an unflagging ambition to take George to the top of the wrestling world. Together, the couple worked out the details of George's character transformation, and it was in early–1940s Oregon that "Gorgeous" George Wagner would be unveiled.

And in 1949, Capouya says, the *Washington Post* declared Gorgeous George "The Biggest Thing in TV" (5).

Much of George's success was rooted in his efforts at self-promotion. Unlike many wrestling characters of his day and countless characters since then, Gorgeous George was not the creation of any wrestling promoter but was a creation of the wrestler himself, with the help of his wife Betty. As Capouya writes, "He and Betty did it all on their own. Unlike the Hollywood movie stars George would later rub egos with, he had no studios supplying him with scripts and directors, or choosing his parts.... They became the writers, directors, publicity agents, wardrobe supervisors, and key grips of their own feature presentation" (4).

According to Dwight Garner, in a Sept. 19, 2008, *New York Times* report on Capouya's book, "The first thing Gorgeous George liked to do, when he arrived in town for a match, was to alert the news media and then head for the nearest women's beauty parlor to tune up his blondeur. He'd modeled his pin-curled hairstyle on actresses like Betty Grable and Gene Tierney, and he knew that doing interviews with his head under a hot croquignole machine—this in an era when John Wayne represented the masculine ideal—was good hokum."

According to www.cagesideseats.com, on at least one occasion in Southern California, George "rented a convertible, drove to the corner of Hollywood and Vine, and began throwing money at passers-by. No one at the time understood the value of the press like Gorgeous George, and he used both newspapers and television to propel him to superstardom."

In the arenas, Gorgeous George never failed to rile a crowd by marching to the ring to the strains of "Pomp and Circumstance." Entrance music for wrestlers was otherwise unheard of in those days, though it has all but become a cliché for wrestlers of the present era. In the ring, George would spend minutes fretting over the referee's intention to put his hands on George as part of the customary pre-match inspection. His valet, who had appeared to the audience long before George showed his face, would be busy perfuming the ring with a spray gun. George would toss roses and "Georgie pins"—gold-plated bobby pins—to members of the snarling crowd. He'd hurl a few insults at his opponent or the audience ... and then, when he was good and ready, he'd lock up with his frustrated opponent before usually finessing or cheating his way to victory.

Over the course of his three-decade career—most of it as Gorgeous George—George Wagner won several titles, including two regional world heavyweight championships and the Pacific Coast Junior Heavyweight championship, recognized for years as a major title in Oregon. After making his name known nationally by traveling around the country, mingling with local celebrities and press, and then by parlaying his success and notoriety in the Midwest to major exposure on the DuMont Network, Gorgeous George relocated to Los Angeles in the early 1950s and took his wrestling career and celebrity to even greater heights. During his career he faced off against such fellow legends as Dick the Bruiser, Bruno Sammartino, and Whipper Billy Watson—at times with his golden locks on the line—and perhaps his best-remembered rivalry was with Lou Thesz, the no-nonsense grappler, who acknowledged in his autobiography, *Hooker,* that he had respect for Gorgeous George (ch. 8).

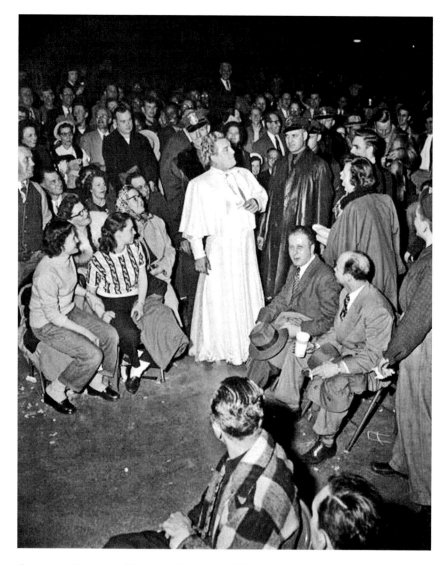

Gorgeous George could mesmerize a crowd from the moment he appeared on the arena floor until long after his match was over. In some cases, what went on in the ring seemed to take second place to the psychology George would unleash on crowds and opponents before his matches got underway.

George shared Thesz's reputation for being a shrewd businessman, and at his peak Gorgeous George earned more money than any other American athlete with the possible exception of Joe DiMaggio. Aside from being an A-list entertainer himself, he was acknowledged as a significant influence by other A-listers including James Brown, Bob Dylan, and Muhammad Ali, and George's influence was obvious on many wrestlers who followed him, including Rogers, Flair, and "Macho Man" Randy Savage, who during his highly successful 1980s/1990s run in the WWF used the same "Pomp and Circumstance" music for his ring entrances that Gorgeous George had used in the 1940s and 1950s.

Apparently due to bad investments, George's finances fizzled late in his career. On top of that, as Garner reports in the *Times*, "the demons that had chased Gorgeous George caught up with and pummeled him. He became an alcoholic; he lost his looks; women claiming to have had children with him began climbing out of the woodwork." And then, less than two years after his retirement due to a liver condition, George, aged 48, died of a heart attack.

While the legend of Gorgeous George lives on largely as a result of his nationally broadcast television appearances from Chicago, Los Angeles, and Toronto, his connection to the Pacific Northwest should not be forgotten. Indeed, while George Wagner may have come into the world in 1915 in a small Nebraska town before moving with his family to Iowa and then Texas, the "Human Orchid" Gorgeous George was born through a lot of ambition, determination, and hard work about 27 years later in Oregon and returned many times to the Northwest to wrestle in both the Oregon and British Columbia territories, long after becoming the hottest touring wrestler in the world.

While wrestling in the current era often blurs any distinctions between good and evil, this was far less the case during the Golden Age of the late 1940s and 1950s. Matches of that era—while often just as tilted toward entertainment as matches of the more modern era—usually seemed to represent some aspect of the universal conflict between good and evil, or at least between decency and contemptuousness.

While a first-class heel such as a Hans Schmidt or a Gorgeous George could turn any opponent into a hero for a night, the heel contingent—nationally and regionally—owed much of its success to opponents that fans cared about, believed in, and were eager to get behind.

Lou Thesz was a wrestler fans recognized as the "real deal." He was a well-trained grappler whose appearances on early network television incited a lot of enthusiasm among fans from coast to coast—especially when Thesz was pitted against such vile characters as Rogers, Schmidt, and Gorgeous George, who fans were eager to see on the receiving end of a beating at the hands of a decent, dedicated, and skilled wrestler like Lou Thesz.

But Thesz played another key role during the late 1940s and 1950s. As National Wrestling Alliance (NWA) champion from 1949 to 1956, Thesz often traveled from one NWA territory to another, wrestling in several matches within a territory and capping things off with a title defense against a regional

Lou Thesz and Gorgeous George were two of the most visible wrestlers in the world during the Golden Age of Wrestling. While their styles in the ring could not have been much more different, each complemented the other well as the two had some memorable encounters in the late 1940s and 1950s.

favorite or territory champion. As world champion, Thesz defended the NWA title against heel and fan favorite alike, and while fans knew Thesz's reputation and respected his success and ability, Thesz often faced opponents the fans were rooting for to take his title. Thesz sometimes roughed things up in order to get fans solidly behind their local challenger, but he was always noted for his ability to bring an air of professionalism and legitimacy that could rub off on any regional promotion or wrestler. While Thesz seldom lost, he usually left a territory in better shape by virtue of having shown that the top regional wrestler he had barely beaten—or wrestled to a heart-rending draw—had proven he was a real world title contender who could well win the coveted NWA title the next time the world champion came to town.

One such contender, and a highly respected wrestler, was Luther Lindsay. Lindsay was an African American from Virginia, and he is credited by some with being a Jackie Robinson–like figure in the world of American professional wrestling.

Reflecting American society of its day, professional wrestling was plagued for decades by the same racial segregation more widely associated with other American sports. While Americans were familiar during the era of segregation with mainstream African American sports figures such as Joe Louis and Jesse Owens, African Americans were for the most part denied the opportunity to compete at the highest level of sport open to people who were white. Many black athletes were denied the opportunity to compete at all, and others were shunted into the "opportunity" to compete only against other people of color.

Segregation in sport began to crumble when figures like baseball's Jackie Robinson, football's Kenny Washington, basketball's Earl Lloyd, and tennis star Althea Gibson crossed the color barriers in their respective sports in the late 1940s and early 1950s. As far as ring sports were concerned, pro boxing—while inconsistent during the early part of the 20th century with regard to racial integration—was largely integrated by the 1930s. Wrestling, however, was a different story.

There are reports of African American competitors participating in the early carnival era of pro wrestling, and it seems safe to presume, given the "take on all comers" nature of carnival wrestling prior to the 20th century, that some African American grapplers appearing at carnivals took part in racially integrated wrestling contests. One such wrestler was Viro Small, who, according to www.originalpeople.org, was likely born into slavery in South Carolina just a few years before the Civil War. During the 1870s and 1880s, Small wrestled at county fairs in New England. Small also wrestled in New York City, and it appears he competed in racially integrated matches.

Reginald Siki—namesake of a more famous African American wrestler of a generation later—was a successful grappler of the 1920s and 1930s who was known to participate in integrated matches, particularly in Southern California. Few other names come up, however, in any search for evidence of real integration in American pro wrestling prior to World War II. For the most part, wrestling was fiercely segregated during the first half of the 20th century—and especially so in the Old South.

As far as the Pacific Northwest is concerned, the first African American wrestler to enjoy significant success in the region was George "Seelie Samara" Hardison, a Georgia native who had a strong career from the late 1930s to the mid–1950s and a run as a headliner in Thye's Western Athletic Club—including a best-of-three-falls victory over Thesz in Portland—in 1945 and 1946, a period in which Samara had success in Oregon, Washington, and British Columbia. In many ways Samara, whose lifetime contribution to wrestling seems underappreciated, could be considered a trailblazer for

Luther Lindsay, whose own reputation as a trailblazer has stood up over time.

Lindsay, a wrestling star from the early 1950s to early 1970s, spent his childhood in Virginia and North Carolina. Though he became a skilled college wrestler and football player, laws of the time prevented him from competing against white athletes—which set the tone for much of Lindsay's professional wrestling career, including periods where, deprived of the opportunity to face white opponents, he was billed as the "Negro heavyweight wrestling champion."

But with segregation unraveling in the United States in the 1950s, Lindsay was the first African American wrestler to compete in racially integrated matches in at least two southern states, Texas and Tennessee. As far as Tennessee was concerned, although that historically significant match—in Knoxville against Ron Wright—took place in the late 1950s, Lindsay wrestled in segregated matches in the Volunteer State as late as 1965, in the Memphis wrestling territory, one of the last in the United States to desegregate.

Lindsay had considerable success in wrestling territories that did not practice segregation. One such territory was outside the United States—in Calgary, Alberta, center of a territory best remembered as Stampede Wrestling, owned and run for over three decades by Stu Hart, a tough-as-nails wrestler himself and father of seven wrestlers, including 1990s five-time WWF World Heavyweight champion Bret "Hitman" Hart. Stu Hart also featured Samara in his territory at times in the 1950s.

Lindsay's first encounter with Canada had preceded his pro wrestling days, as he played two seasons of professional football in Canada after college. He proved to be a popular, successful wrestler in Canada, winning major titles both as a singles and tag team wrestler in Calgary, and Heath McCoy, author of *Pain and Passion: The History of Stampede Wrestling*, says that Stu Hart held Lindsay in the highest regard as a grappler and friend.

During most of the early part of Lindsay's career—while wrestling's popularity across the United States was at a peak—he was based in the Pacific Northwest, appearing regularly in Oregon and Washington. Like Hart's promotion in Canada—which extended over the border, spilling over into eastern Washington—Don Owen's wrestling territory was integrated and was enjoying good business. One reason for its success was the popularity of Lindsay.

While the Pacific Northwest is often regarded as a bastion of tolerance and a model for race relations, such has not always been the case. Oregon had seen a great deal of discrimination against African Americans and other minorities in the years before Don Owen began promoting. According to www.portlandoregon.gov, the KKK was a powerful force in Oregon during the 1920s, with Governor Walter M. Pierce "overtly supported by the Klan and [promoting] the Klan's agenda" and the state legislature "dominated by members of the Klan." In 1926, www.portlandoregon.gov reports, "Oregon repealed its Exclusion Law, which barred Blacks from the state," and in 1927 "the Oregon State Constitution was finally amended to remove a clause denying Blacks the right to vote."

Few African Americans lived in Portland during the Depression, but that changed with a rise in employment opportunities during World War II. Some skilled jobs, however, were withheld from black people, as were union benefits. Portlandoregon.gov reports that, during the wartime influx of African Americans, "with this rise in diversity in populations came signs throughout Portland: 'We Cater to White Trade Only.'"

Discrimination against blacks continued after World War II. Segregation and unfair policies, even in the public sector, made housing a challenge for many African Americans in Portland during most of the 1950s—and, some would argue, long after that. Segregation continued in some Portland schools long after the landmark Brown v. Topeka Board of Education ruling in 1954 suggested segregation was on the way out. Most surprisingly, perhaps, Oregon did not ratify the post–Civil War 15th Amendment to the U.S. Constitution until 1959. And then, during the 1960s, Portland and the Northwest could not avoid some of the racially motivated rioting more often associated with other areas of the country.

Despite challenging circumstances when he arrived in Portland in 1953 after barely a year's experience as a professional wrestler, Luther Lindsay quickly established himself as a respected grappler and fan favorite throughout much of Oregon and Washington. Following in the footsteps of Samara, Lindsay crossed color lines and made such an impact that, within months of arriving in the Northwest, he was the local favorite touring NWA champion Lou Thesz would face during a run through the Pacific Northwest in the summer of 1953—with Lindsay quietly making history as the first African American challenger for the NWA championship. From 1953–1955 Lindsay and Thesz wrestled several times in major cities of the Northwest—including Portland, Seattle, and Tacoma—and each time, Lindsay held his own against the champion, with their matches often going to a draw. Lindsay's ability— and Thesz's—to give an air of credibility to matches between the local favorite and a highly respected champion who was prominently featured on national television helped raise the stock of pro wrestling in the Pacific Northwest, and Lindsay's credibility and crowd appeal also contributed positively at a time when racial problems in the Northwest and across the United States were getting ironed out. If he had wrestled in a later period, Lindsay may well have been an integrated World Heavyweight champion and not simply a "Negro heavyweight wrestling champion." But as it was, he was a longtime Northwest favorite who, over the course of his 20-year career, challenged at least four reigning NWA world heavyweight champions.

While Lindsay wrestled across the United States and internationally and was instrumental in furthering integration in pro wrestling during the 1950s, he was not a performer featured on national network television.

The best-known African American wrestler nationally during the wrestling surge corresponding with the rise of network television in the United States was Bobo Brazil, a native of Arkansas who was raised in the Midwest. Brazil, born in 1924 and debuting as a pro wrestler in the late 1940s, was the first African American main event-level wrestler to benefit from prominent exposure on national network television. While he helped pave the way for future nationally known African wrestling stars such as Reggie "Sweet Daddy" Siki (no relation to earlier wrestler Reginald Siki), Dory Dixon, "Sailor" Art Thomas, and Bearcat Wright, Brazil was the one who made a national name during the 1950s' dismantling of segregation. While Brazil wrestled in segregated territories at times in his career, he became a hugely popular symbol of integration in wrestling during the 1950s via network broadcasts of his ring battles against such nemeses as Killer Kowalski, future Northwest mainstay Don Leo Jonathan, Washington State native Johnny Valentine, and Brazil's greatest career rival—and longtime employer in the Detroit territory—The Sheik. Brazil also passed on to many fellow African American grapplers the "move" he used in winning countless matches: the "coco-butt" or head butt, long associated with African American wrestlers and playing into the stereotype suggesting people of African descent had unusually thick skulls. Brazil was still at the height of his career when he made a few memorable appearances in British Columbia in 1968.

Other key early TV network wrestlers on the babyface ("good guy") side were almost as unorthodox as some of the leading heels of the day. One wrestling hero who clearly stood out from the pack was Ricki Starr, a dancer and real-life friend of Gorgeous George's who employed an arsenal of ballet-type wrestling moves fans hadn't seen before and which brought them to laughter, if not tears, during numerous contests between the dainty Starr and a variety of roughhousing opponents. While hardly the he-man sort of hero many fans were most comfortable with, Starr showed little of the bombast or arrogance of a Gorgeous George and was clearly a fan favorite who appealed to a national audience and wrestled in some main events in Oregon and British Columbia during the 1950s.

An enormously popular babyface in the 1950s was Antonino Rocca, who became one of the biggest names ever in the Northeast. Rocca, an Italian expatriate raised in Argentina, began his wrestling career in 1947, according to Brian Solomon's WWE Legends, working for a South American promotion associated with former world champion wrestler Stanislaus Zbyszko. A year later, Rocca made his wrestling debut in the United States (Solomon, 20).

Rocca proved a big hit from the start. As Solomon reports, "Rocca wowed fans who had never seen an athlete of his type in a wrestling ring. In an era when wrestlers never left the mat and often clinched in holds for minutes at a time, Rocca brought a new, fast-paced excitement.... His flashy repertoire of aerial maneuvers like dropkicks, hurracanranas [sic], and victory rolls dazzled spectators" (20).

After wrestling briefly in other parts of the country, Rocca established his base in New York City, where "Toots" Mondt—two decades after the breakup of the Gold Dust Trio—was back to being a major power broker in wrestling. During the 1950s Rocca regularly headlined shows in Northeast arenas as an Italian ethnic hero, but he was also booked out by Mondt to appear on other promoters' wrestling cards nationwide, usually as a headliner. Though Rocca appeared regularly in Chicago and the Midwest, it was often in opposition to shows run by Fred Kohler. Yet Rocca became a star at the Marigold Arena, and the DuMont Network—by broadcasting his matches from the Marigold along with some of his other matches from the East Coast—made him a star nationally. While his skills as a grappler were seldom taken seriously, Rocca was a revolutionary entertainer in the wrestling business who, according to Solomon, "literally changed what pro wrestling was for the generations that followed" (20)—and whose influence in the Northwest was perhaps best seen in the form of 1960s/1970s high flier Erich Froelich or Fijian wrestler Jimmy Snuka, who dazzled fans in both the Portland and Vancouver territories in the 1970s before heading off for main-event success in other promotions, most notably the WWF.

One DuMont-era wrestler whose legitimate grappling skills were seldom called into question was Verne Gagne, a Minnesota native who, according to the Professional Wrestling Hall of Fame and Museum website, was a multi-sport star in high school and a state wrestling champion.

Gagne, attending the University of Minnesota, was a four-time Big Ten heavyweight wrestling champion, first winning the title in 1944 "before having his college career interrupted by military service," according to *Minneapolis Star Tribune* sportswriter Joel A. Rippel in his book *Minnesota Sports Almanac: 125 Glorious Years* (309). Gagne returned to the University of Minnesota after World War II, proceeded to win three more Big Ten heavyweight championships, and pulled off the uncommon feat of winning consecutive NCAA championships in 1948 and 1949.

Like many other wrestlers of his day, Gagne ventured into pro football before hitting the road as a pro wrestler. His amateur credentials—including a spot as an alternate for the 1948 Olympic freestyle wrestling team—made him a hot prospect who was slotted into feature matches everywhere he wrestled. Gagne established his wrestling base in Chicago when DuMont wrestling was at its peak, and he became a popular attraction based on his ability to make matches appear credible, even when he was paired with some of the more outlandish performers of his day.

"Scientific" matches pitting Gagne against clean-cut, sportsmanlike rivals such as Thesz, Wilbur Snyder, and Édouard Carpentier also played well on early national television, satisfying fans who leaned more toward the sport-oriented side of wrestling than the theatrics. Gagne maintained a solid though perhaps unspectacular style of wrestling throughout his three-decade career, winning numerous world championships, particularly in the Minnesota-based American Wrestling Association (AWA) he cofounded and would own in part or in whole during most of his wrestling career and for a decade afterward—until the early 1990s, when many wrestling territories in the U.S. fell to the WWF juggernaut.

As far as the Pacific Northwest is concerned, Gagne—while apparently making only one brief appearance in the region during his career—engaged in numerous 1950s and 1960s battles across the U.S. Midwest and sometimes in Montreal and Winnipeg, Manitoba, against Northwest greats Don Leo Jonathan and Gene Kiniski, with the latter defeating Gagne in mid–1961 to kick off a brief run as AWA World Heavyweight champion. Gagne also had a long association with 1960s/1970s Winnipeg promoter Al Tomko, who would become promoter of Vancouver's All-Star Wrestling for over a decade from the late 1970s through the late 1980s. But Gagne's greatest imprint on the Pacific Northwest was undoubtedly through having a hand in training numerous wrestlers—including regional heavyweight champions Bulldog Bob Brown and Buddy Rose and future world champions Ric Flair, Curt Hennig, Sergeant Slaughter, and the Iron Sheik—who would all wrestle in the Pacific Northwest at some point in their careers.

Another wrestler with an amazing 30-year career was New Zealander Pat O'Connor, a big favorite on 1950s network TV who went on to win the NWA championship before that decade was over and followed that up with a three-month run—at least, on paper—as the inaugural AWA World Heavyweight champion in 1960. O'Connor, who employed a ground-based style, was noted for putting on solid, believable matches with both babyface and heel opponents while throwing in an assortment of flashy moves such as the spinning arm lock and the spinning leg lock. Both through his appearances on early national TV in the United States and Canada (as a regular performer on Toronto-based cards broadcast on the CBC's *Saturday Night Wrestling*) and, later, his NWA title defenses against opponents including Shag Thomas, Kurt von Poppenheim, "Tough" Tony Borne, Gene Kiniski, and Don Leo Jonathan, O'Connor was a wrestler fans in the Pacific Northwest got to know well.

"Whipper" Billy Watson was already a celebrity in Canada and a well-known wrestler in the United States prior to becoming an attraction on

Wrestling from Marigold. He had started learning the ropes in Europe while still a teenager, earning his nickname in the United Kingdom for frequently "Irish whipping" his opponents into the ropes. In his early twenties, Watson returned to his native Ontario and soon became a major wrestling figure and local celebrity in Toronto, where he did more than anyone else to establish Maple Leaf Gardens as more than a hockey arena. When 1950s network television in Canada brought Toronto wrestling to a nationwide audience, Watson became a celebrity all the way to the West Coast.

Watson won the National Wrestling Association (not National Wrestling Alliance) World Heavyweight championship in 1947, losing it two months later to Thesz. But nine years later, on March 15, 1956, Watson turned the tables by capturing the prestigious National Wrestling Alliance (NWA) Heavyweight title from Thesz and becoming the number one touring wrestling attraction in North America.

During his eight-month reign as NWA champion, Watson defended the title against familiar faces such as Gorgeous George, Hans Schmidt, Killer Kowalski, Pat O'Connor, Buddy Rogers, Bobo Brazil, and top Northwest contenders Gene Kiniski, Don Leo Jonathan, and Luther Lindsay. He also defended the title in Vancouver against Thesz and future NWA champion Dick Hutton.

In the early 1960s, several years after losing the NWA title back to Thesz, Watson wrestled regularly in the Vancouver territory, winning multiple tag team championships and, for nearly two years, holding the Western Canada version of the British Empire Heavyweight championship while in his mid-forties.

During the previous decade, Watson had been less successful at making his mark in Seattle—not as a wrestler but as a promoter. In 1955, the year before winning the NWA championship, Watson bought the existing Seattle wrestling territory from NWA promoter Bob Murray.

Murray, recalled many decades later by Dean Silverstone as "strictly a hardcore businessman," had been involved in promotion in Seattle during the 1930s in association with Musty Musgrave. From there—with a break during wrestling's lengthy shutdown in Seattle in the 1940s—Murray promoted events in the Emerald City in partnership with Ted Thye's Western Athletic Club. But then, according to www.legacyofwrestling.com, "Murray broke away from Thye and began to deal with Jerry Meeker, who ran a booking office out of Great Falls, Montana." What seemed to drive Murray's switch from Thye to Meeker was the latter's association with the NWA, as Murray, an NWA promoter himself, was likely under pressure to end his association with Thye, who was never admitted to the organization. Murray continued promoting in Seattle as the NWA came under investigation in the 1950s by the U.S. Department of Justice for alleged monopolistic and exclusionary policies, and it appears Murray was eager to sell his promotion by the mid–1950s.

After taking over in mid–1955, Watson was a low-profile figure in his own promotion, instead depending largely on wrestlers from the Toronto and Calgary territories—possibly, www.legacyofwrestling.com reports, because Toronto promoter Frank Tunney and Calgary promoter Hart may also have been in on the purchase of the Seattle territory from Murray. But while Watson and local promoter Ken Kenneth booked proven commodities such as Thesz and Gorgeous George on the Seattle cards, it wasn't enough, and the promotion was sold a year later to Idaho promoter Neal "Tex" Hager, who had an office in Spokane and in the 1950s promoted wrestling events in Washington cities including Tacoma and Seattle as well as Spokane. According to www.wrestling-titles.com, Hager's circuit also included Kennewick, Pasco, Chehalis, and Walla Walla, where he staged wrestling shows in association with local promoters Ivan Mickailoff, Luke Dailey, Glen Detton, and Jack Kennedy and Dale Haddock. Looking back at Hager decades later, Silverstone recalls him as a "mini Vince McMahon" who ran an extensive, thriving territory for his day, both inside and outside Washington. "He had so many irons in the fire," Silverstone says.

As far as Watson is concerned, perhaps featuring himself on his shows would have saved his promotional venture, but 1955–1956 was not the best time to be an NWA promoter, and besides, putting more focus on saving his territory may have slowed or even prevented Watson's winning the NWA World Heavyweight title and rising for a time to the top of the wrestling world as a performer—fueled in large part by the reputation he had earned through his appearances on early network television.

6

Regional Promotions on Television

Wrestling in the Northwest may have taken an entirely different turn had another power broker stepped in to take over the Seattle promotion from Bob Murray in the mid–1950s. Thye, who was a major critic of the NWA's power tactics—which made it extremely difficult for an outsider to maintain a foothold in any promotional area an NWA promoter considered his own— hoped Johnny Doyle, who had been a big-time California wrestling promoter, would be the one to relieve Murray of his Seattle-based promotion.

Doyle—the son of James G. Doyle, a former publisher of the *Seattle Post-Intelligencer*—was involved in wrestling promotion on the East Coast during the Depression before relocating to Southern California around 1940. In California he got into arena management, but www.legacyofwrestling.com reports that, after becoming a booking agent, "Doyle represented about 98% of professional wrestlers in Southern California in 1950, including Gorgeous George, Baron Michele Leone, Primo Carnera, and Antonino Rocca."

In early 1950 Doyle was offered a spot for a Saturday night wrestling show to be televised in the Hollywood–Los Angeles market. Hollywood in the early 1950s was drawing national attention as a television center, and *Hollywood Wrestling*, after two years of success in the local market, went on to become a hot commodity in the early days of TV syndication via the Paramount Television Network, a loose network of affiliates whose lifespan roughly coincided with the DuMont Network's.

Oregon's first TV station, KPTV (now a Fox-TV affiliate in Portland), went on the air on Sept. 20, 1952, and soon started broadcasting *Hollywood Wrestling*, which also appeared on Tacoma's KMO-TV (renamed KTVW-TV in 1954). While Doyle's successful run in TV syndication certainly provided him the opportunity to leave his fingerprints on wrestling in the Northwest, his influence may have risen to an altogether different level had he taken over Murray's promotion in the mid–1950s and turned his attention toward making Seattle a major wrestling center, as he had done with Hollywood.

Southern California under Doyle was only one of many strong NWA regions in the early 1950s. NWA territories were springing up around the United States, and by 1956—the year the NWA's troubles with the government came to a head—the National Wrestling Alliance comprised 35 member territories in the United States, along with one in Mexico, one in Canada—Stu Hart's Big Time Wrestling (later Stampede Wrestling)—and one in Japan.

The Japanese promotion—called the Japan Pro Wrestling Alliance—was the creation of Rikidozan, who began his transition to professional wrestling—a little-known form of sport or entertainment at the time in Japan—after retiring from sumo at age 25 in 1950. According to www.legacyofwrestling.com, "Rikidozan met up with a contingent from the United States, which was headed by Joe Louis, and began to train for the pro-wrestling ring."

Rikidozan relocated to the United States, making his debut as a pro wrestler on Oct. 28, 1951. Based mainly in Hawaii and California at the start of his career, Rikidozan quickly became a major attraction, and within three months of his debut, he wrestled Lou Thesz to a draw. Rikidozan toured the United States, gaining valuable experience in the ring and learning the ins and outs of the business he would put on the map in Japan.

In mid–1953 Rikidozan established the Japan Pro Wrestling Alliance, which hit it big by most often sticking to a simple formula—the local hero, Rikidozan, would defend the nation's honor by battling toe-to-toe with a menacing challenger, often a well-known main event wrestler from North America—and this formula proved to be a huge hit on television.

As Lee Thompson reports in *Sport, Memory and Nationhood in Japan: Remembering the Glory Days*, "[Rikidozan's] active career from the mid–1950s to the mid–1960s [1953–1963] coincided with the first 10 years of television in Japan, and broadcasts of his matches—especially those with foreign (often identified as American) wrestlers—were hugely popular." Thompson continues,

> The phrase kuroyama no hitodakari (a black sea of heads) is used to describe the huge crowds that would gather in front of television sets in outdoor locations to watch his matches in the years before most households owned their own devices. From 1957, a leading producer of television sets, Mitsubishi Electronics, sponsored a weekly [program] featuring Rikidozan's bouts on the Nippon Television channel. In annual surveys of TV ratings reported by the Dentsu advertising agency, professional wrestling broadcasts received the highest ratings for five of the nine years between 1955, when ratings were first compiled, and 1963, the year of Rikidozan's death.

Thompson points out that, with the World War II devastation still central in Japanese minds, Rikidozan embodied "the theme of Japanese spirit and technology overcoming perceived physical inferiority vis-à-vis foreigners. That is, the foreign opponents that Rikidozan faced were usually perceived as being much larger, and he defeated these wrestlers in a burst of righteous indignation using his patented weapon from the arsenal of Japanese martial arts: the karate chop" (130–131).

Little known at the time, however, was that Japan's favorite son and defender Rikidozan was not Japanese at all. Kim Sin-rak, born in what would become North Korea after the partition of the peninsula, "had first come to Japan in 1939 as a strapping teenager, brought by a touring sumo wrestling scout from Nagasaki, who signed him on with the Tokyo Nishinoseki stable" of sumo wrestlers, according to Robert Whiting's *Tokyo Underworld: The Fast Times and Hard Life of an American Gangster in Japan* (102), which is not primarily about Rikidozan or wrestling but goes into some detail concerning the alleged seamier side of Japan's greatest wrestling hero.

Rikidozan's relocation to Japan happened when Korea was under brutal Japanese occupation and Korean culture and people were largely regarded by the Japanese as infinitely inferior to the Japanese. Whiting writes,

> The feeling among those in the Nishinoseki stable was that the public would not accept a Korean in what was known as the sport of the Emperor and was seen as the epitome of the national ethos. It was thus heretical to claim that a Korean, or anyone of any other nationality for that matter, could defeat a Japanese sumoist. As a result, the public fiction was concocted that young Kim had been born Mitsuhiro Momota, the pure-blooded son of Minokichi Momota of Omura, Kyushu—the scout who had discovered him. Later hagiographies would even describe, in amazing detail, free of the slightest trace of irony, a fabricated childhood and a fictional athletic career at Omura High School [102].

Rikidozan's "lifelong deception," as the Jan. 16, 2005, *Newsweek* article, "Korean to the Core," called it, was kept up throughout his career as a pro wrestling impresario and performer until his 1963 death at age 39 due to complications following a nightclub stabbing. According to Whiting, revelation of Rikidozan's actual background to the public "would, by his own calculation, have cost him 50 percent of his fan base due to anti–Korean prejudices long held among the Japanese" (101).

Of course, fabricated ethnicities and identities have nearly always been a staple of pro wrestling. In the Pacific Northwest, for example, many fans would have been surprised to learn that 1970s Northwest stars Steven Little Bear and Ivan Koloff—the latter having appeared several years earlier in British Columbia and Oregon as "Irish" Red McNulty—were no more Native Canadian or Russian than Hans Schmidt was German, the Sheik was Syrian, or Rikidozan was Japanese. But Rikidozan took his fictional character to the very height of his profession and is still viewed by many—considering that he almost single-handedly generated interest in pro wrestling in a country that has been a hotbed of the sport ever since and which has provided numerous opportunities to Northwest wrestlers—as the most important pro wrestler ever. In any case, national exposure on television was instrumental in his success, just as exposure on nationally broadcast wrestling shows from Chicago, New York, and Los Angeles launched or fired up many successful wrestling careers in the United States during the early years of network and syndicated television.

Just as vital as nationally broadcast programs to the overall health of wrestling were the locally broadcast wrestling shows that began proliferating throughout the United States. The first such program in the Pacific Northwest appears to have been scored by Seattle promoter Tex Porter in 1948. Porter, according to 1970s Washington State promoter Dean Silverstone at www.1wrestlinglegends.com, had begun his wrestling career in 1927 for promoter Sailor Jack Woods in Medford, Oregon, and wrestled in California, Hawaii, and Seattle prior to promoting matches around Seattle, often in partnership with Murray. According to Silverstone, Porter's early foray into locally televised wrestling proved "so popular in the area that a whole troupe of promoters emerged, all running the area at the same time."

Five years after Porter's introduction to the Northwest of locally televised wrestling, Don Owen—well established as the promoter of Portland's most popular weekly entertainment event, Pacific Northwest Wrestling—received a visit from representatives of the Heidelberg Brewing Co. of Tacoma, Washington.

The Heidelberg Brewing Co. was the result of the 1949 restructuring of Columbia Breweries, first called the Columbia Brewing Co. after its founding in 1900. During national Prohibition—and even four years earlier, when the state of Washington supposedly went dry—Columbia, like other breweries, had to lie low. Known for 16 years as the Columbia Bottling Co., Columbia switched its focus, according to www.brewerygems.com, to the production of soft drinks and nonalcoholic beer. By 1933 the company, renamed Columbia Breweries, was back in the business of producing beer.

After weathering challenges of the Depression and wartime, Columbia changed its name to the Heidelberg Brewing Co. in 1949, four years after the end of war with Germany. Thanks in part to an advertising blitz, Heidelberg enjoyed a surge in popularity and underwent some ambitious expansion in the early 1950s, and within five years of taking on the new name, the Heidelberg Brewing Co., according to www.brewerygems.com, "was now the largest brewery north of San Francisco and west of Milwaukee."

This was the context in which representatives from the Heidelberg Brewing Co. came calling on Don Owen at his farm in Springfield, Oregon, in 1953. Owen had ambition to rival Heidelberg's, and this had resulted in his carving out a strong wrestling territory in the early years of the NWA, though he hadn't ventured into weekly television yet. Regular TV exposure had greatly benefitted promoters in other areas—including Porter in Seattle—but television had not come to Oregon until KPTV went on the air in 1952. By then Owen certainly knew how to put on a crowd-pleasing show, yet the majority of KPTV viewers likely regarded the network or syndicated wrestling they saw on TV as more "major league" than the local product. One way of dispelling that perception would be for Owen to get his wrestling product on television.

All of this would suggest a perfect marriage between a rising brewery eager to increase its exposure and a hot local entertainment ticket ready to rise to another level. Heidelberg saw Owen's Pacific Northwest Wrestling as another kind of ticket—a ticket to even further growth in visibility and market share in the brewing industry—and the company representatives who came to visit Owen at his farm offered to sponsor a weekly television show featuring Owen's wrestlers.

Some reports suggest Owen had something else on his mind and was not too impressed when his visitors made their offer. According to John Terry, at OregonEncyclopedia.org, Owen recounted, years later, "My clothes were all dirty and covered with manure. I told these guys, 'I'm tired; I've been up all night with a sick cow. I haven't got time for you.'"

Even so, *Heidelberg Wrestling* debuted on KPTV on July 10, 1953. Initially broadcast live in prime time, picking up the action from Owen's Friday night events in Portland, *Heidelberg Wrestling* switched to a taped format and an 11 p.m. Friday time slot once network programming began to dominate prime time.

The setting of the show was the Portland Armory Annex, a classic Romanesque-style building dating back to 1891, when it was built to provide additional training space to Guardsmen housed in the nearby main Armory building, which had opened three years earlier. The Armory Annex, which still stands, has worn many hats since 1891—most recently serving as a theater facility in Portland's Pearl District—but from 1953 to 1968 the Portland Armory Annex was best known as the setting of Don Owen's weekly wrestling show, first brought to the air on KPTV under the sponsorship of Heidelberg Breweries. Sponsorship of the show would shift in ensuing years, most notably to Portland furniture salesman and television pitchman Tom Peterson, but the Heidelberg Brewing Co.—sold to Canada's Carling Brewing Co. in 1958— played a vital role in kicking off a television institution in Oregon and the Northwest that, ultimately, would last 38 years.

After two years on KPTV, Owen's *Heidelberg Wrestling* found a new home on CBS affiliate KOIN-TV, where it was renamed *Portland Wrestling*. KOIN would broadcast *Portland Wrestling* until 1967, featuring a roster of popular wrestlers including "Tough" Tony Borne, Shag "King Toby" Thomas,

Gory Guerrero, Stan "the Man" Stasiak, Pepper Gomez, Ed Francis, Luther Lindsay, Kurt von Poppenheim, Lonnie Mayne, and Dutch Savage—all made larger than life through their appearances on television.

Joining Tex Porter and Don Owen in the small circle of 1950s-era wrestling promoters in the Pacific Northwest to magnify their product through television was Harry Elliott. Elliott, a Louisiana native, had been a member of the wrestling team at the University of Oregon and went on to be a wrestling coach at that institution. According to Silverstone in *"I Ain't No Pig Farmer!,"* Elliott coached Don Owen's brother Elton when Elton was a student at the University of Oregon (30).

While coaching at the collegiate level, Elliott ventured into pro wrestling as both a referee and part-time wrestler. By 1938, Silverstone reports, Elliott, no longer a collegiate coach, "had begun to dabble in ring promotion" (30).

Harry Elliott's early work as a referee, pro wrestler, and promoter was in association with Herb Owen's promotion. During the 1940s Elliott worked in the heavy construction industry, but Silverstone reports,

Ed Francis was a highly popular wrestler and multi-time champion during Pacific Northwest Wrestling's early years on television. After an outstanding mid–1950s/early–'60s run in the Northwest, Francis began a second career in wrestling as the promoter for Hawaii's Mid-Pacific Promotions.

By 1949–50, Elliott was still wrestling, part-time, professionally, and working a fairly large number of shows as referee for Don Owen and brother Elton, who were carrying on the promotions begun by their father. In subsequent years, Elliott continued working for Owen's booking office, and ran spot shows [one-nighters, outside the weekly or regular event venues] in places like Astoria [OR] and southwestern Washington.... By late 1951, Harry Elliott was listed as the matchmaker of the weekly Portland armory shows.... He continued his association with the Owens, both as a referee and promoter of spot shows, until near the end of the decade, when he launched a pro-wrestling rebirth of sorts in Seattle [30].

After venturing out on his own as a promoter, Elliott maintained his association with Don Owen by booking his wrestlers out of Owen's Portland office. As Owen had done, Elliott secured a deal to introduce his product to a weekly television audience, and beginning in 1957, CBS Tacoma affiliate KTNT-TV televised Elliott's Friday night wrestling events from the "basement arena" of Seattle's Civic Auditorium. In 1960 the show moved to Seattle's CBS affiliate, KIRO-TV, with KIRO sports director Ron Forsell serving as one of the commentators. During the early days of the hour-long broadcast, preliminary matches from Elliott's Civic Auditorium shows would air the same night, Friday, at 11 p.m., until the program was moved up half an hour to 10:30 p.m.

Silverstone—whose own start in the wrestling business was as the writer and seller of programs at Elliott's live shows—reports in *Pig Farmer* that Elliott's KIRO broadcast moved to Tuesday nights, a four-day delay, in September of 1960. From Tuesdays, Silverstone reports, the show moved to 6:30–7:30 p.m. Saturdays "as a lead-in to the immensely popular *Perry Mason* show. That broadcast slot led to the huge ratings *Northwest Championship Wrestling* achieved in the market" (31). And the show, Silverstone adds at www.1wrestlinglegends.com, "would be seen through all of Washington State and parts of Oregon, Idaho, Montana, Utah, Wyoming, Colorado, and parts of British Columbia."

Silverstone reports, in *Pig Farmer*, that Elliott moved his broadcasts from the Civic Auditorium's basement arena to Seattle's Senator Auditorium (formerly, Eagles Auditorium) and then, in 1962, to the Masonic Temple in Seattle's Capitol Hill area. For special shows expected to attract unusually large crowds, Elliott moved events to the Seattle Center Arena or, "once a month in the mid-[1960s]," according to Silverstone, to the much larger Seattle Center Coliseum (later renamed KeyArena), best known, starting in 1967, as the home of the NBA Seattle SuperSonics (31–32).

Running other wrestling events most nights of the week to go along with—and to take full advantage of—his popular *Northwest Championship Wrestling* TV broadcasts, Elliott continued to book his wrestlers out of Owen's office in Portland. As a result, says Silverstone at www.1wrestlinglegends.com, "Portland had to double their staff." In addition, Silverstone—who went on to referee matches and run spot shows in association with Elliott—says, in a June 26, 2006, *SLAM! Wrestling* report following Elliott's death at age 101, that Elliott "made Don Owen a ton of money because Don Owen was able to get better boys [wrestlers] into the area because Harry actually had the best payday of the entire week. They would work Seattle on Tuesday, and of course they worked Portland … the reason Don was able to get so much great talent through the years was because Washington was paying half the bills."

From his current-day perspective, Silverstone refers to Elliott as an "undiscovered gem" to present-day observers looking back on earlier eras of Northwest wrestling. Matt Farmer, meanwhile, says, "Harry should be looked at as one of the most successful promoters in Northwest wrestling history."

On TV and at house shows, Elliott featured wrestlers such as Borne, Lindsay, Poppenheim, Thomas, Stasiak, and Mayne—all top-tier wrestlers in the Northwest—along with numerous others who headlined or filled key spots, including a young Antonio Inoki, who appeared as Kazimoto for about six months from late 1964 to 1965 before returning to Japan and putting together a career that likely places him behind only Rikidozan in terms of the impact an individual has ever had on the wrestling industry in Japan. According to Greg Oliver, who wrote the June 26, 2006, *SLAM!* report, in 1966 Elliott promoted an event at the Seattle Coliseum, headlined by a Thesz–Kiniski NWA title defense, that drew a crowd of over 15,000. Yet the very next year, and despite a solid decade of success for *Northwest Championship Wrestling*—described by Silverstone, at www.1wrestlinglegends.com, as "perhaps, the best live show of its kind ever produced"—a change in CBS management resulted in the cancelation of *Northwest Championship Wrestling* in 1967 and, the following year, Elliott's decision to trade a career in wrestling for a new start in real estate.

7

The Parker-Fenton Era

In British Columbia the promoter of note in the 1950s was ex-wrestler Cliff Parker, who had been a popular performer for the Vancouver-based Big Time Wrestling and Pender Wrestling Club promotions during the late 1930s and through most of the 1940s. As a promoter in the 1950s, Parker employed a mix of regional talent and bigger-name wrestlers and, according to Nevada's *Wrestling in the Canadian West*, "had no difficulty filling the seats [during] one of the longest runs as a promoter in the country's history" (44). Parker also booked talent out to Washington-based wrestler-promoter Cliff Olson, who ran shows in cities such as Tacoma, Olympia, and Aberdeen during the 1950s and into the 1960s.

Unlike other leading Pacific Northwest wrestling promoters of the 1950s Don Owen and Harry Elliott, Parker had no notable television exposure during that decade. Yet, while fans in British Columbia had been exposed to "major league" wrestlers and wrestling promotions based in both Canada and the United States via network and early syndicated television, Parker enjoyed a strong decade using performers such as Buddy Knox, Pepper Gomez, Frank Stojack, Ivan Kameroff, Stu Hart—already well into his promotional career in Calgary—and Kurt von Poppenheim, who could also be seen by many fans in southern British Columbia on Elliott's *Northwest Championship Wrestling*, which spilled over into the province.

In 1960 Parker partnered with Alberta native Rod Fenton, who had wrestled in western Canada, the United States, and internationally in the 1930s and 1940s before becoming a promoter in the early 1950s in Arizona. Fenton is widely credited with introducing fellow Albertan and University of Arizona football standout Gene Kiniski to professional wrestling and booked Kiniski's first match, in Tucson, in February of 1952. Later that year, however, Kiniski returned to Alberta and played briefly for the Edmonton Eskimos, his hometown's professional football team, before returning to pro wrestling a year later.

Kiniski became a major star, particularly in California, Texas, and central

Canada, during the early years of his career. His was a well-known face on television, especially in Canada, where some of his Toronto appearances were featured prominently on Canadian Broadcasting Corporation (CBC) wrestling broadcasts in the mid to late 1950s, and he wrestled occasionally in Vancouver beginning in 1957. Even early in his career, Kiniski was a regular challenger for the NWA title, and by the early 1960s he held two other versions of the world championship, most prominently the World Heavyweight title of the American Wrestling Association (AWA), cofounded by Verne Gagne.

Fenton and Kiniski were back together in the early 1960s. Kiniski, recognized as one of the brightest lights in wrestling, had established a new home base in Vancouver, where he was already winning regional championships and continuing to challenge for the NWA world title. Fenton, meanwhile, was proving himself an important partner to Cliff Parker. According to Nevada, Fenton is regarded as the person most responsible for the Vancouver promotion's securing a TV deal in 1962 with Vancouver's CHAN-TV. As had been the case with the Owen and Elliott promotions further south in the Pacific Northwest, Nevada says "things started to take off" when the Parker-Fenton promotion got on television (45).

Fenton also finalized a professional relationship with Elliott, who was doing strong business in Seattle and other parts of Washington when Fenton joined the Parker promotion in Vancouver. The two promotions shared some talent, and the Vancouver office regularly promoted events in Washington cities such as Tacoma and Bellingham while hitting the major centers of Vancouver and Victoria along with smaller cities in British Columbia every week.

Though he was in demand elsewhere and frequently wrestled outside British Columbia, Kiniski was a key figure in establishing the popularity of Parker-Fenton's *All-Star Wrestling* program, which helped spike business in much the manner *Portland Wrestling* and *Northwest Championship Wrestling* had done in Oregon and Washington. Featured with Kiniski on *All-Star Wrestling* were fellow Vancouver transplant Don Leo Jonathan and, at various times, Whipper Billy Watson, Killer Kowalski, Bearcat Wright, Sweet Daddy Siki, and Haystack Calhoun—all of whom had enjoyed significant TV exposure in the U.S.—and other well-known grapplers, including Oregon's Tony Borne; John and Chris Tolos; Abdullah the Butcher; and the Fabulous Moolah, who held women's world titles for about two decades over the course of a long career and defended the NWA World Women's championship in British Columbia at times during the 1960s. Such wrestlers also appeared on programs taped for a time in Victoria and aimed at a fairly small regional viewership and not the much wider audience associated with *All-Star Wrestling.*

While Nevada reports that "Cliff Parker was, on paper, the promoter for the duration of this company's run" (46)—that is, until its sale to a new

promotional team in 1968—
Nevada and Silverstone agree
that Fenton was the de facto
promoter in the Vancouver
territory during most of the
1960s. Silverstone reports, in
Pig Farmer, that Fenton bought
out Parker's share of the company in 1961 (93). Comparing
the two major Vancouver promoters of the period, Don Leo
Jonathan, who made his permanent home in the Vancouver area during the Parker-
Fenton era, remembers Parker
as "a pretty square down-to-
earth guy." Fenton, meanwhile,
was "all business," Jonathan
says.

The company was suc-
cessful throughout the Parker-
Fenton era, but business
reached a new level when the
promotion's main attraction,
Kiniski, won the NWA World
Heavyweight championship
from Lou Thesz in St. Louis
on Jan. 7, 1966. As Nevada
reports, "Hosting the world
champion, the Vancouver

Don Leo Jonathan was an agile giant and one of
the outstanding wrestlers of his era. During the
early 1960s Jonathan, an avid outdoorsman,
made his permanent home in British Columbia.

booking office was thrust into the spotlight as Kiniski appeared at home to
turn away the challenges of Thesz, Don Leo Jonathan, John Tolos, Abdullah
the Butcher, and more." Nevada adds, "In addition to his marquee status,
Kiniski is believed to have been a [secret] partner in the promotion while
Rod Fenton was at the helm" (46).

It was not uncommon for a headlining wrestler to be a secret partner
in a wrestling promotion, and numerous other main eventers—including
familiar names like Thesz, Gagne, and Watson—had booked, run, or owned
wrestling promotions behind the scenes, or at least without knowledge of
their behind-the-scenes roles volunteered to the public.

While it has been suggested that Fenton did not pay his wrestlers nearly
as generously as Elliott did, some of the biggest names in wrestling passed

through the Vancouver territory in the mid to late 1960s. Even so, 1968 would spell the end for one more prominent wrestling promoter in the Pacific North-west. In Elliott's case, it was the loss of television that proved fatal, but as far as Fenton was concerned, all seemed well with his promotion and its televi-sion program when he called it quits in 1968.

As Silverstone reports in *Pig Farmer*, Fenton's wife had been diagnosed with terminal cancer and wanted to be buried in Arizona (93). As a result, Fenton sold his share in the Vancouver territory to Sandor Kovacs, described by Silverstone as having "paid more dues in professional wrestling than any-one I ever knew" (96). Kovacs had been active for many years as a wrestler and for a time as a booker (a "booker" determines matchups, winners, losers, champions, and a promotion's overall direction), and his would become the name most publicly associated with the "glory days" of Vancouver wrestling in the late 1960s through the late 1970s. Kovacs was not the only force behind Northwest Wrestling Promotions/All-Star Wrestling during the height of Vancouver wrestling, as he had two prominent secret partners: Gene Kiniski, still NWA champion at the time of Kovacs' takeover in 1968; and, perhaps surprisingly, Oregon promoter Don Owen.

8

Dominance of the NWA

While the "big three" of Don Owen in Portland, Harry Elliott in Seattle, and the Parker-Fenton tandem in Vancouver clearly ruled the roost when it came to Northwest wrestling in the late 1950s through most of the 1960s, there were other promoters jockeying or struggling to carve out or maintain small shares of the wrestling business in the region. This was not an easy task for competitors to the big three, as the Northwest was considered part of the NWA's backyard. Owen had been a member in good standing since 1951, Elliott in Washington was his associate, and Parker-Fenton ran a territory in which the NWA champion made regular title defenses and, when Kiniski held the title, made his professional home and even seemed to have a hand in running the territory. Simple economics and the politics of wrestling made the mounting of any viable opposition to the big three highly improbable.

Late wrestler Jim Wilson (no relation to Jim "Wilson" Londos) and coauthor Weldon T. Johnson report in their self-published book *Chokehold: Pro Wrestling's Real Mayhem Outside the Ring* that, when the organization was under investigation by the U.S. Justice Department for alleged antitrust breaches in the mid–1950s, "the NWA provided wrestlers for at least 500 regularly scheduled (usually, weekly) wrestling shows in the US and hundreds of *spot* shows" (244). According to Wilson and Johnson, longtime NWA president and St. Louis promoter Sam Muchnick "proudly told the Justice Department the NWA *controlled wrestlers for 95% of regular arena wrestling shows and all televised shows*" (244, italics original).

According to Wilson and Johnson, the NWA's "chokehold" on rival promoters involved NWA promoters' banding together in order to eliminate outside opposition. As far as the Northwest is concerned, *Chokehold* reports that the Justice Department determined "NWA promoters withheld wrestlers from *outlaw* promoter Ted Thye of Portland" (244–245). Thye, whose original promotional venture in Oregon had, by most accounts, been taken over by Herb Owen through apparently questionable means long before the NWA was established, was one of many promoters whose complaints led to the Justice

Department's investigation of the NWA. Thye's Oregon-based Western Athletic Club had promoted events and booked wrestlers in much of Oregon, Washington, and parts of British Columbia since the 1930s. Thye also promoted events in Australia on occasion.

Concerned about possible blacklisting of himself and wrestlers appearing on his shows, Thye occasionally communicated with NWA president Muchnick, and he applied unsuccessfully for membership—or, according to www.legacyofwrestling.com, withdrew his application—in 1951, the year Don Owen joined the organization. After Seattle's Bob Murray was admitted to the NWA the next year, www.legacyofwrestling.com says "the Pacific Northwest was completely blanketed by the NWA, and Thye was a confirmed independent." In his complaint, www.legacyofwrestling.com continues, "Thye told the DOJ [Department of Justice] that he was 'squeezed' out of all arenas in Oregon and Washington."

Thye and others opposing the NWA had a powerful ally in Thye's brother, Senator Edward Thye of Minnesota, formerly the state's governor, who, Silverstone reports in *Pig Farmer*, "complained to the Justice Department about the NWA's 'monopolistic' practices" (105). Once the Justice Department's investigation of the NWA was underway, the alliance essentially backed down—or, in Silverstone's words, "capitulated, to avoid stringent prosecution and penalties ... promising to be good thereafter" (105). The Justice Department investigation ended when the NWA removed from its bylaws rules formalizing promoters' exclusive right to their territories and calling for the blacklisting of wrestlers and independent promoters operating in opposition to NWA interests. According to www.kayfabememories.com, "the feds, happy with this, dropped their investigation of the NWA and its members."

Kayfabememories.com continues, "However, history has proven that nothing changed. While the NWA members agreed to remove the specific wording, they did a back room deal where they would all still recognize the dropped rules." As a result, running shows in opposition to the NWA remained difficult, and Thye—facing challenges from the Portland Boxing and Wrestling Commission as well as the NWA—did not remain in the wrestling business for long after the federal government dropped its investigation of the NWA's practices. When, as www.legacyofwrestling.com reports, the Department of Justice launched a 1958 inquiry into alleged monopolistic practices in Oregon and Washington aimed specifically at Don Owen and not the entire NWA, the FBI interviewed Thye before the Department of Justice's Antitrust Division determined that complaints against Owen were a local matter and not something the federal government should pursue. Thye essentially faded from the wrestling scene shortly after.

A few other independent promoters made serious efforts to run wrestling shows in the U.S. Northwest in the 1950s and 1960s. One such promoter, C.L. McPherson, formerly an assistant to Thye's ex-partner Virgil Hamlin, to Muchnick in St. Louis, and later, to Thye himself, tried running events in Bellingham in the early 1950s. According to www.legacyofwrestling.com, Thye blamed the NWA for opposing McPherson's efforts, bankrupting McPherson, and contributing to his suicide.

Also in the early 1950s, wrestling events were promoted in Pendleton, Oregon, by Jack and Maury Kennedy under the banner of "High Class Boxing and Wrestling." According to www.legacyofwrestling.com, "in October 1954, the Pendleton Recreation Hall, which was leased by the Kennedys for their sports events, was tremendously damaged by fire," and it appears this may have precipitated the demise of the Kennedys' small promotion, which was probably of little or no concern to the NWA.

In Victoria and Nanaimo, BC, Mike Bulat's Thunderbird Wrestling Promotions lasted just a few months in 1957, during which time the promotion seemed to coexist amicably with Parker's Vancouver promotion, which in the 1950s did not have formal ties to the NWA. The two promotions shared some talent, although Nevada notes that Bulat's cards in Victoria featured international attraction and Washington State native Johnny Valentine, who was not appearing in Vancouver. Nevada reports that Thunderbird Wrestling's premiere on Feb. 26, 1957, at the Victoria Ballroom, featured a young Reggie Siki, the future "Sweet Daddy" Siki, whose flamboyant character seemed to draw some inspiration from Gorgeous George. Siki had debuted as a wrestler in 1955 and already made a name in the Northwest by appearing frequently, sometimes in main events, around British Columbia, Washington, and Oregon. Nevada further reports that Vancouver promoter Parker took over Victoria wrestling in the summer of 1957, while Bulat went to work in Alberta as the Edmonton representative for Stu Hart's Big Time Wrestling (51–52).

The most intriguing opposition to one of the big three Northwest promoters of the late 1950s to late 1960s was a promotion that never got off the ground. The protagonist was Pacific Northwest ring veteran Kurt von Poppenheim, who had an interest in running events out of Portland.

As Wilson and Johnson report in *Chokehold,*

> Poppenheim worked as a top *heel* … for many years in the NWA's Pacific Northwest circuit with his blond crewcut and clipped goatee, a Prussian monocle and a ring robe decorated with the Iron Cross. He was a main event star and Pacific Coast champ in Portland, Seattle, Tacoma, and Bremerton. Then Poppenheim applied to the Portland … Boxing and Wrestling Commission in 1963 for a license to promote in Oregon…. The Portland Commission told Poppenheim it had authority to license whichever bookers and promoters it chose, and it had already chosen the NWA's Don Owen. The Owen-controlled Portland Commission said, "The issuance of a second wrestling matchmaker's license at this time would not be in the best interests of wrestling in the Portland area" [270–271].

Poppenheim proceeded to sue not only the Portland Boxing and Wrestling Commission but others, reports Silverstone in *Pig Farmer*, including the individual commission members, Don Owen, the NWA, and the Mount Hood Radio and Television Broadcasting Corporation, which carried Owen's *Portland Wrestling* (Silverstone, 260–261). Poppenheim lost his suit in the Circuit Court of Oregon, *Chokehold* reports, and all the way up to the Oregon and U.S. Supreme Courts (Wilson, 271). In all, litigation lasted eight years.

Silverstone, who spoke in person years later with Poppenheim about the latter's plans to promote wrestling in Oregon in the 1960s, concluded that "it was obvious that Kurt may have achieved success had he employed stronger attorneys to represent him" (261). According to Silverstone, on several occasions when Poppenheim lost an appeal, the court pointed out improprieties and suggested Poppenheim seek out better representation. Silverstone says, in *Pig Farmer*, "The representatives Kurt had defending him were inexperienced and never furnished the court with the information they had requested" (261).

Reportedly, Poppenheim was not intent simply on establishing a small alternative wrestling promotion in the Portland area. Kayfabememories.com, quoting Silverstone, suggests Poppenheim was working to line up major wrestling names in order to mount serious opposition to Owen and the NWA. Had he been successful in getting his operation off the ground, the history of professional wrestling in Oregon and the Northwest, especially in the 1960s, might have been vastly different. But as history stands, the late 1950s to late 1960s era was dominated in almost every way by the "big three": Owen in Oregon, Elliott in Washington, and Parker-Fenton in British Columbia.

9

All-Star Wrestling's Golden Age, 1968–1977

Prior to buying out Rod Fenton's share of the Vancouver wrestling promotion in 1968, Sandor Kovacs had a solid if unspectacular career in the wrestling business.

Kovacs, born in Hungary, immigrated to Canada as a child, living in several Ontario cities but primarily in St. Catharines, about a 90-minute drive from Toronto and 45 minutes from Buffalo, New York. According to Greg Oliver in a July 2, 2004, *SLAM! Wrestling* report following Kovacs' death, Kovacs knew no English when he arrived in Canada at about age 10, but "an introduction to Greco-Roman wrestling when [Kovacs was] in school in St. Catharines under coach Cliff Chilcott proved to be a universal translator."

Kovacs enlisted in the Royal Canadian Navy during World War II, and Oliver reports that the young officer was stationed in the relative safety of Halifax, Nova Scotia, thanks to his experience and interest in wrestling. Kovacs' wife Betty, Oliver reports, recalled years later that "[her husband's] commanding officer was intrigued by the wrestling bit, so he wanted to keep him there."

During his Navy service, Kovacs met Stu Hart, also in the Canadian Navy, and the meeting proved pivotal in Kovacs' life. According to Oliver, "Kovacs tried different work after the war ended, including working in an auto factory, and as a tool and [die] maker. But his mind drifted back to Hart and his determination to go to New York and make it as a pro wrestler. Kovacs followed his friend to the Big Apple, and took a room with Hart and an Englishman who would wrestle as Lord James Blears."

Kovacs made his professional wrestling debut on the U.S. East Coast in 1946, and there are reports of his having wrestled competitively against the likes of Hart, Blears, and other mid-card opponents in cities such as New York, Washington, Baltimore, and Philadelphia during the earliest part of his career. Within a year of his pro debut, Kovacs returned as a wrestler to

Canada, making appearances in Toronto. He went on to wrestle throughout the United States and Canada, and in 1950 Kovacs main-evented against Antonino Rocca in both New York and Chicago. Over the course of over two decades as a wrestler, Kovacs, normally on the light side at about 220 pounds, earned victories against some of wrestling's bigger names, including Hart, Blears, Danny McShain, Donn Lewin, Chris Tolos, Danny Dusek, Joe Blanchard, and future world champion Nick Bockwinkel. During his long career, Kovacs also faced or teamed with top names such as Guy Larose (the future Hans Schmidt), Reggie Lisowski (the future Crusher), Fred Blassie, Bearcat Wright, Killer Kowalski, Buddy Rogers, Fritz von Erich, Lou Thesz, and Northwest legends Stan Stasiak, Don Leo Jonathan, and Kovacs' future business partner Gene Kiniski.

Kovacs had some experience as a booker in Montreal and in Hart's Alberta territory before venturing to the Northwest in the 1960s. Although *SLAM! Wrestling* records that Kovacs appeared early in his career in Portland, Oregon, Kovacs was a relative newcomer to the Pacific Northwest when, in his early forties, he started wrestling in British Columbia in late 1962, often going back and forth between British Columbia and Alberta over the next few years. In Oliver's *SLAM!* report on Kovacs' life, Kovacs' widow Betty explains the couple's decision to settle in Vancouver for good in the mid–1960s: "We had a son, and he was turning school age, and we were still gypsying around … it was time to put this child in a regular school. So we arrived in Vancouver after doing a stint in Calgary. We arrived in Vancouver, and were really en route to Hawaii. We had been to Hawaii before we had this child and loved it. But I felt a little isolated on the island, so we decided to stay in Vancouver.

"About two years later," she continues, "the [Vancouver wrestling promotion] came up for sale. So we borrowed a bunch of money from the bank, and off we went. He [Kovacs] bought it with two partners," Kiniski and Don Owen.

Kovacs, who added to his experience as a booker during the Parker-Fenton era in Vancouver, had Parker's strong backing as his and Fenton's replacement at the helm of Vancouver wrestling. According to Nevada, Parker wrote a letter in late 1967 to the Vancouver Athletic Commission in which he "wholeheartedly endorsed Kovacs as the successor to carry the territory forward" (58).

Looking back decades later, Nevada suggests the role Owen played in the promotion is not altogether clear. But what *is* clear is that Owen often made the trip north from Portland and was publicly acknowledged as co-promoter, with Kovacs, of some wrestling shows in Vancouver. Nevada says, "Perhaps this can be attributed to the strong ties between the two booking offices and the regular exchange of talent between the two [centers]" (58).

While Owen is generally considered to have been a co-owner of the Northwest Wrestling Promotions/All-Star Wrestling promotion along with Kovacs— and Betty Kovacs' recollection seems to bear that out—Nevada reports, "Those active at that time such as Don Leo Jonathan, do not believe that Owen had a financial stake in Vancouver's wrestling operations" (58).

Kiniski's role in the Kovacs-era Vancouver promotion does not appear to have changed significantly from his role alongside Fenton, except that any doubt about his ownership stake during the Kovacs era is erased. During the apparently seamless transition from Fenton to Kovacs—no doubt in part because Kovacs had taken on administrative duties under Fenton—Kiniski remained the hometown-based world heavyweight champion who attracted a lot of major wrestling names and attention to All-Star Wrestling. Though Kiniski had numerous wrestling obligations throughout North America and abroad during his run as NWA champion from Jan. 7, 1966, to Feb. 11, 1969— nearly a year into the Kovacs era—he remained very active as a wrestler in Vancouver.

His ownership role with the promotion, however, was not acknowledged to the public, as was usually the case when big-name wrestlers had such double duties in wrestling companies. To the public, Kiniski was a wrestling star; Owen, largely unknown to the Vancouver public, was simply the promoter of another territory who featured some of the local wrestlers in his own Portland territory and sometimes co-promoted shows in the Vancouver territory; and Kovacs was the sole promoter of All-Star Wrestling.

Northwest Wrestling Promotions/All-Star Wrestling was a staunch NWA territory during the Kovacs-Kiniski-Owen era, especially at the start. During its first two years under Kovacs, the territory did not even have a local or regional heavyweight champion, which was a rarity among wrestling territories, some of which had more champions than the average fan could keep up with. The reason Vancouver was different at the start of the Kovacs era, of course, was the availability of Kiniski to defend the NWA title against top challengers in his home territory. That meant, in a sense, that Northwest/All-Star's territorial championship was represented by the top contender to Kiniski's NWA title—and an upcoming NWA title challenge in Vancouver— or even by the NWA belt itself.

Among Kiniski's top challengers in Vancouver were Don Leo Jonathan, Dutch Savage, John Tolos, Haystack Calhoun, Bearcat Wright, Abdullah the Butcher, Dean Higuchi, and Bobby Shane. All were credible challengers who had already done well in the wrestling business or, based largely on the strength of their showings in All-Star Wrestling, went on to major achievement elsewhere or seemed certain to do so.

Jonathan, a Utah native known as the "Mormon Giant," was the son of a wrestler described on the Professional Wrestling Hall of Fame and Museum website as the "hymn-singing, psalm-shouting Brother Jonathan, who tossed opponents from pillar to post while in the midst of a Bible quotation." During brief periods from the mid–1930s to the early 1940s, Brother Jonathan appeared in Washington, Oregon, and British Columbia on shows promoted by Thye's Western Athletic Club. On one those visits to the Northwest, "Brother" Jonathan Heaton was accompanied by his six-year-old son, the future international wrestling star Don Leo Jonathan, who, eight decades later, fondly recalls spending a night with his father in Saanich, BC, at the home of First Nations wrestling star Chief Thunderbird. Looking back on that late–1930s visit, Don Leo Jonathan recalls Thunderbird as a gracious host who "took good care of us."

Alberta native Gene Kiniski played professional football before being introduced to professional wrestling by Tucson promoter Rod Fenton in 1952. Nearly a decade later, the two would reunite in Vancouver, where Fenton promoted and Kiniski was a major attraction for much of his career and a co-owner of the regional wrestling promotion for well over a decade. From 1966 to 1969 Kiniski was the National Wrestling Alliance World Heavyweight champion, at the time generally considered the top wrestling title in the world.

After serving in the U.S. Navy, the younger Jonathan, still a teenager, debuted as a wrestler in 1950, often teaming with his father in California and Colorado during a period Jonathan recalls fondly, as he—like many children of traveling wrestlers from generations past—did not see a great deal of his father when he was growing up. Barely a year after his pro debut, Don Leo Jonathan was a name wrestler appearing on the U.S. East Coast, and in January of 1952 he wrestled for the first time in Madison Square Garden.

Throughout his career, Jonathan was a globetrotter who achieved success everywhere he wrestled. Perhaps best remembered for his ring encounters with Jean Ferré (later André the Giant) and Édouard Carpentier in Montreal, WWWF champions Bruno Sammartino and Pedro Morales in the U.S. Northeast, wrestler-promoter Shohei "Giant" Baba in Japan, and Kiniski, Jonathan was a skilled, powerful, agile 6'6", 300-pounder in an era when there were few wrestlers of that size. First wrestling in Vancouver in 1960, Jonathan put down permanent roots in the city a few years later not only because Vancouver was a prime wrestling center surrounded by abundant natural blessings but also because it was a convenient base from which to set out on his frequent air travels. "The polar routes saved a lot of time," he says. "In a few hours I could be in Europe. That's the biggest reason I moved here." While Jonathan became a fixture in the Northwest during the Parker-Fenton period and was already in his forties during most of the Kovacs era, he was a mainstay of the territory and a key reason for its success during the Kovacs years.

Dutch Savage was another name already well established—especially in the Pacific Northwest—at the start of the Kovacs era. Like Jonathan, Savage, who had wrestled around the U.S. for a few years prior to settling in the Northwest, had been a main eventer and tag team champion in British Columbia during the Fenton era. Savage is perhaps best remembered as a large, rugged wrestler who instituted the "coal miner's glove match," finished off opponents by jamming his thumb into their throats, and enjoyed a long run as one of the most popular wrestlers during the height of both the Portland and Vancouver territories.

Prior to emerging as a star singles wrestler in Vancouver, John Tolos was best known as a member of the "Canadian Wrecking Crew" tag team with his brother Chris. The Tolos Brothers were also known as the "Hamilton Wrecking Crew," in tribute to their hometown of Hamilton, Ontario, which spawned a surprising number of wrestlers who were prominent between the 1950s and 1970s and, as a result, has often been referred to as a "wrestling factory" of that era.

The Tolos Brothers won numerous championships in the 1950s and 1960s, including several versions of the world tag team championship and the WWWF United States tag title in the eastern U.S. When Chris ventured out as a singles wrestler mainly in the U.S. Midwest in the mid–1960s, John came to Vancouver and captured the regional Canadian Tag Team championship with new partners, most prominently Tony Borne. In late 1966 the Tolos Brothers reunited in British Columbia, and in 1967 they were the most successful tag team in Fenton's promotion.

Chris did not stay long in Vancouver, leaving around the time Kovacs took over. But during the first two years of the Kovacs era, John—then known by Jim Londos' old nickname, the "Golden Greek"—was very successful both as a singles and tag team wrestler, and was a familiar face on the *All-Star*

Wrestling television show. His interviews were strong, his arrogant character struck a chord, and his matches—often dominated by moves such as body slams, flying knee drops, and his "corkscrew" (where he simply rubbed his knuckle into an opponent's temple)—while perhaps unspectacular, were considered entertaining.

After becoming both one of the most despised and most popular wrestlers in the Northwest, in 1970 John Tolos packed his bags and went to Southern California, where he had wrestled earlier in his career. Tolos achieved his greatest success as a wrestler during his 1970s run in California. Recognized as the top heel in Los Angeles during the first half of the 1970s, Tolos feuded with fellow Los Angeles legends Fred Blassie and Mil Mascaras, and according to *Wrestling Observer Newsletter* editor Dave Meltzer, quoted by Claire Noland in a June 1, 2009, *Los Angeles Times* article following Tolos' death a few days earlier, "He played the role of an arrogant, good-looking, well-conditioned guy. He talked big…. He inflamed the crowd so much, he came off as a real superstar in L.A."

Tolos wrestled a few matches in Vancouver from 1971 to 1975 before returning in 1976 and briefly holding the promotion's heavyweight title. Over the course of his career, he wrestled in numerous territories, and after retiring as a wrestler in 1984, he resurfaced as a wrestling manager, most notably in the WWF. Still, Tolos is probably best remembered by veteran fans of Vancouver wrestling for his work during the early Kovacs era.

Haystack Calhoun, while not usually regarded as a serious contender for major wrestling championships, had been a popular attraction in several territories since making his wrestling debut in 1955. A Texas native, Calhoun, born William Calhoun, was a larger-than-life character—billed at over 600 pounds, though he usually weighed in the 400s—a straightforward, scuffling, no-nonsense country boy who, in fact, was known as "Country Boy Calhoun" before a demonstration of his strength—tossing bales of hay on the popular TV show *Art Linkletter's House Party*—earned him the nickname "Haystack," a moniker that stuck to the end of Calhoun's life and beyond—as Silverstone says, "His tombstone reads 'Haystack Calhoun.'"

Dressed in coverall shorts and a T-shirt, Calhoun played a bumpkin from Arkansas. As Steve Slagle reports on the Professional Wrestling Online Museum website (www.wrestlingmuseum.com), "With his trademark good-luck horseshoe chained to his neck, the barefooted hillbilly struck a [chord] with television's huge wrestling audience, many of whom still lived in rural areas of the country…. As charismatic as he was heavy, the mammoth Calhoun made a lasting impression on a huge percentage of the U.S. population, even those who did not necessarily follow professional wrestling," and parlayed his popularity into commercial endorsements and a role, as himself, in the popular 1962 film *Requiem for a Heavyweight* starring Hollywood heavyweights Anthony Quinn, Mickey Rooney, and Jackie Gleason. As a result of his considerable exposure and unforgettable persona, Calhoun, whose matches usually ended with a "big splash" onto his opponent, was one of the most sought-after and most-traveled wrestlers from the late 1950s through the 1970s.

Calhoun made several tours of the Pacific Northwest in the 1960s, appearing in main events in Oregon, Washington, and British Columbia. Twice—once in the Fenton era and once after Kovacs took over the promotion—he held the Canadian Tag Team championship with Don Leo Jonathan, and while based in Vancouver in 1968, Calhoun was a top contender for Kiniski's NWA Heavyweight title. After leaving the Northwest later that year and touring the United States for the next several years—during which time he won a share of the WWWF World Tag Team championship—Calhoun returned to Vancouver in 1974 for a brief, final run in the Northwest for one of the most memorable characters of the Kovacs era.

Bearcat Wright and Abdullah the Butcher also appeared in Vancouver during both the Fenton and Kovacs eras. Before wrestling throughout the Northwest in the 1960s, Wright was a well-established wrestler who, much like Bobo Brazil and Sweet Daddy Siki, had crossed the color barrier and achieved considerable television exposure and success in the United States. After challenging Kiniski for the NWA title in Vancouver and having multiple tag team title runs in both the Fenton and Owen promotions, Wright returned to British Columbia for a brief though successful stay in the early 1970s.

Meanwhile, Abdullah the Butcher, billed as a Sudanese madman but actually played by an African Canadian from Windsor, Ontario, was still a fairly young wrestler on the rise when he was an attraction for both Fenton and Kovacs in the late 1960s. From Vancouver, where he was a two-time tag team champion and an NWA title challenger, Abdullah went on to become one of wrestling's major stars and top heels over the next two decades, playing a crazed 400-pounder who was as nasty as they came, never spoke English in public, and loved to carve his opponents' faces with a fork he kept hidden in his trunks. It was a simple formula, but it propelled Larry "Abdullah the Butcher" Shreve—who for many years was a restaurateur in Atlanta—to great success across the United States and Canada and to legendary status in Japan.

Dean Higuchi was a popular and well-respected wrestler throughout the Northwest during most of the 1960s, the early 1970s, briefly in the mid–1970s, and then, late in his career, from 1981 to 1983, after the Kovacs-Kiniski-Owen era in Vancouver was over. During periods when Higuchi was not wrestling in the Northwest, he was a successful wrestler in his native Hawaii and in key territories in Texas, Georgia, and Northern California, but he gained most of his visibility as a wrestler during a two-year run in the

WWWF, where as Dean Ho he held a share of the tag team championship for six months in 1973–1974.

Higuchi was a competitive bodybuilder and gym owner in Honolulu, and wrestlers using his gym influenced his decision to pursue a career in wrestling. According to Steven Johnson at the *SLAM! Wrestling* website, Higuchi's gym "became a regular stop for wrestlers passing through the area on the way to Japan."

One of those wrestlers was Dick "The Destroyer" Beyer, one of the biggest wrestling stars of the 1960s in the United States and, especially, Japan. From 1963 to 1965 the Destroyer was a top star in Pacific Northwest Wrestling, holding both the territory's heavyweight and tag team titles more than once during that period. According to Johnson, Beyer was instrumental in training Higuchi to be a wrestler, and Higuchi concurs, saying, "I owe my experiences to him. The guy was great, showed me everything and then some."

As a newcomer to wrestling in the early 1960s, Higuchi was a regular performer in Portland, Seattle, and smaller cities in the U.S. Northwest. During his rookie year, he had his share of losses but earned victories over some well-known wrestlers, including Pat Patterson, Mad Dog Vachon, and Kurt von Poppenheim. Higuchi spent the first six years of his career wrestling mainly in the U.S. Northwest and Hawaii before coming to Vancouver in 1968 and settling in the top mix of wrestlers in Kovacs' promotion for most of the next five years.

In an interview in the Dec. 24, 2010, edition of suburban Vancouver newspaper *Langley Today*, Higuchi says meeting Sandor Kovacs in Honolulu led to his start as a wrestler in the Pacific Northwest. Higuchi says, "He brought me to Portland, Oregon, where I started wrestling on the mainland, which [led] me to Vancouver, which is the area Sandor promoted."

Though other reports show Higuchi's career getting underway in 1962, Higuchi tells interviewer David Murray in *Langley Today* that he debuted in Honolulu in 1956. While other reports indicate Higuchi was born between 1938 and 1940 and would have been only 15 to 18 years old in 1956, Higuchi states in the *Langley Today* interview that he was nine years old when Pearl Harbor was bombed near his Hawaiian home. In the interview, Higuchi says that after the bombing, his father "made our whole family stay in the same room for over six months."

Depending on which report is accurate, Higuchi was either about 30 or well into his mid-thirties when he hit his stride as one of the top wrestlers in British Columbia in the late 1960s. With an arsenal including karate chops and power moves such as bear hugs, Higuchi finished off most of his opponents with a standing full nelson. Occasionally, he gave power demonstrations on *All-Star Wrestling*, and he introduced the "judo jacket match" to *All-Star Wrestling* viewers and live fans in British Columbia. In the early years of

Kovacs' Northwest Wrestling Promotions/All-Star Wrestling, Higuchi was a top local challenger for the NWA title, a four-time co-holder of the regional NWA Canadian Tag Team title, and one of the most popular attractions in the territory.

Bobby Shane's story was altogether different. Born in St. Louis in 1945, Shane debuted as a wrestler in the mid–1960s, wrestled briefly in the Northwest, traveled the central and southern U.S., and then resurfaced in Vancouver in 1968. While he never held a title in the Pacific Northwest, Shane won local or regional championships about 20 times during his nine-year career.

In Vancouver, Shane, on the smallish side for a wrestler, often played the role of a sympathetic, undersized, inexperienced, seemingly overmatched youngster going up against a much larger and rougher opponent such as Kiniski, Stan Stasiak, or Abdullah. It was a formula that worked well in Vancouver, though in other areas Shane would more often play a sneaky, arrogant heel who for a time claimed to be the "king of wrestling," a role Jerry Lawler would later bring to a national and international WWF/WWE audience. Shane was especially successful in the southeastern United States, where he won numerous titles from 1967 to 1973.

Shane was only 29 when the small plane he was aboard with several other wrestlers crashed into Tampa Bay on Feb. 20, 1975. The plane was en route from Miami, where Shane had wrestled the night before, to Tampa, and Shane was the only wrestler to die in the crash.

As a result, Shane has long been considered one of the great "what if...?" characters in wrestling. Future multi-time world heavyweight champion Ric Flair went down in a small plane crash with fellow wrestlers later the same year as Shane's crash, recovered from serious injuries, and went on to become one of the most storied wrestlers in history. It has been pointed out that Shane, whose career was on a similar trajectory to Flair's at the time of his crash, might also have risen to the top of the wrestling world had he been given the opportunity. In any event, while Shane's association with wrestling in the Pacific Northwest did not last long, he is remembered as an engaging, entertaining performer. Shane is also acknowledged in Silverstone's *Pig Farmer* (63–71) as a friend and influence who helped prepare Silverstone to achieve his dream of running a wrestling territory in Washington State, which Silverstone would go on to do from 1973 to 1975.

Challenges to Kiniski's NWA World Heavyweight championship by Jonathan, Savage, John Tolos, Higuchi, and other top regional contenders were major attractions during the early part of the Kovacs era, as the NWA title was considered a holy grail to wrestlers and fans in the territory. With the NWA champion—a part-owner of the promotion—based primarily in Vancouver, fans in British Columbia enjoyed more than their share of NWA title defenses during Kiniski's reign. But after Kiniski stepped down as NWA champion—losing the title in Florida to Dory Funk, Jr., on Feb. 11, 1969—a void in the promotion became apparent. While Funk had wrestled briefly in British Columbia about five years earlier, he had no other connection to the territory, and Vancouver reverted to being just one of many stops on the NWA champion's schedule, which meant far fewer NWA title defenses would be taking place in the territory. To pick up the slack and ensure the promotion maintained a competitive edge, Kovacs and his partners created the NWA Pacific Coast Heavyweight title—the top singles title in the promotion—in February of 1970. While the Fenton and Kovacs promotions had been without a regional singles title for years—since regional titles held by Poppenheim and Kiniski were retired in 1958 and 1963—nearly every other wrestling territory of note had long had its own heavyweight champion, if not several at a time. Owen's Portland territory had long been based on his wrestlers' quest and competition for the NWA Pacific Northwest Heavyweight title, which since its inception in 1957 had been held by big-name wrestlers in the territory and a few national or international stars such as Mad Dog Vachon, Nick Bockwinkel, The Destroyer, and Pat Patterson.

Among the top regional names in Oregon in the late 1960s and early 1970s was Lonnie Mayne, an oddball character who started out in Oregon as a heel but later developed into one of the Owen territory's most beloved wrestlers. Since making his Oregon debut in 1966, Mayne had already held the NWA Pacific Northwest Heavyweight title eight times when Kovacs, Owen, and Kiniski made the call to establish the new NWA Pacific Coast Heavyweight title in Vancouver. A proven commodity with championship credentials, Mayne was brought into Vancouver on Feb. 9, 1970, to defend the new Pacific Coast title—which he had never actually won in the ring—against top Vancouver contender Mark Lewin.

Lewin, though only 32, had already enjoyed a very successful wrestling career dating back to his 1953 debut at age 16. According to Mike Mooneyham in the Feb. 8, 2014, *Charleston Post and Courier*, Lewin says he "was drawn to the profession like a magnet."

A native of Buffalo, New York, with two brothers who also wrestled professionally, Lewin first made his name as a tag team wrestler, teaming with brother Donn to win titles in Maryland and Georgia in 1956 and 1957. In 1958 Mark Lewin formed one of the most successful tag teams in the United States with veteran Don Curtis, and from 1958 to 1964 the Lewin-Curtis team appeared in major arenas and won major championships in the eastern and southeastern United States, in the process beating such big-name teams as the Graham Brothers, Eddie and Jerry; Dick the Bruiser and Hans Schmidt; and the Fabulous Kangaroos, a well-traveled, highly regarded team that would hold the NWA Canadian Tag Team championship in Vancouver several times in 1964 and 1965. Lewin also had success as a singles wrestler during his years teaming with Curtis, and challenged for the NWA World Heavyweight title several times in 1963 and 1964.

Before the Lewin-Curtis team won its final championship in late 1963, Lewin had a run as the NWA Texas Heavyweight champion, defeating Pepper Gomez, a popular wrestler who had held titles in Vancouver between 1953 and 1955. After dissolving his partnership with Curtis, Lewin, billed as a master of the sleeper hold, focused primarily on his singles career, though he also went on to hold tag team titles in California, Toronto, Vancouver, Texas, Australia, and New Zealand. Lewin held numerous regional singles championships over the course of a career spanning well over three decades. Perhaps the pinnacle of his singles career was a 1966 victory in Los Angeles over Lou Thesz for the regional WWA World Heavyweight championship. Mooneyham reports, in

Lonnie Mayne's success as a wrestler in the U.S. Northwest played into his helping establish All-Star Wrestling's new Pacific Coast title in 1970. Before Mayne's loss to Mark Lewin set up Lewin as All-Star Wrestling's new heavyweight champion, the promotion had not recognized a regional singles champion for several years. Following the Feb. 9, 1970, Mayne–Lewin meeting in Vancouver, the NWA Pacific Coast Heavyweight title would be traded over the next several years among top regional contenders including Gene Kiniski, Don Leo Jonathan, Bulldog Bob Brown, Steven Little Bear, and Lewin.

the *Post and Courier,* that Lewin defended the WWA title several months later against South Korea's all-time wrestling legend, Kintaro Oki [Kim Il], before a reported crowd of 48,000 in Seoul.

Lewin's greatest success was in Australia and New Zealand, where he was a megastar both before and after his early–1970s run with All-Star Wrestling. Australia in particular was a hotbed of professional wrestling beginning in 1964 under promoters Jim Barnett and Johnny Doyle. Doyle, the ex-California promoter whose father had been a publisher of the *Seattle Post-Intelligencer,* had entered into a partnership with Barnett in 1959, establishing a wrestling territory covering such far-flung cities as Detroit, Indianapolis, Minneapolis, Denver, and San Francisco. In 1964 Barnett and Doyle saw new opportunity and shifted their base of operations to Australia. Lewin followed and soon became a superstar in Australia, facing opponents such as Killer Kowalski, Mitsu Arakawa, King Curtis Iaukea, and Spiros Arion. By 1966 Lewin held both the IWA (Australia) World Heavyweight and World Tag Team titles, and for the next seven years he traveled between Australia and North America, winning multiple championships on both continents.

Lewin's background made him a legitimate choice to hold the NWA Pacific Coast title in 1970, and he took the title from Mayne in Vancouver on Feb. 9. Lewin dropped the title two months later before regaining it in January of 1972. In the meantime, he won tag team titles in Vancouver and, several times, in Australia.

After Kiniski defeated Lewin for the Pacific Coast championship on April 13, 1970, losing the title in turn to Jonathan, next in line was another memorable character of the Kovacs-Kiniski-Owen era in Bulldog Bob Brown.

Though Brown, a Manitoba native, never reached the professional heights Kiniski, Jonathan, or Lewin did, he was a tough wrestler who amassed over 70 local or regional titles over the course of a long career, achieving his most notable success in the Vancouver, Kansas City, and Canadian Maritime territories. In Vancouver, Brown won the Pacific Coast title each year from 1970 to 1972, and from 1969 to 1972 he held the promotion's tag team title eight times with partners Savage, Kiniski, and John Quinn, a native of Hamilton, Ontario.

Without a doubt, Brown was one of All-Star Wrestling's most colorful characters. Nevada reports, in *Wrestling in the Canadian West,* that Brown, during his first two years on the West Coast, "was fined by the Vancouver Athletic Commission a reported 17 times for various infractions of the established rules and regulations. In 1970 he found himself in serious hot water for punching a fan that was alleged to have burned him with a cigar. The drama played out for weeks before a fine was levied and Brown returned to action" (58).

The only wrestler other than Mayne, Lewin, Kiniski, Jonathan, or Brown to hold the Pacific Coast title between 1970 and 1972 was Vince "Steven Little Bear" Bryant, a Texas native who had spent about a decade wrestling mainly in Georgia, Tennessee, Missouri, and California prior to arriving in Vancouver in early 1970. During the early years of his career, Bryant, whose brother

Richard Bryant also wrestled for a time as a Native North American (Chief Little Eagle), wrestled at times under his real name. He also wrestled as Emil Bryant and, presumably in a career move that ultimately led to his 1970 move to Vancouver, as Steve Kovacs, tag team partner of Sandor Kovacs when the two wrestled in Tennessee from 1961 to 1962. Bryant continued to use the Kovacs name after splitting from Sandor, sometimes shortening it to Kovac, and enjoyed moderate success through the remainder of the 1960s.

Bryant first tried out the Steven Little Bear persona during a brief stay in Stampede Wrestling in late 1969. He continued to have moderate success while with Stampede Wrestling, splitting wins with other heavyweights in the promotion. Then, before having much chance to move up the ladder in Calgary, Bryant/Little Bear rejoined Sandor Kovacs in Vancouver in early 1970.

Bryant's career reached its pinnacle in Vancouver. As Steven Little Bear, billed as a Native Canadian from the Caughnawaga (Kahnawake) reserve in Québec, Bryant quickly ascended to the top mix of wrestlers in Vancouver, regularly facing opponents like Kiniski, Brown, and Quinn. Little Bear earned his first All-Star Wrestling championship, the Canadian Tag Team title, with Jonathan on Nov. 9, 1970.

In all, Steven Little Bear spent four years in Vancouver, capturing numerous titles from 1970 to 1973. Six weeks after losing his first Canadian Tag Team championship in February of 1971, he regained the championship with Higuchi as his partner. From 1970 to 1973 Little Bear held the tag title eight times with partners Jonathan, Higuchi, Lewin, and Savage. His most successful pairing was with Savage, as the team held the Canadian Tag Team title four times in 1972–1973. During the early 1970s, the title was frequently bounced around between teams consisting of the promotion's main-event core of Kiniski, Brown, Jonathan, Savage, Higuchi, Quinn, and Little Bear, and during that period, Little Bear held a share of the Canadian Tag Team championship more times than anyone else.

Little Bear was also a successful singles wrestler throughout his stay in the Northwest. Twice, he won the Pacific Coast title, defeating two-time Pacific Coast champion Kiniski in July of 1971 and three-time champion Brown in May of 1972. Little Bear also appeared regularly in Oregon while working for All-Star Wrestling. He was a main event wrestler in Portland, making appearances around the Owen circuit from 1970 through 1973 and having a brief run with the Pacific Northwest title in November of 1972. Though his Native North American gimmick, complete with war dances and tomahawk chops, would seem dated to many present-day wrestling fans, Vince Bryant as Steven Little Bear was a strong, credible performer during the height of Northwest Wrestling Promotions/All-Star Wrestling in the early 1970s.

After leaving the Northwest in early 1974, Bryant returned to Tennessee, appearing as Steve Kovac and often participating in main events, including a January 1975 loss to NWA champion Jack Brisco that drew over 10,000 fans. After wrestling as Steve Kovacs in Virginia and the Carolinas in 1977, Bryant, later that year, returned to his most successful persona, Steven Little Bear. As Little Bear, he performed successfully in Georgia and the New Orleans-based Mid-South promotion until retiring from the ring in the early 1980s.

While wrestlers such as Kiniski, Jonathan, Brown, Higuchi, Quinn, Savage, and Little Bear represented the core of main eventers in the British Columbia territory during the Kovacs-Kiniski-Owen era, other key wrestlers came into the territory for memorable stays lasting anywhere from a few weeks to a few years.

Among the most widely known wrestlers to make a stop in British Columbia in the early 1970s was Oreal "Ivan Koloff" Perras, who showed up in All-Star Wrestling in mid–1971 after a successful run as a headliner on the U.S. East Coast capped off by a victory over longtime WWWF Heavyweight champion Bruno Sammartino and a brief run as WWWF titleholder. Though Perras was Canadian, "Ivan Koloff" was a methodical Russian strongman during the height of the Cold War; and while some fans in British Columbia drew a connection between Koloff and "Irish" Red McNulty—Perras' character when he was an undercard wrestler in British Columbia in 1966 and 1967—Koloff formed a powerful team with Kiniski and had a memorable three-month stay in the territory in 1971 before going on to enjoy many more years of success in a variety of wrestling promotions.

The following year saw the arrival of a limited but entertaining grappler named Mike Davis, who had debuted as a wrestler five years before landing in All-Star Wrestling in 1972. Davis, a hefty bruiser who weighed nearly 300 pounds, wrestled during the early part of his career in the U.S. Midwest but mainly in the Florida-Georgia area, often under a mask as the Spoiler or the "Big O."

After losing his mask in a stipulation match in Florida, Davis became Beautiful Brutus, a role he may have had visions of when he appeared near the start of his career in California as Mighty Brutus. He was a fairly well-traveled wrestler with some championship experience when—as a bald, beefy brawler looking much older than his 27 years—he first appeared in the Northwest, stopping briefly in Oregon and capturing the NWA Pacific Northwest Tag Team championship as Tony Borne's partner, the Skull, before putting together an impressive resume in Vancouver.

Wrestling as the Brute—a brash, comedic, sometimes philosophizing bully noted for off-the-wall interviews, a high-pitched laugh, and a finishing move called the "pulverizer," which mixed elements of a powerslam and a splash—Davis was a hit in Vancouver from the start. In 1973–1974 the Brute held the Pacific Coast Heavyweight title twice and the Canadian Tag Team championship three times, but he is most remembered in the Northwest for his eccentric persona and entertaining interviews, much as is the case with Lonnie Mayne. Davis played the maniacal Brute so convincingly that many fans of 1970s Vancouver wrestling would undoubtedly be surprised to know Davis was a graduate of Purdue University who, according to a Dec. 22, 2000, article by Ric Russo in the *Orlando Sentinel,* "originally thought about becoming a lawyer and even attended law school [until] his love for professional wrestling kept detouring his other career goals." Fans of the Brute's interviews would also be surprised if they knew, as Jodie Tillman reports in the Sept. 1, 2011, *Tampa Bay Times,* that Davis had a speech impediment, "one that made his face grimace, his head jerk, his words stutter." But as Davis recounts in the same report, "You hand me a microphone and put me on television and oh, boy, could I talk."

After two years in the Vancouver territory, the Brute moved south to California, where he often teamed with Mayne. In January of 1975, the Brute won the San Francisco version of the NWA United States Heavyweight championship from Peter Maivia, grandfather of 1990s/2000s WWF/WWE wrestling champion-turned-Hollywood actor Dwayne "The Rock" Johnson. Six months later, Mike Davis joined the WWWF, where he was given the name Bugsy McGraw and continued to act like a crazed version of the Three Stooges' Curly who, the Sept. 1, 2011, *Tampa Bay Times* article says, "laughed like a ticklish serial killer." One of McGraw's first big victories in the WWWF was in Philadelphia over Dean Ho, the former Dean Higuchi.

As Bugsy McGraw, Davis had successful runs in the WWWF and several southern and eastern NWA territories, and he also wrestled internationally, most notably in Australia and Japan. During the second half of his long career, Davis often played the role of a babyface. After his career started slowing down in the late 1980s, he continued making wrestling appearances for several more years but later settled into a job as a nurse at Tampa General Hospital in Florida.

John Hill of Hamilton, Ontario, was a journeyman wrestler with periods of success and some championship experience prior to his arrival in Vancouver in 1973. Appearing as Guy Hill and Guy Miller, Hill spent the first years of his career mainly in Georgia, Alabama, the Carolinas, and the U.S. Midwest, enjoying moderate success and capturing a couple of regional titles. In 1964 he began wrestling in Indiana, where he made his home for many years. As a mid-carder and sometimes main eventer appearing mainly in the Midwest and in the Toronto area as Guy Mitchell, the Assassin, Guy Heenan, and the Stomper, Hill won several regional tag team championships between the mid–1960s and his 1973 arrival in Vancouver. As Lewin did, Hill also wrestled for the popular World Championship Wrestling promotion in Australia (no connection to the later Atlanta-based World Championship Wrestling) during the mid–1960s, once winning that promotion's IWA World Heavyweight title, as the Destroyer—namesake of Dick Beyer's alter ego—from Bearcat Wright.

Hill, described as "a character actor of a wrestler" in a March 12, 2010, *SLAM! Wrestling* report the day after his death, sometimes wrestled twice on the same show during the first decade of his career—once as a heel under a mask and once as a fan favorite without a mask. According to Steven Johnson, author of the *SLAM!* article, Hill, after witnessing a fan stabbing and critically injuring heel wrestler Pedro Zapata in Alabama in 1962, decided he would wear a mask when called on to wrestle as a bad guy, presumably because it would be safer if he concealed his identity. When Hill first appeared in Vancouver in late 1973, it was under a mask as a villain, Mr. X.

Mr. X was promptly placed in the upper mix of wrestlers in Vancouver, often teaming with the likes of Kiniski, the Brute, and Buck Ramstead, who wrestled for several years as a mid-card babyface and heel in British Columbia and also made appearances in Oregon from 1972 to 1975 and then again when his career was winding down in 1984. Shortly after Mr. X's debut, he and Ramstead won the Canadian Tag Team championship, and by mid–1974 Mr. X held the tag championship two more times with partners Kiniski and the Brute. During that same period of time—on April 1, 1974—Mr. X also captured the Pacific Coast Heavyweight title from respected Winnipeg grappler George Gordienko, who wrestled as Flash Gordon during his 1974 run in Vancouver. During a successful six-month reign as the territory's heavyweight champion—simultaneously holding a share of the tag team title during much of that reign—Mr. X turned back an impressive list of challengers, including the likes of Kiniski, Jonathan, Savage, and John Tolos. Mr. X also challenged NWA World Heavyweight champion Jack Brisco in a Vancouver main event during the middle of X's reign, in July of 1974.

Unmasked after losing the Pacific Coast title to Kiniski in mid–October, Hill became babyface Guy Mitchell and enjoyed a strong end to 1974. Even without the territory's heavyweight title, Mitchell challenged again for Brisco's NWA title in November, and he established himself as the top contender for Kiniski's Pacific Coast championship before recapturing the title on Jan. 20, 1975. Mitchell was a co-holder of the tag team title during part of his second Pacific Coast championship reign, and then, two months after losing the heavyweight title to Jonathan, Mitchell won a share of the Canadian Tag Team title for the fifth time.

While Hill's peak period in Vancouver was 1974–1975, Guy Mitchell remained a strong presence in the Vancouver territory through the remainder of the Kovacs era, winning many of his matches in a steady, workmanlike manner climaxed by a sleeper hold finish. During that period Hill also wrestled in other territories—particularly Dick the Bruiser's WWA in Indiana,

Verne Gagne's AWA, and Sam Muchnick's St. Louis territory—adding to his list of characters Mad Man Mitchell and the masked Strangler. Despite his considerable travels, Guy Mitchell took the Pacific Coast title from Kiniski on March 3, 1977, and he was the first wrestler to capture All-Star Wrestling's major singles title during the Tomko era.

After leaving the Northwest permanently in 1978, Hill adopted—or revisited, as he had occasionally played the role in previous years—the best-known character of his career when he joined the newly named World Wrestling Federation (WWF) as Jerry Valiant, one of the blond-haired Valiant Brothers, and captured the WWF Tag Team championship with "brother" Johnny on March 6, 1979. After losing that title seven months later, Hill continued wrestling for several more years as Jerry Valiant, both in the WWF and in other territories. He also dusted off the Guy Mitchell name on occasion, most notably in Tennessee and Japan. After his wrestling days wound down in the mid-eighties, Hill owned a landscaping company in Indiana and, according to the *SLAM!* report following his death, played Santa Claus for several years at a mall in Indianapolis.

Bill Lehman was a relative latecomer to professional wrestling, arriving in Vancouver near the beginning of 1975 at age 36 with barely a year of matches under his belt. Formerly a star football and tennis player at a small Lutheran college in Texas, Lehman played a season of Canadian pro football with the Saskatchewan Roughriders after graduating from college in 1960. After leaving the Roughriders, Lehman spent eight years as a player—including six as a player/assistant coach—for the San Antonio Toros of the Continental Football League. While in San Antonio, Lehman was trained in professional wrestling by Joe Blanchard, also an ex-pro footballer in Canada, who had a long career in wrestling both before and after settling in the 1960s in San Antonio, where he took over the local wrestling promotion and ran it successfully until the early 1980s.

Lehman debuted as a wrestler in Texas in 1973 and spent the earliest part of his wrestling career mainly in the southern U.S. Most often wrestling as Siegfried Stanke, one of a long line of bald, roughhousing German heels following in the footsteps of Hans Schmidt, Lehman was successful almost from the outset, capturing several regional tag team championships and the NWA Western States Heavyweight championship in 1974.

Changing his ring name slightly to Siegfried Steinke after arriving in Vancouver at the start of 1975, Lehman was placed in the top mix of wrestlers almost immediately, earning his share of victories with an arsenal featuring elbow drops, knee drops, and the "iron grip" or "claw" hold associated with many German wrestling characters over the years. By early May, Steinke held the Pacific Coast Heavyweight title following a victory in Vancouver over Jonathan. An even greater highlight of Steinke's career perhaps came a week later, on May 12, 1975, when he challenged Jack Brisco, though unsuccessfully, for the NWA title.

Steinke stayed in Vancouver for only about two years during the Kovacs era—making appearances in Oregon and Washington as well during that time—but remains a memorable face, presence, and interview practitioner from All-Star Wrestling's heyday in the 1970s. Leaving Vancouver after adding four tag team championship runs to his resume, Lehman wrestled successfully as Siegfried Stanke in Texas, Oklahoma, Kansas City, and Florida before having another successful, though even shorter, run in Vancouver when the Kovacs era was over. After retiring from the ring, Lehman coached high school football in Texas for over 20 years and then returned to his alma mater, Texas Lutheran University, where he coached football and tennis. From 2002 to 2010 Lehman was TLU's head coach in men's and women's tennis. He passed away in 2012.

The long list of Vancouver wrestling characters and personalities during the heyday of All-Star Wrestling spans the whole range associated with that era of wrestling. There were ethnic characters and stereotypes across the board: sneaky Japanese heels, perhaps best portrayed by Kinji Shibuya, a major star in California, and Mr. Saito, a member of the 1964 Japanese Olympic freestyle wrestling team; a representative of British Columbia's South Asian population in Tiger Jeet Singh, best remembered as an Asian Indian wrestling legend in Toronto, where he played a hero, and Japan, where he played a sword-wielding lunatic; intellectual or pseudo-intellectual braggarts such as former Olympian and collegiate wrestling star Dale Lewis and former Canadian Football League defensive tackle and player representative Mike Webster; super-super heavyweights Calhoun and Man Mountain Mike, whose "big splashes" usually spelled the end for opponents; and a revolving-door cast including cowboys, Indians, outlaws, Italian heroes, and strongmen to support the main players such as Kiniski, Jonathan, Savage, and Quinn.

Steady, proficient "workers" like Duncan McTavish, known in Vancouver as the Man of 1,000 Holds—who, while never a main event star, had wrestled in Madison Square Garden before coming to the Northwest—and the acrobatic Erich Froelich—a German native who was anything but a heel during his years mainly as a preliminary wrestler in Vancouver—played an important part in filling out hundreds of wrestling shows in Vancouver, Victoria, and smaller cities during the height of All-Star Wrestling. Other key preliminary wrestlers during the Kovacs era included Jack Bence, a solid wrestler who never held a title during a long career that took him to many territories; Fred Barron, a familiar wrestler throughout the Northwest dating back to the early 1960s; Bad Boy Shields, who later became a high-profile preliminary wrestler in the AWA as the "wrestling truck driver" Bull Bullinski; Igor Volkoff, whose profile gradually rose in Vancouver, reaching its peak after the Kovacs era ended; and Sailor White, a 300-pound, tattooed Newfoundlander who, nearly a decade after an inauspicious stay in British Columbia, worked his way up to becoming a tag team champion in the WWF.

Kovacs' Northwest Wrestling Promotions/All-Star Wrestling drew not only a good share of established wrestlers to Vancouver in the late 1960s through much of the 1970s but also many young prospects hoping to establish their names and credentials in the wrestling business. Of the many young or beginning wrestlers who passed through the Vancouver territory during the Kovacs-Kiniski-Owen era, a few names clearly stand out.

Don Muraco was a well-built 20-year-old Hawaiian who was just starting in the wrestling business when he touched down in Vancouver in the spring of 1970. Introduced to All-Star Wrestling fans as Don Morrow, he was a hit from the start and a natural in the ring. Wrestling as a babyface, Morrow held his own against a variety of ring veterans in Vancouver, and he also appeared regularly for Owen's Portland promotion during his stay in the Northwest. Though he left the Pacific Northwest after just four months, Morrow, during that brief time, gave every indication that he was headed for a long and successful career.

Muraco used the strength of his showings in the Northwest as a springboard to a brief but successful stay in Southern California, as Don Muraco, and then, early in 1971 at age 21, returned to Hawaii, compiling a strong winning record and sharing the ring with accomplished wrestlers including Lonnie Mayne, Bearcat Wright, and Verne Gagne. Later that year Muraco surfaced in the AWA, where several of his early wins were against Jack Bence, who had been one of his first opponents in Vancouver. Muraco quickly moved up to the star level in the AWA before returning to the Northwest and wrestling briefly in Oregon in 1972 and 1973. From there he went on to achieve success and win titles in several U.S. territories from coast to coast, most often as a tough, brash heel. His greatest success came in the 1980s as a roughhousing wrestler applying his reverse piledriver and a variety of power moves to opponent after opponent—in the process, capturing the WWF Intercontinental Championship twice, remaining in the top mix of WWF wrestlers for several years, and establishing his position as one of the most successful wrestlers of the 1980s.

Larry Whistler, a young man trained by East Coast legend Bruno Sammartino, had only several months' match experience—as Larry Zbyszko, in tribute to early pro wrestling superstar Stanislaus Zbyszko—when he arrived in Vancouver in the spring of 1973. Though Whistler, like Muraco, stayed in the Vancouver territory only a few months, he too established a good babyface rapport with fans and gave signs that an excellent career was underway.

Over the course of a lengthy career, Whistler—wrestling exclusively as Larry Zbyszko after leaving the Northwest in the fall of 1973—won titles in several major U.S. wrestling companies. Most notably, he twice held the AWA World Heavyweight championship, in 1989 and 1990. Zbyszko, like Muraco, spent most of his career wrestling as a heel, with the pivotal moment of Zbyszko's career coming in 1980 when he smashed a chair over his trainer and mentor Sammartino to set up a wrestling feud leading to a match in a steel cage at New York's Shea Stadium.

During parts of 1974 and 1975, Bob Remus, a relative newcomer to wrestling who had been trained by Verne Gagne, often wrestled in the middle of cards in the All-Star territory. Remus, in his mid-twenties and tipping the scales at nearly 300 pounds, had moderate popularity and middling success in British Columbia, winning a few big matches but falling short of the top tier in the promotion. He also appeared in Oregon and Washington, as the heel "Beautiful" Bob Remus, for Owen's Pacific Northwest Wrestling during his stay in the Northwest.

Remus, employing several ring names, wrestled in various territories through the remainder of the 1970s, winning several regional championships along the way. But his career rose to a new level in 1980, when he hit upon the persona that would make him one of the most recognized wrestling stars of his day.

As the ultrapatriotic Sergeant Slaughter, Remus, like Zbyszko, achieved notable success in the WWF, the AWA, and the NWA's Carolina-based Jim Crockett Promotions. Often vanquishing hated foreign menaces or traitorous Americans with his cobra clutch finishing hold, Slaughter, while lacking the depth of some of wrestling's more intriguing characters, had a talent for stirring up a crowd in a manner that was perhaps not evident to British Columbia wrestling fans in 1974 and 1975.

Jimmy Snuka, on the other hand, already had experience electrifying crowds when he arrived in Vancouver in the mid–1970s. Snuka, born James Reiher, was a Fijian native who, like Dean Higuchi, had been a bodybuilder in Hawaii—and, in fact, had spent considerable time at Higuchi's gym in Honolulu—before jumping into pro wrestling. Experimenting with several ring names during the first year or two of his career, Reiher started out by wrestling mainly in Hawaii and along the U.S. West Coast. By 1971, the year he arrived in Portland, he was already a hot commodity in wrestling as Jimmy Snuka.

In and out of the Portland territory for the next seven years—and winning both the NWA Pacific Northwest Heavyweight title and a share of the NWA Pacific Northwest Tag Team championship numerous times—Snuka was a huge favorite and an avant-garde wrestler of the 1970s. From his base in Portland, Snuka began venturing north to British Columbia in the middle of the decade, and during the last two years of the Kovacs era in Vancouver, he divided most of his time between the Portland and Vancouver territories.

In British Columbia, Snuka had a brief run in 1976 as a Canadian Tag Team champion with Jonathan.

While Snuka's success in British Columbia did not match his success in Oregon, he was a popular performer for All-Star Wrestling and one who showed every sign of big things to come. During the 1980s Snuka went on to great success in the Crockett territory and, despite limited interview skills, even greater success in the WWF during its days of national and international expansion. In the WWF Snuka was a top-shelf heel, an equally effective baby-face, and, by any measure, one of the leading wrestlers in the world in the 1980s—three decades before he would face tough health and legal challenges as a senior citizen stemming from a cancer diagnosis and the suspicious death of his girlfriend, 23-year-old Nancy Argentino, following a WWF television taping back in 1983. Snuka passed away in early 2017.

Also from the South Pacific, Afa and Sika Anoa'i had been wrestling for less than a year—already winning the Stampede Wrestling International Tag Team championship—before arriving in Vancouver in the late summer of 1973. A couple of burly, wild-haired 300-pounders when those were relatively uncommon, Afa and Sika proceeded to win the Pacific Coast Tag Team title, just a few weeks after their arrival, from Kiniski and the Brute. For the next four years they were in and out of the territory, often headlining as singles wrestlers as well as a team. They also made appearances in Oregon during that period.

After leaving the Northwest, Afa and Sika—usually called the Wild Samoans—struck out into numerous territories, often winning whatever tag team championship was available. Between 1980 and 1983 they held the WWF World Tag Team title three times, taking their arsenal of head butts and Samoan drops to a national stage and helping pave the way for a long line of fellow Samoans and family members to follow them into the ring.

Keith Franke was a 20-year-old sophomore who wrestled as Keith Franks after arriving in Vancouver in mid–1975. His fundamentals were good, and he was a fairly popular mid-card babyface during a year-long stay in Vancouver with appearances also in Oregon and Washington.

After leaving the Northwest, Franke morphed into the edgier, rough-housing, biker-type persona of Adrian Adonis. He honed the Adonis character in Texas and Georgia before returning, as Adonis, to the Northwest after the Kovacs era was over. While in the Northwest, he was an NWA Pacific Northwest Tag Team champion in 1979. But his greatest success came in the major promotions, particularly the AWA, where he formed a championship tag team—the East–West Connection—with an opponent he had faced in Oregon, Jesse Ventura; and the WWF, where he was an upper-card heel and formed another championship tag team—this time, the North–South Connection—with Texas veteran Dick Murdoch.

Beset by weight problems in his early thirties, Adonis adopted a less menacing character when he became "Adorable" Adrian Adonis, an effeminate, cross-dressing 1980s interpretation, perhaps, of Gorgeous George. When his weight got out of control, Adonis was relegated to much smaller wrestling promotions, and tragically, he died along with several other wrestlers while on a wrestling tour in Newfoundland when the car they were riding in hit a moose and plunged into a lake.

During the Kovacs-Kiniski-Owen era in Vancouver, the territory was a veritable magnet for established wrestlers and up-and-comers eager to soak in the Northwest grandeur and put in serious ring time while entertaining receptive audiences around the circuit. Shows at Vancouver's Agrodome usually drew a few thousand fans, while the bigger cards—often highlighted by a meeting between the territory's top contender of the week and the visiting NWA champion—most often drew a few thousand more to Vancouver's Pacific Coast Coliseum. According to Silverstone, some shows packed the Coliseum, which seated over 15,000.

Other cities around the loop were led by Victoria—which on a good week drew a third or half the number of fans as in Vancouver. Other stops like Nanaimo, Chilliwack, and a few small cities or towns within a short drive of Vancouver were more likely to draw in the hundreds.

Cards promoted in northern Washington State—Dutch Savage bought rights to promote there from Kovacs in the early 1970s—drew steadily in Bellingham and smaller cities north of Seattle, so the more capable "money-drawing" wrestlers could usually expect plenty of work in the Vancouver territory during the Kovacs era. But for many wrestlers, the highlight of the week was Tuesday night, when the *All-Star Wrestling* TV show was taped at the CHAN studio.

Though *All-Star Wrestling* had been in production since 1962, the program became enormously popular during the Kovacs era, appearing in syndication in Canada from coast to coast. Not only was Vancouver's wrestling territory a successful one under the Kovacs-Kiniski-Owen leadership, but during that period it could be considered a promotion aimed at a national audience, to some degree like 1950s Toronto wrestling on the CBC or, in the U.S., *Wrestling from Marigold* that same decade on the DuMont Television Network or Vince McMahon's WWF/WWE from its expansion in the 1980s to the present day. *All-Star Wrestling* normally stuck to a simple formula—two relatively lopsided matches called by avuncular, white-haired, non-too-excitable commentator Ron Morrier; interviews building up the coming Monday's card in Vancouver; and in the latter part of the show, a "duration match" filling out whatever time remained in the TV hour—and wrestlers appearing on the program had the potential to become national stars, to catch the attention of the right people, and to watch their careers take off.

The Kovacs era is widely considered the height of Vancouver wrestling, but a changing of the guard took place when Kovacs sold his share in the promotion to veteran Winnipeg, Manitoba, wrestler and promoter Al Tomko in 1977. Perhaps Kovacs had an inkling of where the wrestling industry was headed, as several years later he was the local promoter for Vancouver-area WWF events and, according to Nevada, handled arrangements in the area for closed circuit telecasting of early WrestleMania shows in the days before pay-per-view (59). In any event, Kovacs was out and Tomko was in as an owner-promoter of All-Star Wrestling in January of 1977 for a price Tomko reported as $100,000. And while most reports indicate Tomko shared ownership of the promotion with Kiniski and Owen—as most reports indicate Kovacs had done—there is some disagreement as to what Owen's role in the company actually was by that point.

10

New Home
of *Portland Wrestling*

While the extent of Don Owen's influence on Vancouver's Northwest Wrestling Promotions/All-Star Wrestling territory in the late 1960s and 1970s may not be transparent, such is not the case with Oregon, where Owen was in every way the kingpin of Pacific Northwest Wrestling. Though brother Elton was minority owner and the promoter of shows in some of the territory's outlying cities and towns—earning mixed reviews from ex-wrestlers and others familiar with Elton's contributions to the Owen wrestling empire and the wrestling business in general—Don clearly was his father Herb's successor when it came to setting the vision for Pacific Northwest Wrestling and making the major decisions affecting the operation and future of the company.

When the Blitz-Weinhard Brewing Co. purchased the Portland Armory complex in 1968, Don Owen was forced to find a new home base for the linchpin of his Pacific Northwest Wrestling promotion, the popular *Portland Wrestling* TV program that had been broadcast in some form from the Portland Armory Annex since 1953. After 12 years on CBS affiliate KOIN-TV, *Portland Wrestling* returned in 1967 to KPTV, where it had first appeared as *Heidelberg Wrestling* from 1953–1955. Just months before the sale of the Armory, Owen's promotion lost most of its regional television exposure with the cancelation of Harry Elliott's *Northwest Championship Wrestling*, which had featured Owen's roster of wrestlers and, in effect, greatly increased the size of his territory. With *Northwest Championship Wrestling* no longer on the air, it was vital for Owen to find a good location that would allow the *Portland Wrestling* TV program to continue without a hitch.

He settled on a bowling alley in North Portland, which was converted to a small arena seating about 3,000 and aptly christened the Portland Sports Arena. The new Portland Sports Arena became the setting for Owen's Saturday night *Portland Wrestling* TV shootings, and Owen's investment in the bowling alley proved sound, as the Sports Arena would remain the setting for *Portland Wrestling* for well over two decades.

While a converted bowling alley may not seem the best setting for broadcasting any sporting or quasi-sporting event that doesn't involve knocking down pins, it proved ideal for a wrestling show aimed at conveying immediacy, intimacy, and a strong sense that the Sports Arena was the place to be on Saturday nights in Portland. The Portland Sports Arena provided a homey alternative to wrestling shows taped in larger arenas or nondescript TV studios, as were seen in many other parts of the country. KPTV's *Portland Wrestling*, emanating from the Portland Sports Arena, was a local hit—even in black and white—when it went on the air, first, at 9:30 on Saturday nights before moving up to 8:30 in 1970, and KPTV remained a strong backer of its top-rated local show, all on the basis of a "gentlemen's agreement." Don Owen's son Barry, who was active in the promotion for many years, says, "There was nothing in writing with the station," and that would remain the case during nearly the entire duration of Don Owen's association with KPTV.

It was a simple formula the show followed: usually three matches, two of them preliminary bouts; a TV main event, often two out of three falls; plenty of interviews to build up interest in the next week's matches; and some funny advertising spots by sponsor Tom Peterson, described by John Terry at www.oregonlive.com (*The Oregonian*) as a "furniture/appliance marketing maven ... whose off-the-wall TV spots elevated him to an advertising icon."

While Pacific Northwest Wrestling was only one of a few dozen successful wrestling territories in the late 1960s and 1970s, the territory's wrestlers, featured on *Portland Wrestling*, enjoyed an unusual rapport with fans. The *Wrestling Observer Newsletter*'s Dave Meltzer says, in a Sept. 23, 1999, *SLAM! Wrestling* report by John Molinaro, "The Portland wrestling fans were different in that they knew the wrestlers as people. Watching the show, you could tell it was the same fans who would go to wrestling every Saturday night. They knew everyone and it was a real homey feel."

Washington State-based writer Bryan Alvarez concurs, adding, in the Aug. 11, 2002, issue of his wrestling newsletter, *Figure Four Weekly*, "The first rows of the Sports Arena were filled with the same fans week in and week out, year after year. Unless you were one of those fans, you couldn't sit there, as they were literally permanently reserved. A few times every year, Owen would run shows with discounted ticket prices, so even fans who couldn't afford a weekly ticket could at least show up occasionally to witness live action." According to John Baumer, weighing in at www.kayfabememories. com, a Saturday night at the Portland Sports Arena involved "sitting in the bleachers of an old bowling alley surrounded by thousands of rabid fanatics."

By small to midsized market standards, attendance was strong in Portland

and other cities in the territory, which included Salem, Eugene, Seattle, Tacoma, and a variety of smaller cities and towns for spot shows. Although some of the smaller cities and towns hosting Pacific Northwest Wrestling may not have had much else to offer entertainment-wise, it was on the back of Owen's TV program set in the Portland Sports Arena that interest in his wrestling product was so hot throughout the Northwest.

While the 1967 cancelation of Elliott's *Northwest Championship Wrestling*—taped in Seattle featuring Owen's wrestlers, seen across Washington, and reaching into several other states and British Columbia—threatened to reduce the penetration of Owen's promotion substantially, the Portland Sports Arena shows proved successful and compelling enough that, by the mid–1970s, Owen, with the help of Washington promoter Dutch Savage, was able to rebuild a respectable syndication network. With demand for Owen's television product running high, Saturday night shows at the Portland Sports Arena resulted in two different programs: *Portland Wrestling*, mainly for viewers in Portland and surrounding areas; and *Big Time Wrestling*, mainly for viewers in other parts of Oregon and Washington State in order to build up interest in cards promoted there, but also syndicated—according to Baumer, at www. kayfabememories.com—to stations in Idaho, Montana, California, British Columbia, and Alaska.

What drove the success of the show, hosted by KPTV sportscaster Frank Bonnema, was its intimacy, its simplicity, and its characters—most notably the wacky pitchman Peterson; "Ringside Rosie," Portland's version of the elderly-woman-in-the-audience stereotype seen in many territories at the time; Owen, often portraying the voice of reason in a sea of turmoil; and, of course, the wrestlers themselves, nearly always the source of that turmoil.

Perhaps the most colorful wrestler in the Owen territory during the early part of the Portland Sports Arena era in the late 1960s—or any era—was second-generation wrestler Ronald Mayne, a college football standout in Utah who adopted the ring name "Lonnie" during his earliest days as a professional wrestler in Southern California. Showing great promise in the ring, Lonnie Mayne was only 21 when he migrated up the coast to Oregon in 1966 and soon became a popular face on *Portland Wrestling* and throughout the Pacific Northwest Wrestling circuit thanks to his engaging personality and entertaining brawling style. Mayne wasted little time climbing the ladder in Oregon, and within two short years, as the Portland Sports Arena established itself as the new home of *Portland Wrestling* and the center of Owen's Oregon territory, Mayne was already a five-time holder of the regional NWA Pacific Northwest Heavyweight championship.

Mayne was the dominant performer in Pacific Northwest Wrestling during a spectacular four-year run from 1967 to 1970. During that period he headlined around the territory, establishing an unforgettable arena and television persona and holding the Pacific Northwest Heavyweight title 11 times. While Mayne faced a variety of Northwest fan favorites during the first year or two after his arrival in the Northwest—including multi-time Pacific Northwest Heavyweight champions Shag Thomas, Stan Stasiak, and Pepper Martin—the stocky brawler who would become known for delivering off-the-wall interviews and eating just about anything became the territory's leading fan favorite himself over the course of his dominant run through 1970.

Though he was a sought-after wrestler elsewhere, Mayne continued to wrestle regularly in the Owen territory through 1972. After leaving the Northwest in 1973 to wrestle mainly in other regions for the remainder of his career, he ventured back to Pacific Northwest Wrestling every so often as a returning legend. Mayne's career saw him wrestle in Japan; in Vancouver, helping to establish the British Columbia territory's Pacific Coast Heavyweight championship in 1970; and around the United States, including territories in Hawaii, Georgia, and Texas. In Hawaii shortly after the height of his success in the Northwest in the early 1970s, Mayne shared the ring with renowned grapplers such as Verne Gagne; British star Billy Robinson; Hawaiian star King Curtis; California "Blond Bomber" Ray Stevens; Mexican legend Mil Mascaras; Peter Maivia, grandfather of Dwayne "The Rock" Johnson; and a variety of wrestlers well known to fans in the Pacific Northwest, including former Pacific Northwest champion Ripper Collins; Frankie Laine, a championship tag team partner of Mayne's during Mayne's ultra-hot run in the Owen territory; and a long line of others including Don Muraco, Dale Lewis, Bearcat Wright, Haystack Calhoun, Bulldog Bob Brown, Jimmy Snuka, and Mad Dog Vachon. Picking up where he'd left off in Oregon, Mayne enjoyed a successful 1971 in Hawaii, winning the NWA Hawaii Heavyweight championship from Laine and the regional tag team championship twice with Collins and once more with Sweet Daddy Siki, before having another strong run in Oregon in 1972. In Texas a few years later, Mayne was a headliner facing or teaming with Texas legends such as Terry Funk, Bruiser Brody, and Fritz von Erich, and during a successful 1977 Texas run, Mayne won the NWA Texas Heavyweight championship from 1970s Vancouver star Siegfried Stanke (Steinke) and challenged champion Harley Race at least once, in Dallas, for the NWA Heavyweight championship.

From 1973 until 1978, the year his life was cut short in a traffic mishap, Mayne was a major star in California, headlining at different times—and sometimes simultaneously—in both the Northern California (San Francisco) and Southern California (Los Angeles) territories. In California, Mayne faced many opponents familiar to Northwest fans, including Pepper Martin, Kinji Shibuya, Mr. Saito, Pat Patterson, Don Muraco, Mr. Fuji, and a young Roddy Piper, who would go on to become a Northwest legend on the level of Mayne.

During his years in California, Mayne had multiple runs as the top singles champion in both the Los Angeles and San Francisco territories. He was also a tag team champion in both territories, once capturing the Northern California territory's NWA World Tag Team championship with partner Ray Stevens, a nationally renowned wrestler who had appeared briefly in Vancouver in 1966 and made several appearances in Portland from 1965 to

As charismatic as he was odd, Lonnie Mayne soon grew on Pacific Northwest Wrestling fans after starting out in the territory as a villain. In the late 1960s and early 1970s Mayne had an outstanding championship run in the Northwest, and a few years later he gained national recognition as a featured performer in the World Wide Wrestling Federation, a forerunner of WWE.

1968. The Mayne-Stevens combo won the title in Northern California from Kurt and Karl von Steiger, who had held the Pacific Northwest Tag Team championship seven times during the early years of the Portland Sports Arena. Mayne also enjoyed tag team championship runs in California with Patterson, Dean Ho (Higuchi), and Ron (Sam Oliver) Bass, who were all major stars in the Northwest during the 1960s or 1970s.

In terms of national recognition, the height of Mayne's career was a successful 1973 run in the World Wide Wrestling Federation. As the wacky and newly named "Moondog," Mayne was a top contender to WWWF champion Pedro Morales and a hot opponent of WWWF fan favorites all the way up to Bruno Sammartino. Mayne was tailor-made for the wrestling magazines published in the Northeast that ended up on magazine shelves across the country and made national stars of successful and colorful WWWF wrestlers. Though Mayne did not stay in the Northeast for long, he paved the way for a few fellow "Moondogs" who in later years would surface in the WWF, including early 1970s Vancouver preliminary wrestler Ed "Sailor" White, who in 1981, as Moondog King, was a co-holder of the WWF World Tag Team championship with partner Moondog Rex.

In the Northwest, Moondog Mayne's success as a singles wrestler was easily matched by his record as a tag team wrestler. In all, Mayne was a

17-time NWA Pacific Northwest Tag Team champion, with his final run coming in late 1977—the year before his death a month short of only his 34th birthday—with partner Sam Oliver Bass. Over the course of his career in the Northwest, Mayne formed championship teams with several partners, but his most successful pairing, by far, was with Tony Borne, the only person in the history of Pacific Northwest Wrestling to have held a share of the promotion's tag team championship more times than Mayne did.

Over the course of 14 years from 1958 to 1972, Borne amassed a record total of 20 tag team championship reigns in the Pacific Northwest, including 11 with Mayne from 1966 through 1972. This was to go with nine Pacific

Dick "The Destroyer" Beyer (left) and Tony Borne meet in a match refereed by James "Shag" Thomas. While the Destroyer had the most career success of the three outside the Pacific Northwest, Thomas and Borne—both tag team partners and bitter rivals in Pacific Northwest Wrestling in the 1960s—had tremendous success and popularity in the region over many years.

Northwest Heavyweight title runs in the 1960s—a record certainly justifying *Wrestling Observer* editor Dave Meltzer's assessment of Borne, at www. onlineworldofwrestling.com, as "one of the area's all-time legends."

Borne, originally from Columbus, Ohio, enjoyed moderate success in several areas during the early years of his career, including in the Utah–Idaho– eastern Washington region and in northern Ontario. In those areas he wrestled under his own name, but in his home state of Ohio and in the Mid- Atlantic region, Borne was recast as the more sinister-sounding Ivan Bornov. As Bornov, Borne captured his first two professional wrestling championships, the Ohio Tag Team title with Boris Malenko and the NWA Mid- Atlantic Southern Tag Team championship with a lesser-known wrestler named Karol Fozoff.

Borne became a regular in the Portland territory in the mid–1950s, facing a variety of wrestlers up and down the card, including main eventers like Kurt von Poppenheim, Pepper Gomez, Ed Francis, and Red Bastien, all of whom had held singles or tag team championships in the Northwest. While Borne lost most of his early encounters with opponents of that caliber, his star consistently rose as his roughhousing style captured fans' attention, and Borne won his first title in the Northwest—the Pacific Northwest Tag Team championship—with partner Francis in September of 1958.

Known for his "cannonball jump" finishing move from the top rope, Borne held the regional tag team championship another seven times before capturing the first of his 11 tag team championships with Mayne in 1966. From 1958 to 1966 Borne held the tag title with seven different partners, the best known nationally being Pat Patterson—a major wrestling star for over two decades before joining the WWF/WWE in a behind-the-scenes capacity—and Mr. Fuji, played by Hawaiian Harry Fujiwara, who had a long career as a karate-chopping, salt-throwing Japanese heel before becoming a manager in the WWF. But Borne's most successful and best-remembered championship pairing prior to his teaming with Mayne was with fellow Columbus native Shag Thomas.

In *"I Ain't No Pig Farmer!"* Dean Silverstone says Borne was a key factor behind Thomas' arrival in Oregon in early 1960. According to Silverstone, Borne's recommendation, which carried a lot of weight in the territory, led to Owen's decision to bring in Thomas; and Borne and Thomas—described by Silverstone as "believable heels"—clicked as a team from the start, winning the Pacific Northwest Tag Team championship in March of 1960. The team remained red-hot through much of 1960, winning the title for a second time in November of that year. And then, a month later, according to Silverstone, "the unbelievable happened. Shag and Borne got into a squabble during a match and they were defeated. Each blamed the other for the loss and things got physical between the two of them." The result was a highly successful series of matches during which fans took to Thomas as the good guy, the role he had in the Northwest for the remainder of his career. While Borne remained cast in the role of a tough-as-nails villain, his career later took a similar turn as Thomas' as, eventually, Silverstone says, "the fans loved to hate him so much that they began to love him for what he did" (23–24).

Silverstone also credits Borne with facilitating Mayne's arrival in the Northwest. As Silverstone reports, Lonnie Mayne's father, wrestler Ken Mayne, had met Borne in Columbus in 1947 and, 19 years later, when Borne was a long-established star in the Northwest, called and asked Borne to help his son out (84). While Borne helped the younger Mayne find a spot in Pacific Northwest Wrestling, Silverstone quotes Borne as saying Owen wasn't giving Mayne any matches at first—though that obviously changed sometime before Mayne caught fire as the hottest wrestling attraction in Oregon and Washington and half of the most successful team in the territory's history with Borne (83).

Borne also held the Pacific Northwest Heavyweight championship nine times in the 1960s, all before *Portland Wrestling* made its move to the Sports Arena in 1968. But he remained a huge fan favorite during the height of the Sports Arena years throughout the 1970s and into the early 1980s, teaming on occasion during the latter part of his career with son Matt Borne, who won both the territory's singles and tag championships in the early 1980s.

Another major attraction during the early years of the Portland Sports Arena era was Québec native George Stipich, who had appeared in Vancouver in the late 1950s as Emile Koverly—facing the likes of Luther Lindsay and the famous ballet-style wrestler Ricki Starr—before hitting it big in the Northwest and numerous other areas as Stan Stasiak. Before winning his first Pacific Northwest Heavyweight championship in Portland, from Mad Dog Vachon on June 18, 1965, Stasiak held a few titles, including Stampede Wrestling's NWA Canadian Heavyweight title, which he took earlier in 1965 from Don Leo Jonathan. And then, just three days after winning the Portland territory's heavyweight title, Stasiak captured the first of eight Pacific Northwest Tag Team championships he would hold over an 18-year period. He also held the Vancouver NWA Canadian Tag Team championship twice, in 1968 and 1969, with partner Dutch Savage, who was also Stasiak's partner during a short tag team championship run in Pacific Northwest Wrestling in 1979.

While Stasiak achieved notable success as a tag team wrestler, he is best remembered as a large, powerful, bruising singles wrestler who enjoyed a long and outstanding career. Billed for most of his career from Buzzard Creek or Beaver Creek, Oregon, Stasiak pounded his way to numerous singles titles in Texas, Alberta, and elsewhere—often with his taped-fist "heart punch," which was exactly what it sounds like: a punch to the chest designed to put an opponent down for the three count. In the Northwest, Stasiak held the

Tony Borne (left) and Lonnie Mayne were 11-time NWA Pacific Northwest Tag Team champions between 1966 and 1972. Borne is credited with helping Mayne—at the time a young wrestler short on experience—get started in the Northwest in 1966.

Owen territory's heavyweight championship seven times over a 14-year period and was a tough wrestler fans took to and strongly supported for years.

Stasiak also held two versions of the world heavyweight championship during his career. In 1970 he had a short reign as Australia's IWA World Heavyweight champion, and then, three years later, he briefly held the

WWWF World Heavyweight title as a transitional heel champion between the much longer babyface championship reigns of Pedro Morales and all-time favorite Bruno Sammartino. While Stasiak was a WWWF headliner and championship contender through most of the 1970s, at a national level he is probably best remembered for his nine-day reign as the WWWF world champion in an era when wrestling world championships generally did not change hands nearly as frequently as they would in later decades.

Along with his success in the Northeast, Texas, Toronto, and other areas, Stasiak kept close ties to the Northwest throughout the 1970s and beyond, resurfacing at times in British Columbia and reestablishing himself as a mainstay in Oregon and Washington toward the end of the decade and well into the 1980s, when he both wrestled and did some TV announcing.

Dutch Savage—born Frank Stewart in Scranton, Pennsylvania—already had a few U.S. regional titles under his belt, but his career took off after he arrived in the Pacific Northwest at age 30. He captured a series of tag team championships in Vancouver during the latter years of the Fenton promotion and the early years of the Kovacs-Owen-Kiniski triumvirate. In all, Savage amassed 13 tag title runs over the course of a part-time career in Vancouver spanning nearly a decade and a half from 1966 to 1980 with partners including Kiniski, Brown, Jonathan, Stasiak, Quinn, and—four times—Little Bear. Initially, Savage was cast as a heel, but, as happened with others like Mayne and Borne, the fans were solidly behind him during the vast majority of his run in the Northwest.

While Savage was highly successful in British Columbia, most of his activity and success in the Northwest was in the United States. In the Portland territory, Savage captured his first NWA Pacific Northwest Heavyweight title in 1970 and his first Pacific Northwest Tag Team championship the following year. With impressive movement and a skill set many larger wrestlers did not have—along with a convincing tough-guy character and the ability to speak well and "sell" his upcoming matches in interviews—Savage easily established himself throughout the 1970s as a Northwest wrestling star on a level few have ever surpassed and a headliner up and down the West Coast, from British Columbia to California.

From 1970 to 1977 Savage held the NWA Pacific Northwest Heavyweight title seven times and had notable feuds over the title with Mayne, Bull Ramos, and future Minnesota governor Jesse Ventura. Savage was also co-holder of the Pacific Northwest Tag Team championship a decade-leading 12 times in the 1970s, with partners including Mayne, Little Bear, and—six times from 1973–1978—Snuka. Savage's final run with the Pacific Northwest Tag Team title was with Stasiak in September of 1979, three months before the Savage-Stasiak pairing captured their second and final Canadian Tag Team championship in Vancouver. In both instances, Savage and Stasiak would lose their

Dutch Savage (standing) and Lonnie Mayne were rivals before joining forces in 1972 to capture the NWA Pacific Northwest Tag Team title twice. While both were introduced to Pacific Northwest Wrestling fans as heels in the 1960s, Savage and Mayne would go on to become two of the most successful babyfaces in the promotion's history.

titles to the Kiwi Sheepherders, one of the more violent, "extreme" tag teams of the time, who in the late 1980s would morph into the wackier, more family-friendly Bushwhackers in the WWF.

Like Stasiak, Savage would go on to become a TV commentator in the Portland territory once his wrestling days were largely over. Savage also became a part-owner of Pacific Northwest Wrestling when his ring career was still going strong, and for several years he was the company's promoter for events held in much of Washington State. Having already purchased, from All-Star Wrestling in Vancouver, the rights to promote wrestling events in northern Washington, Savage was a powerful force in Northwest wrestling in several capacities: as the charismatic originator of the "coal miner's glove match" and a top-tier singles wrestler; a 25-time tag team champion in the two major Northwest wrestling promotions of the 1960s and 1970s; a major wrestling power broker with his ownership stake in Pacific Northwest Wrestling and his promotional activities in Washington; and a no-nonsense color commentator during a hot period on *Portland Wrestling* and the syndicated *Big Time Wrestling*.

According to Silverstone, "no-nonsense" is also an apt description for Savage in his promoter's role, as Savage the promoter was noted for throwing his weight around, much in the manner he had done as a wrestler. Overall, Savage is generally remembered as a successful promoter. According to Farmer, "When Dutch was running spot shows in Washington, his side of the territory would often outdraw Don's side." But while respected for his wrestling mind and his ability to run a profitable promotion, Savage is not remembered as the easiest promoter of his era to do business with. "There were very few people who liked him," says Mike Rodgers, a longtime wrestling historian and chronicler of Northwest wrestling.

After a falling-out with Don Owen in the 1980s, Savage cut ties with Pacific Northwest Wrestling before working in real estate and becoming an ordained minister. But he stayed close to wrestling and resurfaced briefly as a commentator on the small Vancouver, Washington–based Championship Wrestling USA promotion's television program in the mid–1990s. An outspoken critic of the direction wrestling had taken since his days in the ring, Savage remained a resident of southern Washington until his death in 2014.

Another all-time legend of Pacific Northwest Wrestling was nearing the end of his career as a full-time wrestler when *Portland Wrestling* made the transition to the Sports Arena in 1968. James "Shag" Thomas, a short, stocky, charismatic African American, had been a huge attraction throughout the Owen territory since 1960 and was probably the top babyface in Oregon from 1961 until several years later when Lonnie Mayne caught fire as a fan favorite. Thomas, master of the head butt associated with many leading African American wrestlers of his day, held the Pacific Northwest Heavyweight championship twice in the 1960s and a share of the Pacific Northwest Tag Team championship 17 times, most notably with Borne, Pepper Martin, Bearcat Wright, and five-time championship partner Luther Lindsay. Though all but one of Thomas' title reigns came before the christening of the Sports Arena, Thomas remained a headliner in *Portland Wrestling*'s new venue, often facing the likes of Mayne, Stasiak, Wright, and Kurt and Karl von Steiger. It was with Lindsay as his partner that Thomas captured the final championship of his career in 1969. Though he retired as a full-time performer in 1969, Thomas was a popular Pacific Northwest Wrestling referee until 1972 and made return appearances as a wrestler as late as 1976. He passed away as a result of a heart attack in 1982 at age 53.

Thomas also had some notable achievements outside Northwest wrestling rings. A graduate of Ohio State University, he worked as a teacher before achieving fame in wrestling. While in college, he was an All-American guard in football, and he went on to play briefly for the Green Bay Packers. Onlineworldofwrestling.com reports that Thomas also served, in a noncommissioned capacity, in the Army Medical Corps. While the vast majority of his success as a wrestler came in the Northwest, Thomas was also a prominent wrestler in other areas, including California, Alberta, the Midwest, Texas, Hawaii, and Georgia, where www.onlineworldofwrestling.com reports Thomas may have been a participant in that state's first interracial match in 1963. Originalpeople.org describes Thomas as a "trailblazer" for African American wrestlers, along the lines of others such as Bobo Brazil, Bearcat Wright, Sweet Daddy Siki, and Luther Lindsay.

Lindsay—born Luther Goodall in Virginia—had a long association with Thomas both inside and outside their storied tenures with Pacific Northwest Wrestling. One reason, according to www.originalpeople.org, is that, during the period of segregation in much of the United States, top African American wrestlers such as Lindsay and Thomas often had no option but to wrestle for "Negro" championships. According to www.originalpeople.org, Lindsay "once claimed to have known Shag Thomas better than any other competitor, because in many territories, the two men had to wrestle each other because they were both black." The two men, however, had significantly different wrestling styles, as Lindsay was less of an entertainer during his matches and was considered, in particular by "hooking" legends Lou Thesz and Stu Hart, as a legitimately gifted pure grappler. Don Leo Jonathan, who says, "I spent a lot of time in the dungeon"—Stu Hart's fabled training ground where countless wrestlers including Lindsay and Jonathan sparred over the years—is quick to describe Lindsay as "a good wrestler."

Lindsay's arrival in the Northwest preceded Thomas' by about seven years, as Lindsay first appeared in both the Vancouver and Portland territories in early 1953, about a year and a half after debuting as a wrestler in Columbus, Ohio, Thomas' hometown. Lindsay had racked up a good record, primarily in and near Ohio, prior to heading for the Northwest, where he quickly established himself as a top wrestler in both major regional territories. Although he wrestled extensively in Oregon, Washington, and British Columbia through the remainder of the 1950s, Lindsay had only single, brief heavyweight and tag team title reigns in the Northwest during that decade, almost certainly because numerous wrestling commitments elsewhere often kept him out of the Northwest for extended periods.

After spending most of 1960 wrestling successfully in Alberta, in the U.S. Midwest, and on the East Coast, Lindsay returned to Pacific Northwest Wrestling in early 1961 to face or team with the likes of Francis, Poppenheim, and future NWA Pacific Northwest Heavyweight champion Billy White Wolf. Lindsay also engaged in a series of matches with reigning Pacific Northwest Heavyweight titleholder "Iron" Mike DiBiase, stepfather of 1980s/1990s WWF headliner Ted "Million Dollar Man" DiBiase. Lindsay won his first NWA Pacific Northwest Heavyweight championship from Mike DiBiase on May 26, 1961, and just two weeks later he also held a share of the Pacific Northwest Tag Team title. Titles continued to come his way throughout the 1960s, and Lindsay had a fourth and final run with the Pacific Northwest Heavyweight championship shortly after the promotion's 1968 transition to the Sports Arena. Before losing the title to Mayne in April of 1969, Lindsay also captured the territory's tag title for the 10th and final time—and for the fifth time with Thomas as his partner.

A challenger to several world champions over the course of his career, Lindsay left the Northwest in 1969 and spent most of the next three years wrestling in the Mid-Atlantic region where he grew up—and where he wrestled until the moment of his death, as he suffered a fatal heart attack during a match in Charlotte, North Carolina, at age 47.

Manuel "Apache Bull" Ramos was a well-traveled superheavyweight who had challenged Sammartino on the East Coast and enjoyed some success, particularly in California and his native Texas, before landing in the Pacific Northwest near the beginning of 1972. Longtime Houston promoter and former Northwest wrestler and promoter Paul Boesch is among those credited with helping Ramos—at the time, a lean boxer—kick off his wrestling career in 1964 at age 16.

Though frequently in and out of the territory—with successful stays in Vancouver and, especially, Texas and several tours of Japan—Ramos was a major attraction in Pacific Northwest Wrestling from 1972 through the end of the 1970s and was perhaps the wrestler who best exemplified the Portland territory's transition from one traditionally featuring lighter heavyweight wrestlers to one having a roster loaded with legitimate heavyweights and even a few superheavyweights. In the Portland territory during the 1970s, Ramos' big-man brawling style, along with moves including "splash" body presses and elbow drops, brought him four heavyweight title and five tag team title reigns to go with a long list of memorable interviews and several memorable feuds, including one with Mayne.

Ramos, an impactful presence from the start in Pacific Northwest Wrestling, recalled his first match in the territory in an Oct. 13, 2004, *SLAM!*

Wrestling report by Greg Oliver. "Lonnie Mayne made Bull Ramos in Portland," Ramos said. "The first match I had was with Lonnie Mayne. When I went in there, they had Indians on one side and lumberjack people on the other side. I went in there and broke Lonnie Mayne's arm ... bones were sticking out of his arm. That is what made Bull Ramos there, I'll tell you that." After Mayne sat out a few weeks, Ramos won their Feb. 1, 1972, Portland rematch, setting himself up for a long and successful stay in the Northwest.

Probably the longest feud of Ramos' career was with Savage, as the two engaged in sometimes bloody matches all over the Oregon-Washington circuit over a six-year period. Ramos captured his first NWA Pacific Northwest Heavyweight title from Savage in April of 1972 and his first share of the Pacific Northwest Tag Team title from a team including Savage in June of 1973. From there, Ramos and Savage proceeded to trade victories through most of the remainder of the 1970s. In all, Ramos won five of his nine career titles in Pacific Northwest Wrestling at the expense of Savage. Though both men played the parts of bitter rivals and enemies to perfection for years, decades later Savage had the highest praise for Ramos' professionalism and credibility as a big-time heel. Ramos, meanwhile, in the Oct. 13, 2004, *SLAM!* report, recalled his long series of matches with Savage: "Dutch and I, anytime we met it was a sellout. Anytime we came together, people came to see us in Oregon. Then we started going to Washington, and in Washington, the same thing—sellout after sellout." Savage, describing the hard-hitting nature of his matches with Ramos, added, in the same report, "We really convinced the folks in the front as well as the back rows because we laid the lumber to one another and neither of us ever complained."

Ramos had another major feud spanning several years in the 1970s with Jimmy Snuka, With an arsenal of flashy, crowd-pleasing moves not often seen in the Northwest—or in any American or Canadian wrestling market at the time—the high-flying Snuka was an ideal babyface to throw to the stout and surly Ramos, who was about a decade older and showed every day of that and more. Ramos was the perfect heel to evoke crowd support for Snuka, and the Ramos-Snuka feud was a big ticket-seller around the Northwest on and off for years and established once more that Ramos was an effective heel who could draw large crowds to arenas and rile them when they got there.

Ramos' career started to wind down after he left the Northwest in the late 1970s. By the early 1980s, after an impactful career that took him to several countries, Ramos returned to the Houston area, where he had grown up, and—perhaps appropriately—got into the wrecking business. In 2006 he died at age 68 of an infection following a long bout with diabetes.

Snuka, meanwhile, held the Pacific Northwest Heavyweight title six times during a three-and-a-half-year span between late 1973 and early 1977. He also held the Pacific Northwest Tag Team championship seven times—

Bull Ramos (front) and Dutch Savage were noted for violent brawls—often with the Pacific Northwest Wrestling Heavyweight title at stake—all around the Portland territory in the 1970s. The title changed hands between the two four times during the decade, which also saw the pair and their partners exchange the territory's tag team title four times.

including six times with Savage over a five-year period as the two combined to form one of the most successful tag teams during the first decade of the Portland Sports Arena era.

Two other teams achieving similar success during the early Sports Arena

era consisted of prima-
rily tag team specialists
and were not the result of
major singles stars join-
ing forces and jelling, as
had been the case with
teams such as Savage-
Snuka and Mayne-Borne.
On many Pacific North-
west Wrestling cards in
the late 1960s through
the mid–1970s, tag team
encounters—with poten-
tial for a level of mayhem
no referee was likely to
contain—were a focal
point and the most
chaotic part of the show,
and two teams composed
of tag team specialists
were largely responsible
for that.

Kurt and Karl von
Steiger were one of the
most successful pairings
in the United States for
about a decade beginning
around the time Pacific
Northwest   Wrestling
moved its television base
from the Armory annex
to the Portland Sports

Dutch Savage and Jimmy Snuka (right) were noted
for vastly different styles in the ring, but the two
meshed well and definitely had staying power. Over a
five-year period (1973–1978) the popular pair managed to win the Pacific Northwest Wrestling Tag Team
championship six times. Both also had multiple runs
during that period as the Pacific Northwest Heavyweight champion.

Arena in 1968. Although both von Steigers had been wrestling professionally
for the better part of a decade prior to their arrival in Oregon, during most
of that time they were not yet brothers—and not yet German. By birth the
von Steigers were no more German—and every bit as Canadian—as Golden
Age trailblazer Guy Larose, who played the evil Hans Schmidt. Greg Oliver
and Steven Johnson, in their book *The Pro Wrestling Hall of Fame: The Tag
Teams*, describe the von Steigers as "Canadian boys from Winnipeg who acted
German" (244).

Both were active early in their careers in Winnipeg's Madison Wrestling
Club. Kurt von Steiger—known by his real name, Arnold Pastricks—also

wrestled for the Norland Wrestling Club, a small, short-lived promotion during the late 1950s/early 1960s era when several small wrestling clubs were operating around Winnipeg. After wrestling for several years in and around Winnipeg, Pastricks ventured south in the mid–1960s to territories in Oklahoma, Texas, and Georgia, where he wrestled as Kurt Steiger and Kurt von Steiger, losing most of his matches but growing into the character for which he would be remembered.

Meanwhile, Karl von Steiger, wrestling under his real name of Lorne Corlett, was one of the top grapplers in the Madison Wrestling Club from 1960 to 1965. In 1960 he won a share of the promotion's Middleweight Tag Team championship with fellow Manitoban Orest Antonation, who, wrestling as Bill Cody, made several tours of the Vancouver territory and appeared occasionally in Oregon in the 1970s. During one of his stays in British Columbia, Cody was co-holder of the Canadian Tag Team title for a month in 1979.

In 1963 Corlett held a second Madison Wrestling Club Tag Team title, this time as a heavyweight. His partner was fellow Manitoban and future Vancouver headliner Bob Brown, who held 10 Madison Wrestling Club championships in the early years of his career.

Corlett held the Madison Wrestling Club's Heavyweight title for a period in the mid–1960s. As a singles wrestler, he also appeared in the mid–1960s on AWA cards held in and near Manitoba, including those promoted in Winnipeg by Al Tomko, a Winnipeg wrestler who, during periods in the 1950s and 1960s, promoted events for the Madison Club and eventually bought into the club. Like some of the other Madison Club wrestlers, Corlett had the opportunity to appear on AWA cards, perhaps through his association with Tomko, who, besides promoting Madison Club shows, became promoter of AWA events in Winnipeg in 1966. Another wrestler appearing on AWA cards in Winnipeg, in early 1967, was Kurt von Steiger—former Madison Club wrestler Arnold Pastricks, who, after two years on the road fitting into his new persona, was back trying it out in front of a hometown crowd. Shortly after his final appearance with the AWA in Winnipeg in February of 1967, Pastricks hit the road again, this time with new "brother" and tag team partner Lorne Corbett, now known as Karl von Steiger.

The von Steigers honed their act in Stampede Wrestling in 1967 before heading west to Vancouver, where they had middling success before traveling down the coast to Portland in the summer of 1968. In Pacific Northwest Wrestling, they were quickly placed in the top mix, competing against the likes of Mayne, Bobby Shane, Stasiak, Lindsay, and Borne; and barely two months after debuting in Oregon, the von Steigers captured their first NWA Pacific Northwest Tag Team championship from the team of Mayne and Beauregard in the main event of an Oct. 12, 1968, show in Portland.

Fans hated the von Steigers—a pair of bald, roughhousing, elbow-smashing, spike-helmeted "Germans" from Manitoba, one of whom was of Polish descent and, reportedly, had close relatives incarcerated by the Nazis during World War II. In all, the von Steigers won seven Pacific Northwest Tag Team titles from 1968 to 1971 to go along with a variety of titles they held in other U.S. territories from the late 1960s through the late 1970s. Perhaps most interestingly, as Oliver and Johnson report in *The Pro Wrestling Hall of Fame: The Tag Teams*, the von Steigers briefly held the AWA Tag Team championship—at least in the minds of Northwest fans—when former NWA Pacific Northwest Heavyweight titleholder Maurice "Mad Dog" Vachon and his brother Paul "Butcher" Vachon agreed to drop the AWA Tag Team title in Portland as they left the U.S. for a 1971 tour of Japan. According to Oliver and Johnson, the Vachons were supposed to regain the title from the von Steigers upon their return to the U.S., which they did, before heading back to Verne Gagne's Minnesota-based AWA and continuing to defend the title as if they had held it all

The von Steigers

Kurt (left) and Karl von Steiger were one of the top tag teams in North America during the first decade of the Portland Sports Arena. Before adopting their German characters and migrating to the West Coast, Arnold "Kurt von Steiger" Pastricks and Lorne "Karl von Steiger" Corlett spent several years developing their skills during the "wrestling club" era in their native Manitoba.

along. According to Dutch Savage, as quoted by Oliver and Johnson, "This made the Von Steigers hotter than ever. Verne never knew what was going on" (244).

To fans in the U.S. Northwest in the late 1960s and early 1970s, the von Steigers represented a foreign menace and a reminder of events that had transfixed the nation a generation earlier. But the arrogant and diabolical Manitobans playing Germans also provided wrestling fans a measure of escape from events transfixing the nation during the early years of the Portland Sports Arena era. While Cold War references often figured into wrestling storylines during much of the 20th century, promoters during the Vietnam War era generally kept references to Vietnam to a minimum. As a result, while perhaps indirectly reminding fans of the conflict gripping the United States during the early years of the Sports Arena, the von Steigers provided a welcome escape from some sobering events of the day—much as *Portland Wrestling* provided television viewers a welcome respite from the wartime images and reports from Vietnam that had Americans glued to the nightly news in the late 1960s and early 1970s.

Another dominant tag team during the early era of the Portland Sports Arena was formed as a tribute to one of the most prominent and innovative tag teams of the late 1950s and 1960s, the Fabulous Kangaroos. The original version of the Fabulous Kangaroos, composed of the Australian duo of Al Costello and Roy Heffernan, achieved national and international success, holding numerous titles over a seven-year period, including—four times from 1964 to 1965—the Vancouver territory's NWA Canadian Tag Team title.

Bursting on the scene in Pacific Northwest Wrestling in the summer of 1971 was a new tag team, the Royal Kangaroos, comprising real-life cousins Jonathan Boyle, aka Jonathan Boyd, and Norman Lowndes, aka Norman Charles III. The Royal Kangaroos made an immediate impact by putting an end to the von Steigers' seventh and final reign as NWA Pacific Northwest Tag Team champions in early July.

Prior to teaming in the Pacific Northwest, both members of the Royal Kangaroos had wrestled individually for a few years, mainly in their native Australia. Boyd was the first to gain notice in the Northwest, introducing his compact frame, menacing look, and brawling style to fans around the Owen circuit in the early spring of 1971 while competing in hard-hitting matches for a few months against the likes of Stasiak, Borne, Snuka, Mayne, and, individually, the von Steigers. Boyd quickly established himself as a top singles contender in Pacific Northwest Wrestling, and in June he had an unsuccessful title challenge in Salem against NWA World Heavyweight champion Dory Funk, Jr. While Boyd's initial reign, the following month, with the newly arrived Charles as an NWA Pacific Northwest Tag Team champion was brief, Boyd followed it up—just a week after losing the tag team title—by ending the second and final Pacific Northwest Heavyweight Championship title reign of Kurt von Steiger, who had a measure of success as both a tag team and singles wrestler in Pacific Northwest Wrestling to rival Boyd's.

Boyd held the NWA Pacific Northwest Heavyweight title twice in 1971 and once more late in the decade, but he is best remembered as half of the Royal Kangaroos, who, like the von Steigers, were one of the top regional tag teams in the country during the early years of the Portland Sports Arena. Top-of-the-card heels throughout the territory, the Royal Kangaroos held the Pacific Northwest Tag Team championship four times during a one-year period starting in July of 1971 by employing a variety of power moves and every sneaky tactic in the book, including the use of a boomerang—from the Fabulous Kangaroos' old playbook—as a backup weapon whenever necessary.

The Royal Kangaroos left the Pacific Northwest in late 1972 and spent most of the next two years in the Mid-Atlantic and southeast regions, where they continued to headline and win championships. Boyd and Charles also made successful visits to Japan and the Australia-Pacific region before returning to Pacific Northwest Wrestling in late 1974. Back in the Northwest, the pair quickly picked up where they had left off and, in February of 1975, captured the Pacific Northwest Tag Team title from Savage and Snuka before dropping the title to the same team 10 months later in a Christmas night main event in Seattle.

After another brief Pacific Northwest Tag Team title reign along with further championship reigns in Georgia, California, and Stampede Wrestling, Boyd and Charles disbanded the Royal Kangaroos in the summer of 1977. Boyd resurfaced in Portland almost immediately, quickly falling back into the mix of top wrestlers, and he enjoyed great success in 1978, for a period that year simultaneously holding the Pacific Northwest Heavyweight title and the Pacific Northwest Tag Team championship with Savage. Both of those championship runs highlighted the importance of Boyd to the promotion, as in each case his title loss facilitated a changing of the guard by helping establish a young Roddy Piper as a credible titleholder to Pacific Northwest Wrestling fans and, eventually, an all-time favorite in the region. While he would never hold another title in the Northwest following his tag team title loss to the Piper–Tim Brooks combo on New Year's Eve 1978 and his heavyweight title loss to Piper on Feb. 17, 1979, Boyd enjoyed continued success for nearly another decade with occasional appearances in the Portland and Vancouver territories and numerous title runs in southern states such as Texas, California, Georgia, Tennessee, and Alabama. Charles, meanwhile, while not enjoying the same level of longevity or success following the disbanding of the Royal Kangaroos in 1977, earned further titles in Stampede Wrestling and the southeastern U.S. before calling it a career a few years later.

Other champions of the early Portland Sports Arena era included two-time heavyweight champion Roger Kirby; three-time heavyweight titleholder Ripper Collins; the masked Rasputin, played by Scotsman Frank "Black Angus Campbell" Hoy, who briefly held the heavyweight title; and heavyweight champion Mr. Fuji. Most of those wrestlers also held the Pacific Northwest Tag Team championship at some point in the late 1960s or early 1970s, as did Billy White Wolf, a Native American babyface character and real-life Iraqi native who had multiple runs as both the Pacific Northwest Heavyweight champion and co-holder of the territory's tag team title before taking his Native American character east in 1976 and winning the WWWF Tag Team championship with real-life Italian American Chief Jay Strongbow—who in 1959 and 1960 had wrestled as a mid-carder in Pacific Northwest Wrestling under his real name, Joe Scarpa. In the early 1990s, during the lead-up to Operation Desert Storm, Adnan Bin Abdulkareem Ahmed Alkaissy El Farthie, the former Billy White Wolf, returned to the WWF as hated Iraqi character General Adnan, an associate of then-traitorous G.I. Joe–type character Sergeant Slaughter, played by mid–1970s All-Star Wrestling/Pacific Northwest Wrestling alumnus Bob Remus.

While Billy White Wolf was one of many Native American wrestling characters played by a nonnative, he was probably the only such character played by an Iraqi. In the 1960s White Wolf was a popular wrestler and six-time titleholder in Pacific Northwest Wrestling. In the 1970s Adnan Bin Abdulkareem Ahmed Alkaissy El Farthie took his White Wolf character to the World Wide Wrestling Federation, but in the early 1990s Gulf War era he would resurface in the WWF as an Iraqi villain.

On a national scale, the best-known grappler—also a multi-time heavyweight champion—

to emerge from 1970s-era Pacific Northwest Wrestling was Vietnam War Navy SEAL Jesse Ventura, who trained to be a wrestler in his native Minnesota before hitting the road and arriving in the Northwest very early in his wrestling career.

After getting his feet wet for a few months in the Kansas City territory, Ventura made appearances in both the Vancouver and Portland territories in late 1975. While he definitely showed promise in Vancouver, Ventura was almost immediately slotted as a main eventer in Portland and throughout the Pacific Northwest Wrestling territory, and it was there that he did most of his wrestling through the remainder of the 1970s.

Ventura won his first NWA Pacific Northwest Heavyweight title from Snuka in January of 1976. A week after losing the title to Savage in April, Ventura won his first Pacific Northwest Tag Team championship with partner Bull Ramos—whose straight-ahead, anything-but-pretty persona seemed at odds with Ventura's arrogant, flashy, bodybuilder character—from Savage and Snuka. In late June of 1976, shortly after the Ventura-Ramos pairing lost the tag team championship to the Royal Kangaroos, only to recapture it a few days later, Ventura regained the heavyweight title from Savage.

Savage and Snuka were among Ventura's chief adversaries in Pacific Northwest Wrestling, and Ramos was perhaps his best-remembered tag team partner, as the two made a successful odd-couple pairing. Ventura also formed a successful tag team with fellow Minnesotan "Playboy" Buddy Rose, who arrived in Portland in May of 1976, won the territory's tag team title twice with Ventura by January of the following year, and would go on to become perhaps *the* wrestler 21st-century fans looking back at Pacific Northwest Wrestling most readily associate with the heyday of the promotion.

As far as Ventura is concerned, after achieving major success in the AWA and WWF during the 1980s, he became a popular wrestling color commentator, playing off his flamboyant wrestling persona; a semi-successful Hollywood actor and television personality; the mayor of a Minneapolis suburb; most notably, the governor of Minnesota leading into the 21st century; and someone has shown the ability to work his way back into the news on occasion long after his single term as governor of Minnesota came to an end in 2003.

The Portland territory's proximity to British Columbia and Don Owen's association with both territories ensured frequent appearances in Portland and around the Pacific Northwest Wrestling circuit by Vancouver-based wrestlers from the late 1960s through the 1970s. Erich Froelich, for example, made numerous trips south to compete in preliminary and mid-card matches for Pacific Northwest Wrestling. Other mainly preliminary wrestlers commuting from Vancouver to fill out cards in the Portland territory included

Jack Bence, Tony Orford, Butts Giraud, Bob Harmes, and John Foley, who would resurface as a heel manager in the Vancouver territory in the 1980s after a successful stint as manager J.R. Foley in Stampede Wrestling.

Up-and-comers in British Columbia who also appeared on Pacific Northwest Wrestling cards during the Portland Sports Arena's first decade included future standouts Bob "Sergeant Slaughter" Remus; Don Muraco; Keith Franke, who wrestled in the Portland territory as Keith Franks in the mid–1970s before returning a few years later as Adrian Adonis; Larry "Zbyszko" Whistler; Afa and Sika Anoa'i, the future Wild Samoans; and Bobby Shane, whose appearances with Pacific Northwest Wrestling barely extended into the Sports Arena era but who had success in several territories and showed rare promise as a young wrestler until his life was cut short in 1975.

Vancouver headliners such as Don Leo Jonathan, John Tolos, Bulldog Bob Brown, Dean "Ho" Higuchi, and John Quinn made successful visits to Pacific Northwest Wrestling during the early years of the Portland Sports Arena; and Steven Little Bear, who wrestled regularly in Oregon during the height of his success in Vancouver, won both major Pacific Northwest Wrestling titles in late 1972 and early 1973.

As far as Gene Kiniski was concerned, his greatest contribution to Pacific Northwest Wrestling came as a result of his visits to the territory as the touring NWA World Heavyweight champion during the late 1960s. Portland, Salem, and Eugene were the sites of numerous Kiniski NWA title defenses against the likes of Stasiak, Borne, Mayne, Thomas, Patterson, Lindsay, White Wolf, Jonathan, and Wright. Most of those wrestlers were well established as regional champions in the Owen territory, and the opportunity to challenge for the NWA title was probably a bigger feather in any of their caps than the regional title was. In the days of diehard NWA territories, a regional title clearly played second fiddle to the world championship, and Kiniski's frequent visits to Oregon gave Pacific Northwest Wrestling fans a taste of the big time and—with each credible showing by Borne, Stasiak, Lindsay, and the others—confidence that their local promotion and its top wrestlers were among the best in the world.

Kiniski's successor as NWA champion, Dory Funk, Jr., traveled to the Northwest to face the challenges of NWA Pacific Northwest Heavyweight champions Mayne, Savage, Kirby, Kurt von Steiger, Stasiak, Boyd, and Ramos and title contender Mike "The Skull" Davis during an outstanding four-year reign as world champion. Subsequent NWA titleholders Harley Race, Jack Brisco, and Terry Funk turned back the challenges of a battery of Pacific Northwest Wrestling standouts, including Stasiak, Ramos, Snuka, Savage, Mad Dog Vachon, Boyd, and Ventura. While the challengers from Pacific Northwest Wrestling always fell a bit short in their quest for the NWA World

Heavyweight title, a strong showing against the world champion normally labeled a top wrestler in the territory as the real deal and ensured his place in the top mix of wrestlers in the region for months or even years afterward.

The lifting of a 30-year ban on women's wrestling in Oregon in 1975 brought some fresh air to the promotion, with female wrestlers such as Sue Green, Paula Kaye, Jean Antone, Betty Niccoli, and British Columbia native Sandy Parker mixing it up—sometimes in mixed tag team matches with male partners—in Portland and other stops on the circuit in the mid–1970s.

The success of Pacific Northwest Wrestling from the late 1960s through the 1970s was driven by entertaining, sometimes over-the-top characters placed in often compelling situations usually requiring some form of fisticuffs to settle a score. Through an assortment of larger-than-life characters with the ability to involve audiences in the competitors' personal issues, Don Owen presented the hottest ticket in most cities and towns around the territory. Of course, it was the power of a television product with few frills—*Portland Wrestling* and the syndicated *Big Time Wrestling*—that sold fans on coming out to the arenas. That spoke volumes about the ability of Owen and the wrestlers themselves to create characters and situations intriguing enough to sustain a hit local and regional TV show year after year during the height of Pacific Northwest Wrestling. There was nothing spectacular about the voice of commentator Frank Bonnema, but, like Vancouver's Ron Morrier during the heyday of *All-Star Wrestling*, Bonnema seemed the perfect fit for *Portland Wrestling*. The real stars of the show over the long haul, though, were probably the former bowling alley repurposed in 1968

Maurice "Mad Dog" Vachon, who displayed some of the same eating habits as Lonnie Mayne, was an outstanding amateur wrestler before beginning his professional wrestling career in the early 1950s. A native of Québec, Vachon was a six-time NWA Pacific Northwest Heavyweight champion in the 1960s, a decade that also saw him hold the AWA World Heavyweight championship four times. Vachon remained active until the 1980s, when he was well into his fifties. Vachon also had significant success as a tag team wrestler, most notably with real-life brother Paul "Butcher" Vachon.

as the Portland Sports Arena and the legion of dedicated fans who showed up week after week to watch the gladiators go at it.

Unfortunately, relatively little video footage survives from either the pre–1972 black-and-white era of *Portland Wrestling* or the next several years of TV shootings from the Portland Sports Arena, as Owen, like other dollar-conscious wrestling promoters of his day, taped new episodes over existing ones rather than spending a modest amount of money to purchase new tapes. Without a doubt, though, images of many brutal battles and the antics of a steady stream of unforgettable characters remain etched in the memories of some older fans of late-1960s and 1970s *Portland Wrestling* to the present day.

11

Life of an "Outlaw" Territory, 1973–1975

Although Oregon and British Columbia were the main centers of activity during pro wrestling's 1970s glory days in the Pacific Northwest, there was also plenty of wrestling activity in Washington State during that decade. While wrestling in Washington had taken a hit with the demise of Harry Elliott's *Northwest Championship Wrestling* in 1967, the industry managed to stay afloat in the Evergreen State until Dutch Savage bought promotional rights in Washington—particularly, the northern part of the state—from Vancouver promoter Sandor Kovacs in about 1972. A few years later, in 1976, Savage bought a share—widely reported as a third—of Pacific Northwest Wrestling and focused on running a full-fledged promotion in Washington using a talent pool based mainly in Portland, which was also the setting of the regionally syndicated television show that brought fans out to see the stars of Pacific Northwest Wrestling in major Washington centers such as Seattle, Tacoma, and Spokane.

Although NWA promoters did not always see eye to eye in the 1970s—or ever, for that matter, since the inception of the organization in 1948—members did for the most part stand behind fellow member NWA promoters and their "right" to exclusivity when it came to promoting wrestling events within their designated territories. That did not necessarily prevent new promoters from appearing in NWA territories, as agreements with NWA promoters sometimes enabled satellite promotions to function in areas the NWA had granted to member promoters. This was the case with Savage, who promoted many events in Washington State during the 1970s with the full blessing of NWA promoters Owen and Kovacs. As if to highlight his unblemished relationship with his neighboring promoters, Savage remained a main event wrestler for both Pacific Northwest Wrestling and All-Star Wrestling during times when much of his energy was focused on his promotional activities in Washington.

In the previous decade, Harry Elliott had been a successful promoter in Washington and, like Savage in the 1970s, maintained an excellent relationship with the promotions in Oregon and British Columbia. Booking wrestlers, including main eventers, mainly out of Portland, Elliott ran a profitable promotion spanning much of Washington, and his *Northwest Championship Wrestling* TV show reached virtually every population center in the state. But things started to unravel in 1967, when Seattle's KIRO-TV, *Northwest Championship Wrestling's* flagship station, made the call, as Silverstone reports in *Pig Farmer*, to move the venue for Elliott's TV tapings from the inner-city Masonic Temple to the much smaller, 200-seat Norway Center. According to Silverstone, KIRO called for the move due to concerns about gang and criminal activity near the Masonic Temple, especially after a KIRO truck sent out to televise a wrestling show was invaded and employees in the truck were assaulted (96).

As Silverstone—an associate of Elliott's at the time—describes it, moving the television tapings constituted a downgrade from an arena-like setting for Elliott's show to a more sedate, studio-like setting. "Switching from a house-show tape to a studio-type tape," he says in *Pig Farmer*, "really hurt the quality of the show, and television ratings began to drop" (96).

Subsequently, the show was canceled, and Elliott soon left the wrestling business. For a brief time, Silverstone reports, Elliott was the "front man" or promoter of record in Seattle for the Kovacs promotion, which had purchased from Elliott the right to hold spot shows in Seattle. According to Silverstone, tapes of Vancouver wrestling, with dubbed-in commentary by Silverstone and station announcer Carl Seidel, were broadcast weekly on Tacoma's KTVW-TV (now KCPQ) to tout upcoming matches in Seattle and Tacoma. But incursions into the Seattle-Tacoma area were by no means a priority for the Kovacs promotion, which was doing well in British Columbia and, without solid TV penetration in the major Washington cities to drive attendance, doubled down on its efforts in British Columbia rather than investing significant resources in running Washington shows. Silverstone, who had been a jack-of-all trades for Elliott—writing and selling programs fans would purchase at the arenas, promoting spot shows in smaller towns, and refereeing—started traveling weekly to Vancouver, where he sold his programs to fans attending All-Star Wrestling's major Monday night shows and filled in occasionally as a referee. Each week, he reports in *Pig Farmer*, he returned to Washington with a videotape of *All-Star Wrestling*, which would be broadcast on KTVW. But the station's weak signal at the time and an aversion to running money-losing shows soon led the Kovacs promotion to discontinue running events around Seattle (97–98).

Silverstone reports in his book that he was contacted in 1972 by a friend, program manager Jim Neidigh of KTNT-TV—an independent Seattle channel and former DuMont Television Network affiliate—about the possibility of supplying a wrestling show to air on the channel. According to Silverstone, Neidigh, who had worked for KIRO when *Northwest Championship Wrestling* was pulling strong ratings on the station, favored giving a similar wrestling boost to his new station, although KTNT itself lacked the ability or resources to produce its own wrestling show. When Silverstone called around to other television stations, he heard the same thing: They'd be happy to give airtime to Silverstone for a wrestling program, but they couldn't produce an original show (Silverstone, 99).

According to his account in *Pig Farmer*, Silverstone, still making weekly excursions to Vancouver, asked promoters Kovacs and Kiniski for permission to have the weekly videotape of *All-Star Wrestling* air on TV stations in Washington other than "that Mickey Mouse station in Tacoma." As Silverstone describes it in *Pig Farmer*, he proposed to Kovacs and Kiniski, "Let me take that tape to other stations and I'll re-open Washington for you. The only thing you'd have to do would be to edit special promos onto the tape geared to Washington spots." Silverstone reports Kovacs and Kiniski liked the proposal, but the third partner in the promotion, Don Owen, vetoed it, thereby delaying Silverstone's longtime dream of running a promotional office for wrestling in his home state of Washington (99–100). Soon after, Savage purchased the Washington promotional rights from Kovacs, in effect filling the role Silverstone had sought to fill.

Undeterred, in early 1973 Silverstone visited Spokane ABC affiliate KXLY-TV—another former DuMont Network affiliate—and asked to see a station employee he had known while working for Elliott. When his old acquaintance, James Agostina, appeared, Silverstone requested help producing a wrestling show he hoped to broadcast in Seattle and Spokane. According to Silverstone, Agostina indicated that, while KXLY did not have the means to produce a wrestling show, a sister station in Yakima, Washington, could perhaps accommodate Silverstone. Silverstone reports that he thanked Agostina, drove "directly to the Spokane International Airport ... [and] booked a seat on the next available flight to Yakima, which was about 200 miles southwest of Spokane" (Silverstone, 111–112).

After arriving in Yakima, Silverstone quickly worked out details with KAPP-TV regarding production of a program that would be guaranteed airtime in Spokane, Yakima, and Kennewick on Saturday or Sunday afternoons. Arrangements with further stations would be left up to Silverstone, who reports in *Pig Farmer* that he struck deals with TV stations in Bellingham and Wenatchee, Washington; Lewiston and Boise, Idaho; and Pendleton, Oregon; along with Tacoma's KTVW and Seattle's KTNT, the station that had started him on this adventure. Silverstone reports, "Every possible market in the state of Washington would be able to view at least one hour of [his program] *Super Star Championship Wrestling* each and every week. Don Owen's wrestling program ... could not be seen by people living in Pendleton, but they would pick up *Super Star*, which was broadcast in northeastern Oregon. People living in southern British Columbia would be able to view the Bellingham broadcast" (114).

An interesting note is that KAPP's Yakima studio was so small that any matches to be taped there would have to take place in a 14×14–foot ring, which would provide only about half the area of a more standard 20×20–foot ring of the sort modern-day fans are used to seeing on television. Though Silverstone had other, larger rings he intended to use at the house shows in the new territory he envisioned, he had to purchase a smaller ring suitable for the KAPP studio.

He had plenty else to do, including getting a promoter's license, hiring wrestlers, buying a truck to transport equipment, putting together a TV show, and lining up towns for his house shows. Confident in his ability to work things out quickly and concerned that rival promoters might try to move in on his home state, Silverstone informed the 10 TV stations planning to broadcast his new program that he would begin supplying them with tapes by the start of the new television season in September of 1973.

Silverstone made good, getting his Washington promoter's license and then a license to promote in Pendleton, Oregon, far enough from Don Owen's recognized territory that his request to run shows in Pendleton was granted. He hired former Seattle sportscaster Bill O'Mara—who had called matches on television two decades earlier for Bob Murray's promotion—as his television announcer, secured John Quinn as a main event wrestler, and headed for the southern U.S. to look for wrestlers to bring up to the Northwest to work for Super Star Championship Wrestling. As Silverstone explains at www.1wrestlinglegends.com, "Wrestling fans [in the Northwest] were tired of seeing the same crew over and over again. I wanted to bring in new faces that had never been there."

Silverstone hired a crew including southeastern U.S. wrestlers Rip Tyler; Eddie Sullivan; Arman Hussian, known a few years earlier in British Columbia as Armand Hussein; Eric "Great Gama" Verbel, better known elsewhere as Jack Evans and not to be confused with Stampede Wrestling's "Great Gama," who appeared, usually as Gama Singh, in British Columbia and Oregon in the 1970s; Greg Lake; and Don "Lumberjack Luke" Morrison, a Kelowna, BC, native who was wrestling in the Gulf Coast area and was eager to return to the Northwest. After arranging or purchasing everything needed for kicking off his new wrestling promotion, Silverstone had his first *Super Star Championship Wrestling* taping at Yakima's KAPP studio in early September of 1973. The weekly tapings began on Fridays but switched, two months later, to Wednesdays, which, as Silverstone points out in *Pig Farmer*, "would allow plenty of time to bicycle [transport] the tapes to the other stations that aired the show" (125).

With some Northwest-based backup talent to supplement his collection of headlining and mid-card wrestlers, Silverstone established a weekly pattern of cards in Seattle, Tacoma, and Spokane to go along with his weekly TV tapings and house shows (the same night) in Yakima, where, once the promotion got rolling, "we sold out the [3,000-capacity] Yakima armory almost every week. There were occasions when we drew less, but we never had a house less than 1,500 people" (135). Rounding out the week were spot shows in numerous Washington towns, as well as Pendleton, Oregon, and locations in western Idaho. Shows outside Washington were normally held on Sundays because a Sunday-wrestling ban was in effect in Washington at the time.

One particularly hot rivalry in Super Star Championship Wrestling was a program Silverstone likens to the Shag Thomas–Tony Borne rivalry that had played big in Pacific Northwest Wrestling in the early 1960s. Much as Borne and Thomas had been a dominant heel tag team in Pacific Northwest Wrestling, Sullivan and Lumberjack Luke played a similar role with Super Star Championship Wrestling. And then, as had happened in 1960 with Thomas and Borne, their partnership dissolved during the heat of a tag team battle.

In the case of Sullivan and Luke, during a televised match in March of 1974, the pair laid a beating on Goldie Rogers, who worked preliminary matches for Pacific Northwest Wrestling and All-Star Wrestling as well as Super Star Championship Wrestling in the 1970s. As Rogers bled profusely, Sullivan and Luke had different opinions about whether they should administer further punishment to Rogers. While Luke was in favor of dishing out more brutality, Sullivan decided enough was enough. As Silverstone reports in *Pig Farmer*,

> With the blood streaming down Goldie's face, Luke was … ready to finish him off, but Eddie could take no more…. Eddie came into the ring through the ropes and surprised Luke with a sock to the jaw that lifted the 260-pound wrestler four feet above the ground. The surprised Luke became irate and charged after Sullivan, who had turned his attention to the prone, unconscious Goldie Rogers. Luke brought his boot down onto Eddie's neck, after which the two began to battle. The fans in the bleachers became energized and the dressing room emptied to separate the two [142].

Silverstone continues, "Six hours later, at the house show held at the Yakima armory, the entire audience knew Eddie was a babyface; and that was before the tape had aired on television. The incident had spread by word of mouth, and when Eddie entered the armory that night, he was swarmed by the fans. We had created the strongest babyface possible and we were about to make money" (142).

It was a simple formula but one that, when played out masterfully—as it was in the case of Borne–Thomas and Sullivan–Luke—could set a wrestling territory on fire. Silverstone describes the first week of the two-month-long Luke–Sullivan program: "We sold every ticket (and then some) in all seven cities and drew more than 12,000 people, which generated $35,000 gross. When concession and program sales were added, the figure topped $38,000" (144)—which was excellent for a territory the size of Super Star Championship Wrestling in 1974.

That same year, Luke was involved in an incident Silverstone describes in his book and at www.1wrestlinglegends.com as "perhaps the biggest promotional surprise in Northwest history," when, according to *Pig Farmer*, "an unplanned incident that took place on television mushroomed into a great deal of publicity for Super Star Wrestling" (216).

Silverstone reports that "Luke's persona was that of a he-man from the Canadian wilds. He criticized Americans for being soft and lazy and said their employment was [characterized] by non-intelligent jobs. One day, while doing an interview in Yakima with Bill O'Mara, he said he objected to having to wrestle in front of the local people, who were common 'pig farmers'" (216).

At www.1wrestlinglegends.com, Silverstone continues, "The tone of [Luke's] voice and the way he referred to the local people as a bunch of pig farmers [ensured] that the listening public was outraged." Silverstone adds, "His remark about pig farmers caused such anger from the viewers that the TV station [KAPP], before sending out the tapes for the other stations, actually 'bleeped' the words 'pig farmer' all five times from his interviews. After the tape was played in each market, the viewing public was curious as to what had been said and apparently they swamped the television station and sports editors of newspapers to find out what that no-good bum had said."

Silverstone continues, in *"I Ain't No Pig Farmer!"*—which obviously drew its title from this incident—"Suddenly, we had press and TV coverage galore. The same newspapers which had steadfastly refused to even print wrestling results ... were reporting Luke's comments like he was the one responsible for the Watergate break-in. All the TV stations wanted Luke to appear on their newscast and talk shows, and every radio station in the state wanted Luke for their talk radio programs" (217). All that publicity and notoriety kept ticket sales strong through the remainder of 1974 and into 1975.

While Luke—who passed away in 2009—is probably the wrestler most closely identified with Super Star Championship Wrestling, other key wrestlers in the promotion included Quinn, Paddy Ryan—like Quinn, a native of the Hamilton, Ontario, "wrestling factory"—Ripper Collins, Don Fargo, Luke Graham, Whipper Watson, Jr., Duke Myers, Sullivan, 450-lb. "Tiny" Frazier, Ron Dupree, Chris Colt, Karl von Brauner, Lake, 6'9" veteran and international star Tex McKenzie, and Sandy Parker, a British Columbia native who in the 1970s was a popular touring female wrestler across the United States and Canada.

Fueled by Luke, Quinn, Sullivan, Ryan, Dupree and Colt as the Hell's Angels, and a strong supporting cast, Super Star Championship Wrestling was doing well enough in Washington to draw the attention of NWA promoters to the immediate north and south. Silverstone reports, in *Pig Farmer*, "All of a sudden, in November 1974, Don Owen and Sandor Kovacs were running shows in a few of our best-drawing towns," including Yakima, Seattle, and Bellingham (194).

Looking back more than four decades after the fact, Silverstone recalls other signs that his independent promotion was in the sights of the National Wrestling Alliance. "I had athletic commission inspectors calling me," he says. According to Silverstone, the commission told him there had been complaints about Super Star Wrestling's violation of some entries in Washington State's decades-old "Rules and Regulations of Professional Wrestling" handbook, particularly when it came to matches involving the Hell's Angels, Colt and Dupree, and their tendency to take the action out of the ring onto the floor. "It all stemmed from phone calls from the NWA attempting to curtail my houses," says Silverstone, who credits the same two wrestlers who had been fingered by the NWA and the state commission—Colt and Dupree, described by Silverstone as "big moneymakers"—with helping provide him the ammunition to point out to inspectors and the commission that Super Star Championship Wrestling was drawing good crowds and, as a result, contributing generously to the state's coffers. "Five percent of our gross went to the state," Silverstone says.

Colt and Dupree continued their mayhem, and Washington fans continued to support the homegrown Super Star Championship Wrestling promotion, which seemed to maintain the upper hand throughout Washington well into 1975. But sadly, Dupree—who retired as a wrestler in early 1975 due to heart problems—passed away in October of that year while ring announcing a Collins–Ryan match for the promotion in Tacoma.

A few months earlier, in July, Silverstone learned that KAPP-TV would be relocating several months later and the studio hosting *Super Star* tapings would be demolished. While KAPP made it clear that it wanted *Super Star* tapings to resume once the station's relocation to a new studio was complete, there would be a nine-week period near the end of 1975 when there would be no facility available for the tapings. After determining that it would be virtually impossible to maintain interest in his wrestling product without sticking to his weekly television schedule—and after determining it would be too costly and risky to move tapings to a different location until the new KAPP studio was available—Silverstone decided to close down Super Star Championship Wrestling in December of 1975. For four decades afterward, he focused on his other passion—music—as the owner of a popular record store, specializing in hard-to-find titles, in Seattle.

12

The Tomko Takeover

Al Tomko, who took over Sandor Kovacs' share of Vancouver's All-Star Wrestling territory in January of 1977, may have been relatively unfamiliar at the time to West Coast wrestling fans, but he was anything but a newcomer to the wrestling business.

Like the von Steigers and Bob Brown, Tomko began his wrestling career at an early age in Manitoba. He was still in his teens when, as prowrestling. wikia.com reports, "he started out as a wrestler in his hometown of Winnipeg in the 1950s [precisely, 1950] with his own promotion, the Olympia Wrestling Club." According to Nevada's *Wrestling in the Canadian West*, "Tomko opened the Olympia Club out of the basement of his Elmwood home with the ambition to train wrestlers and bodybuilders" (48). Nevada says Tomko's main interest at the time was in weight training and bodybuilding, and it appears Tomko had limited involvement in wrestling or training wrestlers while he owned the Olympia Club. While the Olympia Wrestling Club was the training ground for a few wrestlers who broke into the professional ranks, the club started to decline after a couple of years, and Tomko shut it down.

In 1954 Tomko resurfaced in the larger Madison Wrestling Club, the Winnipeg-based promotion that served as a training ground for the von Steigers, Brown, and Moose Morowski, who was a headliner in British Columbia at times from the late 1960s all the way to the late 1980s. Tomko also appeared in mid–1950s events promoted by Winnipeg's Crescent Boxing and Wrestling Club, and in the late 1950s he wrestled for Winnipeg's Brooklands Wrestling Club, earning a victory over Brown in April of 1958.

Tomko spent over a decade wrestling for the Madison Club, where, prowrestling.wikia.com reports, he became "one of that promotion's top heels," although the only title Tomko held during that period was a mid–1960s tag team championship with Stan Mykietowich, the future Moose Morowski. In 1966 Tomko became the Manitoba agent for Verne Gagne's AWA, and a year later Tomko purchased the Madison Club for a reported $5,000. Nevada reports that, while Tomko strongly denied it, "it is [rumored] that the purchase was ordered by Verne Gagne himself to eliminate any competition to his growing monopoly on the territory, as the Madison Club was drawing strong weekly crowds and challenged the AWA's growth" (50). Tony Condello, who wrestled for the Madison Club in the 1960s before kicking off a long career as an independent promoter, says, "[Gagne] put up Al Tomko to buy out the Madison Club…. He ran maybe one or two shows and then shut it down" before turning his full attention to the AWA.

Tomko was also an active wrestler in the late 1960s, working for Stampede Wrestling as the masked Cosmo #1 and for the AWA in the Manitoba-Minnesota area mainly as Leroy "Crazy Legs" Hirsch, a name Nevada reports Tomko attributed to a meeting with an ex–NFL player who had the same name (55). In 1969 Tomko ventured to the Northwest, appearing for the first time in Oregon and, for a few months, wrestling as a mid-carder in British Columbia.

During most of the 1970s Tomko stayed close to his Winnipeg base, promoting events for the AWA; starting up another small promotion and providing a training ground for local wrestlers; and wrestling on occasion in Manitoba and in nearby U.S. cities where the AWA held shows.

Nevada says Tomko's new promotion—Central Canadian Championship Wrestling, established in 1972—was a reaction to the efforts of Condello to establish a professional relationship with the AWA. Nevada writes, "When … Tomko learned of Condello's aspirations, he contacted the AWA owner, Verne Gagne in Minneapolis, telling him to avoid the Italian entrepreneur, warning (falsely) that he was connected to the Montreal Mafia. Needless to say, Gagne was not interested in doing business with Condello in any manner after this discovery" (Nevada, 63). As well, "Tomko was encouraged to commit some of his energies to promoting his own product independently of his obligations with the AWA" (Nevada, 68), presumably to keep the efforts of Condello—who was viewed as a promoter in opposition to the AWA—in check.

Condello, who says he was stopped at the U.S. border while heading south expecting to sign a deal with the AWA, confirms that Tomko "told Verne Gagne … Tony Condello belonged to the Montreal Mafia." Afterward, Condello says, "Every time I saw Verne Gagne in Winnipeg, he stayed away from me."

Using a mix of name wrestlers—most notably, AWA star Baron von Raschke and Winnipeg native George "Flash Gordon" Gordienko—along with a selection of Winnipeg journeymen, a young and rising Roddy Piper, and Tomko himself—appearing as the Zodiac—Tomko focused on promoting shows in areas of Manitoba outside of Winnipeg. According to Nevada, "This was done so that his independent cards did not interfere with his Winnipeg promotion of the AWA and to combat Condello's advances in the territorial war." Nevada also reports that Tomko was able to secure a weekly Central

Canadian Championship Wrestling program on CKX-TV in Brandon, Manitoba (68).

Despite Tomko's long relationship with the AWA, things were hardly perfect between the Minneapolis-based organization and its Winnipeg representative. According to Nevada, "Tomko had expressed his unhappiness with reported [cancelations] and changes to advertised talent scheduled to appear in Winnipeg, causing Tomko to lose credibility with his sponsors and fanbase in Winnipeg." Whether or not this was a key factor in his decision, Tomko ended his association with the AWA in 1977 when he left Manitoba, Nevada says, "without making arrangements to turn over the lease agreement for the Winnipeg Arena," in effect, shutting the AWA out of its established Winnipeg venue until Tomko's successor as AWA rep was issued a lease of his own (56).

Tomko was lured out of Manitoba when Sandor Kovacs, who had enjoyed a very successful nine-year run promoting All-Star Wrestling in British Columbia, decided to sell his share of the promotion. Though business was strong in the territory to Kovacs' last day with the promotion, it has been speculated that Kovacs saw a hard time ahead for regional promotions such as his own. In any event, Tomko bought out Kovacs' share of All-Star Wrestling and moved halfway across Canada to the Pacific coast, arriving in Vancouver in early 1977.

With Kiniski and Owen apparently maintaining their interests in All-Star Wrestling, the transition from the Kovacs era to the Tomko era seemed relatively seamless. Kiniski continued to wrestle main events in the territory, as did other established names such as Quinn, Jonathan, Mitchell, Savage, and Snuka. Another key wrestler was John Anson, a Vancouver native who, as Karl von Shotz, had held half a dozen tag team titles elsewhere as the German heel partner of Hamilton, Ontario, native Bill "Kurt von Hess" Terry. Hess had success in several territories and wrestled occasionally in British Columbia and Oregon, especially in 1976 and 1977, one time winning the NWA Canadian Tag Team championship with Quinn.

Anson arrived in All-Star Wrestling in the summer of 1976. By the time Tomko arrived in 1977, Anson was a two-time Canadian Tag Team titleholder, once as a babyface and once as a heel—though in no way German. Anson continued to play a key role during the early part of Tomko's promotion in Vancouver, as did Paddy Ryan; Igor Volkoff; Mike Sharpe, yet another product of Hamilton, Ontario, who would go on to become a high-profile mid-carder and "jobber" (or loser of most of his matches) in the WWF; and Erich Froelich, who had been in and out of the territory ever since debuting as a wrestler—in British Columbia—in 1960.

Brought into All-Star Wrestling in the late 1970s were established wrestlers including Moose Morowski, formerly Tomko's Winnipeg tag team partner Stan Mykietowich; Yaki Joe, better known outside British Columbia as Mexican veteran Francisco Flores; Siegfried Steinke, back for one more championship run in Vancouver after successful stays in Florida and, especially, Texas; and Adrian Adonis, who earlier in the 1970s had wrestled in the territory as Keith Franks. André the Giant—the most popular wrestling attraction worldwide in the late 1970s—was also brought in occasionally for major shows in Vancouver.

Don Leo Jonathan's outstanding career extended into the early years of Al Tomko's ownership of the Vancouver wrestling promotion. One of the most respected figures in the history of Northwest wrestling, Jonathan was an international superstar who displayed remarkable skills for a big man and was in demand by promoters around the world. In the early 1960s Jonathan, a second-generation wrestler and native of Utah, established his home in British Columbia, which he has called home ever since.

Though perhaps not to the same degree as a few years earlier, All-Star Wrestling attracted some grapplers who would go on to major stardom elsewhere. Besides Adonis—clearly, by the late 1970s, on his way to becoming one of the outstanding wrestlers of his era—such names included the Iron Sheik, who would become WWF champion in the lead-in to the Hulk Hogan era; Bruce "Butch" Reed, who went on to become a championship-caliber wrestler in many territories; and Jake Roberts, a wrestler in his early twenties who spent most of 1978 honing his skills in British Columbia.

Roberts, born Aurelian Smith, Jr., was a second-generation wrestler. The original Aurelian Smith was a giant Texan who wrestled in numerous territories over many years as Grizzly Smith. The elder Smith wrestled in the Vancouver territory in 1968 and, as Ski Hi Jones, shared a brief Canadian Tag Team title run with fellow giant Don Leo Jonathan.

Jake Roberts followed his father into professional wrestling in the mid–1970s, appearing mainly in the southern U.S. and the Midwest before arriving in Vancouver in early 1978 and quickly finding his way into the top mix of wrestlers. Though he would go on to spend most of his career as a top heel, Roberts was a babyface in the Vancouver territory and one of the most popular up-and-comers the territory saw during the 1970s. A few months after his debut in British Columbia, Roberts was selected as André the Giant's tag team partner when the latter was brought in to headline a Vancouver show in July of 1978.

While Roberts was positioned near the top during his entire stay in British Columbia, some observers believe Tomko, Kiniski, and Owen missed the boat as far as Roberts was concerned. Nevada reports on a rivalry that took place in the spring of 1978 between veteran Morowski—wrestling under a mask as the Black Avenger—and the rising Roberts. As Nevada reports, a cage match was held for the first time ever in Vancouver, as Tomko sought, in Morowski's words, to "keep with the times." According to Nevada, "The feud culminated in the unmasking of the Avenger, establishing Roberts as a main event talent" (70).

Nevada quotes Morowski: "They could have built the territory around that guy, he was that good.... What'd they do? They had Kiniski beat him the next week. They wasted it, after all we'd done to build him up. I left for Japan and found out when I came back [that] Jake had left for Calgary" (70). Roberts adds, in Greg Oliver's April 14, 2010, *SLAM! Wrestling* report on Kiniski's death that same day, "Moose basically led me through the process and made me a star, and got me over. In the process, we got to where the PNE [Pacific Northwest Exhibition Gardens] was selling out, which they hadn't done in years. At that point, Gene says, 'Damn, I'd better come back in and wrestle again, they're having sellouts.' ... Next thing, I wrestled Kiniski and he beat me two straight [falls]."

Roberts' first championship came in Stampede Wrestling just a few months after his late–1978 departure from Vancouver, and he piled up his share of singles titles in major territories over the next seven years and a few more titles late in his career. Roberts earned a lasting reputation as a skilled worker, an engaging speaker, and an unforgettable character and master of ring and crowd psychology as Jake "the Snake" Roberts, whose career culminated in a hugely successful WWF run in the late 1980s and early 1990s. Though Roberts' personal battles are well-documented, he is widely considered one of the best wrestlers of his era never to have won a world championship, and such potential was evident when he wrestled in British Columbia during most of 1978.

Other names featured in Tomko's All-Star Wrestling during the late 1970s included Salvatore Martino, a Belgian native who held the newly named Canadian Heavyweight title and a share of the Canadian Tag Team title before going on to gain some recognition as 1980s WWF mid-card and preliminary wrestler Salvatore Bellomo; Eugene "Buck" Zumhofe, a Minnesotan who had his share of mid-card victories in British Columbia before wrestling in AWA preliminaries throughout the 1980s and, in 2014, getting sentenced to 25 or more years in jail as a result of sex charges; Don Wayt, a tough 300-pound Texan who held both major titles in All-Star Wrestling before retiring young and returning to Texas, where he became a prison chaplain; Ed "Moondog" Moretti, a California native who borrowed Lonnie Mayne's nickname and went on to enjoy several title runs in All-Star Wrestling during the 1980s; Bobby Jaggers, a rugged native of Vancouver, Washington, whose share of the Canadian Tag Team title in 1979 represented just one of at least 30 regional championships—including several in Pacific Northwest Wrestling in the mid–1980s—he would hold during his career; Chris Colt, a favorite of Silverstone's remembered by Moretti as "one of the most underutilized wrestlers in the business" who was "as good as anyone in the world" and by Silverstone, in *Pig Farmer*, as "a unique, interesting, one-of-a-kind individual" and "a cult figure amongst professional wrestling historians and fans" (184); and Tomko himself, who got into the ring occasionally during his early years of promoting in Vancouver but gave little indication of things to come a few years later.

Adding to the depth of Tomko's roster in the late 1970s and early 1980s was his use of key wrestlers from Owen's Portland territory. Appearing on *All-Star Wrestling* and on house shows mainly in and around Vancouver were Pacific Northwest Wrestling notables such as all-time favorites Piper, Snuka, Rose, Stasiak, Ramos, and Savage, along with others such as 1980s 12-time NWA Pacific Northwest Heavyweight champion Rip Oliver; Rick Martel, who in the 1980s would hold titles in All-Star Wrestling, Pacific Northwest Wrestling, the AWA, and the WWF; Jay Youngblood, a Native American character who won multiple titles in Oregon and British Columbia in the early 1980s before gaining national recognition as a World Tag Team champion for Jim Crockett Promotions and passing away, at age 30, in 1985; and the Sheepherders, Bob "Butch" Miller and Brian "Luke Williams" Wickens, the New Zealand duo who, several years after winning the tag titles in both the Portland and Vancouver territories, would become one of the highest-profile teams in wrestling as the WWF's Bushwhackers.

While such formidable backup from Portland certainly made All-Star Wrestling a deeper territory, talent-wise, than it would otherwise have been, some observers feel that was detrimental to the long-term health of All-Star Wrestling. Moretti says, "Owen's [Portland] wrestlers were beating the Vancouver guys on TV. They were making our guys look bad … and it hurt business."

Owen's apparent withdrawal from Vancouver in 1980 does not appear to have improved the situation for All-Star Wrestling. While some main eventers from Portland—particularly Rose, Oliver, and Youngblood—continued to appear in Vancouver and held championships there in 1981, Owen's departure resulted in a drastic reduction of wrestlers traveling from Oregon to British Columbia to fill out—or take featured spots on—the *All-Star Wrestling* TV show or major house shows after 1980. A year or two after Owen's departure, Kiniski would walk away from the promotion as well.

Among Kiniski's matches during his last year or so in All-Star Wrestling were a few tag team contests pairing him with Kelly Kiniski, one of two Kiniski sons who wrestled professionally for a few years in the 1980s in Canada, the United States, and Japan. Kelly Kiniski also made a few appearances in 1981 with Pacific Northwest Wrestling, and younger brother Nick Kiniski followed suit by appearing as a mid-card wrestler in that promotion from late 1985 to 1986.

With Owen and Kiniski out of the picture, Tomko was left to his own devices in his effort to keep the British Columbia territory strong and profitable. He is not remembered, however, as a promoter who was willing or able to spend top dollar to attract established talent. Neil Drummond—both an on-camera and a behind-the-scenes figure for All-Star Wrestling in the 1980s—says, "Al was cheap for sure. He flew by the seat of his pants ... and he liked to make his own stars."

The biggest star Tomko made as the sole promoter of All-Star Wrestling caught many fans and observers by surprise. According to Dutch Savage, quoted in Oliver's Aug. 6, 2009, *SLAM! Wrestling* article the day after Tomko's death, attendance in Vancouver suffered following Owen's departure from the territory, "but Don begged me to help him [Tomko] with the book [or booking—that is, setting out matches and programs for the territory]. So for about five months we slowly got the territory going again. We finally got the houses up and a couple of sellouts at the [Pacific Northwest Exhibition Gardens] and I'll be dipped if he didn't book himself with the champion up there and put him over and take the belt. I wasn't there that week. No wonder he didn't want me up there on that Monday night card; he put the strap on his own waist."

Savage went further: "Incidentally, did you ever see Tomko work? ... He was a nice guy, don't get me wrong, but my granddaughter could [outwrestle] him."

Though that may have been an exaggeration, Tomko was in fact 50 years old when he won his first Canadian Heavyweight title in May of 1982. Over the next four years, wrestling occasionally as a babyface but far more often as a heel, he would win his promotion's top singles title six more times. Tomko also won a share of his promotion's Canadian Tag Team championship five times in the 1980s. That grand total of a dozen Tomko wrestling titles in the 1980s—10 captured after his 50th birthday—contrasts starkly with his earlier record, from the time of his 1950 wrestling debut until he bought into the Vancouver territory over a quarter-century later, of never having won a professional wrestling title or achieved main-event status anywhere outside the old Winnipeg wrestling clubs.

Tomko was far from the only over–50 wrestling promotion owner or part-owner of his era to take advantage of an owner's prerogative to make himself the champion of his own promotion. In Vancouver, Kiniski had held the Canadian Heavyweight title—the Tomko-era version of the old Pacific Coast championship—past his 50th birthday. In the U.S. Midwest, Verne Gagne, owner of the AWA, which had employed Tomko prior to his departure for the West Coast, was recognized as the World Heavyweight champion of his promotion when he was well into his fifties. At that time—in the early 1980s—Gagne's AWA title was widely recognized as one of the top three wrestling championships in the world. Also in the Midwest, owner-promoter Dick the Bruiser held his Indianapolis promotion's top singles title several times after passing age 50. Like Gagne, he was also a co-holder of his own promotion's World Tag Team championship after age 50. In the Detroit territory, meanwhile, owner-promoter The Sheik also held his promotion's top title—the NWA United States Heavyweight championship—several times after passing 50.

There is a notable difference, however, between Tomko and those other owner-champions of his era. Kiniski was a proven athlete—a former professional footballer who had transitioned to pro wrestling in the early 1950s en route to establishing himself as an international wrestling star, an AWA and NWA world champion, a well-known Canadian personality through numerous nationally televised appearances, one of the leading heels of his era, and a West Coast legend before he ever bought into All-Star Wrestling. Gagne was a college football star, a two-time NCAA wrestling champion, an alternate for the U.S. Olympic Freestyle Wrestling team, and a legitimate prospect for the NFL who chose to become a pro wrestler, established himself as one of the top "scientific" wrestlers in the U.S., captured numerous titles before forming the AWA in 1960, and then sold out arenas as the AWA champion for years against the likes of Kiniski, Mad Dog Vachon, Bruiser, Crusher, and Nick Bockwinkel—and, based on his long and successful track record, continued to sell out arenas beyond age 50. Bruiser had played the ultra-tough guy so convincingly for so many years that fans in the Midwest seemed to have little trouble accepting him as a territory champion when he was in his fifties. And the Sheik, while never known for athletic displays or finesse in the ring, had been a main eventer for so long that fans in Michigan and surrounding areas seemed to think nothing of his continuing to hold the U.S.

title when his hair was going gray—and fans remained as eager as ever for the diabolical Sheik to get his comeuppance. Meanwhile, Tomko, unlike those other four, was a relative unknown in the ring and had limited skills to highlight when, near the start of his sixth decade, he opted to feature himself as a championship-level wrestler in his promotion. And while he may have been muscular as a younger man, by the time Tomko was main-eventing in British Columbia, he looked every bit his age in the ring.

Packaging himself as Master Sergeant Tomko—perhaps emulating Northwest alumnus Bob Remus, who was starting to draw national attention as Sergeant Slaughter in the early 1980s—did not seem to make Tomko a much more compelling character. Tomko, however, did have a knack for riling TV audiences and house show crowds, though both were clearly declining by the time Tomko put himself on All-Star Wrestling's center stage.

The *All-Star Wrestling* television program—with a devoted national and regional audience during the height of the promotion and TV show in the 1970s—faced challenges in the early 1980s. The death of popular commentator Ron Morrier in August of 1981 resulted—after a brief period in which John Poser filled in—in the hiring of local radio personality Ed Karl as the new voice of *All-Star Wrestling*. While Karl did nothing to disgrace himself while calling matches for *All-Star Wrestling* for several years, there were many fans in British Columbia and across Canada who were not interested in listening to any voice but Morrier's calling the action for *All-Star Wrestling*.

Another transition for *All-Star Wrestling* came in 1983, when, as Nevada reports, "Tomko changed the format of the twenty year program and started taping television two weeks at a time" (70). From there, says Drummond, the taping schedule became more erratic as Tomko, intent on cutting costs, started taping multiple episodes of *All-Star Wrestling* on the same day or a batch of episodes over a few days—perhaps saving some money but virtually eliminating the up-to-date, week-to-week dynamic that had driven the show for so long.

Tomko did have some talented or established wrestlers on his roster in the early 1980s. Familiar figures, including Dean Ho—back following a successful stay in the WWWF and extensive touring in the 1970s—Morowski, and Bulldog Bob Brown—occasionally returning to Vancouver from his base in Kansas City—were headliners, as were Moondog Moretti; "Diamond" Timothy Flowers, a native of New York State who had success in California before arriving in BC while still in his early twenties and, like Moretti, going on to win multiple titles in Vancouver in the 1980s; and Klondike Mike, a hefty backwoods character and Yukon Eric throwback played by Mike Shaw, who went on to portray numerous characters—most notably, Makhan Singh, multi-time champion in Stampede Wrestling, and Bastion Booger in the WWF—over the course of a successful career. Other key faces in the early

1980s version of All-Star Wrestling included Erich Froelich; Igor Volkoff, who captured the promotion's tag team and heavyweight titles, holding the former with Tomko and losing the latter *to* Tomko; and Buck "Mr. Pro" Ramstead, who won his only Canadian Heavyweight title by defeating Tomko in late 1982. Others filling out the All-Star Wrestling roster in the early 1980s included Jeff "Bruiser" Costa, a young brawler seemingly following in the footsteps of Dick the Bruiser; Terry Adonis (no relation to Adrian), a competent journeyman who perhaps had his greatest career success in Tomko's All-Star Wrestling; Gerry "Rocky" Della Serra, a young Montrealer who would remain active in British Columbia wrestling over the long haul; and Rick Patterson, a Manitoban who debuted in All-Star Wrestling while still a teenager in 1983 and achieved some success there over the next year before eventually going on to his greatest career success as Leatherface in Japan.

Two other young wrestlers arrived in British Columbia in 1983, wrestling there briefly before moving on and becoming major stars in professional wrestling. One, Ricky Rood, left BC in the spring of 1983, became better known as Rick Rude, started building a championship resume, and became one of the most successful wrestlers in the U.S. while appearing in the WWF in the late 1980s, playing a brash ladies' man who, while clearly a cheater, demonstrated excellent ring skills and the ability to work up a crowd. Meanwhile, Michael Hegstrand, who kicked off his wrestling career in British Columbia as Crusher Haig, was a friend of Rood's and a fellow Minnesotan trained to wrestle by Ed Sharkey, probably Minnesota's second most prominent wrestling trainer, behind Verne Gagne. After barely testing the waters in BC, Crusher Haig was never heard from again. Instead, Hegstrand joined forces with Paul Ellering—who had briefly wrestled for Pacific Northwest Wrestling in 1982—and another Hegstrand friend, Joe Laurinaitis, and became Road Warrior Hawk. The Road Warriors, Hawk and Animal, managed by Ellering and noted for a variety of power moves, became a hugely successful tag team across North America and internationally in the 1980s and 1990s, with the first of their many major championships coming less than two months after Crusher Haig's debut in Vancouver.

Tragically, Rood and Hegstrand, two of the best-built wrestlers of their era, died fairly young, as did an alarming number of their wrestling peers from the 1980s and 1990s. Rood's death in 1999 was determined to be the result of a dangerously high dose of mixed medications, and in a 2011 interview on Montreal's Concordia University radio station CJLO—partially transcribed at www.prowrestling.net—Joe "Road Warrior Animal" Laurinaitis blames his former partner's 2003 death, officially caused by a heart attack, on drugs.

While Tomko had a fairly long list of wrestlers at his disposal, his early 1980s shows often featured a succession of somewhat lumbering matches between himself and fellow old-school veterans such as Morowski, Brown, and John Tolos. Those were hardly the sort of state-of-the-art matches that were sometimes on display just a province away in Stu Hart's Stampede Wrestling, which in 1983 featured such notable wrestlers as a young Bret Hart, who would go on to become a multi-time WWF and WCW (Atlanta-based World Championship Wrestling) champion and one of the most highly regarded wrestlers of his era; Davey Boy Smith, a skilled import from Great Britain who would go on to WWF/WWE fame; Tom "Dynamite Kid" Billington, looked back on as a revolutionary wrestler who was years ahead of the wrestling curve in Canada and the United States, and who spent the second half of 1983 in Pacific Northwest Wrestling, holding the promotion's heavyweight and tag team titles during his brief stay in Oregon; David "Dr. D" Schultz, a southern redneck brawler who had spent a few months, sometimes main-eventing, in Pacific Northwest Wrestling in mid–1982, would go on to main-event fame in the WWF, and in many ways seemed a prototype of "Stone Cold" Steve Austin; and "Honkytonk" Wayne Ferris, perhaps not the best technical wrestler on the roster but one who made a lasting impression while growing into the character that would bring him fame as the Honky Tonk Man a few years later in the WWF. Other well-regarded wrestlers on the 1983 Stampede Wrestling roster included future WWF star Jim Neidhart; former Olympic judo bronze medalist "Bad News" Allen Coage, later recast in the WWF as Bad News Brown; and Phil Lafleur, who would go on to wrestle for years as Dan Kroffat in Japan (not to be confused with the 1970s British Columbia–born wrestling star of the same name) and appear for a time in the WWF as Phil Lafon.

Other key figures in 1983 Stampede Wrestling included Atlantic Canada star Leo Burke; future three-time NWA Pacific Northwest Heavyweight champion Mike Miller; Hercules Ayala, a Puerto Rican strongman who mounted a few unsuccessful challenges for the NWA World Heavyweight championship; Archie "The Stomper" Gouldie, better known in the United States as the Mongolian Stomper and widely regarded as one of western Canada's all-time greatest heels; Francisco Flores, a Mexican star who had held titles in several territories, including, as Yaki Joe in 1979, both the heavyweight and tag team titles in Tomko's All-Star Wrestling; Mike Shaw, formerly Klondike Mike in All-Star Wrestling, who in 1983 was gaining heat as a heel en route to greater success in later years as Makhan Singh in Stampede Wrestling and a variety of characters in WCW and the WWF; and the tag team of Duke Myers—a bruising heavyweight and Super Star Championship Wrestling alumnus with several southern U.S. titles to his credit along with several Stampede Wrestling titles—and Kerry Brown, nephew of Bulldog Bob Brown and a capable wrestler in his own right.

Stampede Wrestling also had an excellent relationship with New Japan

Pro Wrestling, the promotion generally regarded as having the most advanced, most athletic wrestling product in the world in the early 1980s. Top Stampede Wrestling stars such as Bret Hart, Bad News Allen, Davey Boy Smith, and especially Dynamite Kid were also stars for New Japan Pro Wrestling. Similarly, Stampede Wrestling had an impressive collection of Japanese wrestlers on its shows in 1983. These included, as regulars, the acrobatic and highly regarded Joji (George) "The Cobra" Takano; Hiro Saito (no relation to former Northwest wrestling star Mr. Saito), who went on to have a long and successful career in New Japan; and Junji Hirata, who wore a Mohawk and wrestled as native North American Sonny Two Rivers in Stampede before dropping the "native" gimmick, growing his hair back, and wrestling for three more decades in Japan. Also appearing in Stampede Wrestling in 1983 were Kuniaki Kobayashi, one of the top junior heavyweights in the world, and two all-time superstars of Japanese wrestling, Nobuhiko Takada and Tatsumi Fujinama. Fujinami would go on to hold the NWA Pacific Northwest Heavyweight title for about two months in late 1988.

Simply put, the talent roster of Tomko's All-Star Wrestling couldn't match up to that of Stu Hart's Stampede Wrestling—and the same was true of the 1983 version of the *All-Star Wrestling* TV show, which noticeably lagged behind many other wrestling programs of the day, including *Stampede Wrestling*, which featured edited-down arena matches, skilled wrestlers, and a strong week-to-week build. That may not have been a major problem to Tomko in the early years of his promoting in Vancouver—though, clearly, his product had begun to decline—as both All-Star Wrestling and Stampede Wrestling were NWA promotions and, as a result, recognized by the NWA as the only legitimate wrestling promotions in their respective territories. In other words, Tomko had little to fear in terms of Stampede Wrestling setting its sights on bringing its live shows and upgraded product to the West Coast.

But then three key things happened. First, in 1982, Stampede Wrestling, with all the connections it needed, left the NWA. Second, *Stampede Wrestling* could be seen weekly on Vancouver television before the end of that same year. And third, Gene Kiniski, according to various accounts, did not like the direction in which All-Star Wrestling was headed and encouraged Stu Hart to run shows in British Columbia.

When Stampede Wrestling held successful shows in Vancouver and Victoria in the spring of 1983, Tomko responded by luring Stampede stars David Schultz and Honkytonk Wayne to Vancouver, where they continued the hot feud they had started in Alberta. According to Nevada, Tomko decided to go further by taking the fight to Stampede Wrestling's home turf, and "part of Tomko's counter-attack against the Hart family enterprise was to schedule a Honky Tonk Man–David Schultz showdown as the main event for his premiere card in Calgary on June 21, 1983." Nevada continues, "He expected this event to draw huge numbers. However, the impact of that debut was greatly reduced when David Schultz withdrew from the appearance" (71).

Nevada writes, in *Wrestling in the Canadian West*, "Though the Calgary debut drew poorly, Tomko made a second attempt in August. The results were equally discouraging" (72). That same month, meanwhile, Stampede Wrestling drew a reported 9,000 fans to an Aug. 25 event in Vancouver featuring Dynamite Kid defending his Stampede Wrestling World Mid-Heavyweight championship; Bret Hart battling nemesis Archie "The Stomper" Gouldie; André the Giant winning a battle royal; and Nick Bockwinkel defending the AWA World Heavyweight title against Schultz, already back in the Stampede Wrestling fold.

All-Star Wrestling in 1983 had nothing to compete with that, and as Drummond—who grew up watching early–1970s *Stampede Wrestling* from his childhood home in eastern British Columbia—puts it, "Stampede took over Vancouver." But Drummond points not only at the arrival on the West Coast of Stampede Wrestling—whose live show and television product Drummond describes as "just outstanding" for the time—but also at the high cost of running events at the Pacific Northwest Exhibition Gardens as a key factor in Tomko's decision to, first, curtail and then eliminate shows in Vancouver. Overall, Drummond says, Tomko saw it as more cost-effective to run his shows in cheaper venues outside Vancouver that typically drew crowds of several hundred. One of Tomko's favorite places for business, Drummond says, was several hundred miles north of Vancouver, on the Queen Charlotte Islands (now Haida Gwaii), where Tomko liked to hold several shows annually in September and was able to rake in some handsome profits with relatively little overhead.

In September of 1983, Tomko took some of his wrestlers—including Flowers, Moretti, Rick Patterson, Mike DuPree, Randy Rich, and Joseph Cagle—on a six-show tour of the Middle East. The tour, apparently arranged in cooperation with a Vancouver-based businessman with ties to Jordan, came on the heels of a match in August at Vancouver's Kerrisdale Arena between Flowers and Tiger Jeet Singh. According to www.kayfabememories. com, "The two incited a small riot and the result was the banning of All-Star Wrestling [for] almost six weeks by the NWA [actually, the Vancouver Athletic Commission] until October of 1983." Kayfabememories.com continues, "Al Tomko wanted to show the fans of BC that his promotion was a world-class operation and they toured Amman, Jordan." Whether or not Tomko succeeded in convincing fans in British Columbia that All-Star Wrestling in 1983 was a world-class wrestling promotion, he at least managed to help provide an unforgettable week—if not a career highlight—to a crew of wrestlers based in the Pacific Northwest who, for one week, got to take their act to an ancient amphitheater halfway around the world. Tomko also managed to capture—and apparently retire—the Jordan wrestling title and the Jordan Tag Team title over the course of what surely was a busy week.

Looking back on the tour, Patterson, a 19-year-old newcomer to wrestling at the time—and, over three decades later, still an active wrestler in Canada and overseas—says, "The fans were so nice. The Jordanian people were so friendly…. It was my very first trip. What a welcome to the wrestling business."

In 1984, when a buyout agreement with the expanding World Wrestling Federation closed Stampede Wrestling's doors, Tomko may have seen reason for hope. And while he continued to promote himself as a main eventer and champion, Tomko apparently saw something to emulate in the new WWF champion at the time, Hulk Hogan, as one of Tomko's most prominent wrestlers in 1984 was Vancouver native Adam "Wojo" Yawrenko, an athletic 6'8", 310-pounder Tomko billed as the "BC Hulk." Tomko dropped the Canadian title to the BC Hulk in May of 1984, though he regained the title when Yawrenko left British Columbia to wrestle overseas. As it turned out, medical concerns limited Yawrenko's ring career to about two years, cutting short a career that may have helped put the brakes to the Vancouver territory's decline, at least temporarily.

But continued decline seemed all but inevitable given the range of wrestling programs available to television viewers in British Columbia by the early to mid–1980s. Stampede Wrestling may have gone down, but many BC viewers had access to weekly wrestling programs from other promotions such as Toronto's Maple Leaf Wrestling, Jim Crockett Promotions (featuring Ric Flair and a strong supporting cast), 1963 Vancouver wrestler Bill Watts' Mid-South Wrestling, the standard-setting WWF, and Gagne's AWA.

The AWA actually ran three shows in Vancouver from January to April of 1985, with Gene Kiniski as the front man, but interest declined over the course of the shows and a fourth event never took place. More successful at planting firm roots in British Columbia was the World Wrestling Federation, which debuted in Vancouver in November 1984, returned for a couple of shows in 1985, and drew particularly strong crowds in 1986.

A major WWF event, promoted by Sandor Kovacs and featuring a Hulk Hogan title defense against 6'10", 360-pound Big John Studd, attracted 16,000 fans to Vancouver's BC Place Stadium on July 5, 1986, and appears to confirm Nevada's observation that "Tomko saw an opportunity to cash in on the popularity of the [WWF]." Perhaps recognizing that fans during the era of a young Hulk Hogan were unlikely to support a 54-year-old champion with an everyman build and limited ring skills, Tomko never booked himself to win another heavyweight championship after the WWF's July 1986 show at BC Place. Instead, as Nevada reports, "Tomko created some characters which had names which were similar, or out and out copies of recognized [WWF] superstars. Some advertising appeared promoting 'Macho Man' Timothy Flowers, 'Hacksaw' Mike Doogan, and King Kong Bundy Jr. [ripoffs of WWF wrestlers Macho Man Randy Savage, Hacksaw Jim Duggan, and King Kong Bundy]" (72). Moretti says, "Tomko, in my opinion, was the Jack Pfefer of his day," referring to an ex–East Coast promoter who worked with Chicago promoter Fred Kohler in the 1960s and became notorious for using wrestlers with sound-alike names such as Hobo Brazil, Bummy Rogers, Benito Sammartino, Slugger Kowalski, Herman Schmidt, and Cha Cha Gabor.

By 1985 Tomko was no longer a member of the NWA—with some reports suggesting he was ejected and others suggesting he left the organization of his own accord—and he no longer had access to name wrestlers that NWA membership could have provided. By this point it is unlikely Tomko would have shelled out the money to bring big-name talent to his promotion anyway. Instead, he stuck with his familiar core of wrestlers, including his WWF knockoffs; added a few wrestlers from the defunct Stampede Wrestling—though none at the star level, as most at that level had gravitated to Japan, the WWF, or other promotions offering better opportunities than All-Star Wrestling did by the mid–1980s; and brought in an occasional new face that he could afford. He also employed his sons, pro wrestling newcomers Todd and Terry Tomko—wrestling as Rick Davis and The Frog, respectively— who both quickly reached the championship level in their father's promotion.

Out of the NWA, Tomko established the fictitious Universal Wrestling Alliance (UWA) as his promotion's governing body, but that change did nothing to reverse the direction in which his company was heading. Neither did the partnership Tomko established with Vancouver businessman Fred Roselli and Drummond, who worked as a referee, manager, and booker in the promotion.

While Tomko's promotion—mainly back to taping television programs weekly and holding its major cards in Cloverdale (Surrey), BC—was far from on fire in the late 1980s, some wrestlers from that period stood out, including three natives of the Pacific Northwest. Two of them, Todd "Oly" Olsen and Steve "Buddy Wayne" Finley, both natives of Everett, Washington, were capable wrestlers who went on to enjoy long careers in a variety of wrestling promotions on both sides of the border in the Pacific Northwest while appearing occasionally in other areas.

Olsen, who trained Wayne to be a wrestler, grew up watching *All-Star Wrestling* in the 1960s and, two decades later, after managing to build his weight up to over 200 pounds, landed a job wrestling for Tomko. Grateful for the opportunity Tomko gave him to break into wrestling, Olsen nonetheless recognized some of Tomko's shortfalls as a promoter. During his shows,

Olsen said, "Al stayed in the dressing room area, not seeing the things that would develop…. I don't think he saw the end product or watched the show." But Olsen, recognized by his peers as a solid wrestler who respected the wrestling business, quickly added, "Al was a funny guy—one of the most imitated promoters." Olsen also said he was invited to stay in Tomko's home while he was starting as a wrestler in Vancouver, and he acknowledged, "I learned everything from him." Sadly, Olsen passed away, at age 58, as a result of a heart ailment in late 2015, shortly after being interviewed for this book.

Meanwhile, Surrey, BC, native John Tenta was a skilled superheavyweight amateur wrestler who, after attending Louisiana State University, joined the sumo ranks in Japan. Starting at the bottom, he began rising quickly before deciding, eight months in, that the rigid life of a sumo wrestler wasn't for him. From sumo, Tenta jumped over to All Japan Pro Wrestling, where he had a fairly successful start to his wrestling career in 1987 and 1988. Tenta also made regular visits to British Columbia during those years, and he was a main eventer for Tomko's UWA, three times holding heavyweight titles in the promotion. By 1989 he was in the WWF, where, as Earthquake, he quickly became a top challenger to Hulk Hogan. The 400-pound Tenta went on to enjoy significant success in the WWF and WCW and, late in his career, a successful return to All Japan Pro Wrestling before a diagnosis of advanced cancer in 2004 ended his career. He passed away in 2006.

In 1988 Tomko, perhaps sensing the inevitable, tried something different—yet again—in order to renew interest in his product when he decided to promote an all-women's wrestling tour. The move wasn't successful, though, and as Nevada reports, "the change to the female-dominated format affected many wrestlers' schedules. Tim Flowers, for one, wasn't supportive of this move," and Nevada says Flowers left the promotion in order to promote some shows of his own (73).

Though Flowers returned to the UWA the following year, little else seemed to be going in Tomko's favor in 1989. While Drummond was doing his best to book matches and events with what he had to work with, interest in the UWA dwindled to the point where few people turned out for the shows and the *All-Star Wrestling* television program—a syndicated hit across Canada not too many years earlier—was on its last legs, with only one TV station east of British Columbia, according to Drummond, still on the bandwagon. Regarding some of the wrestlers Tomko was using near the end of his All-Star/UWA run, Drummond says, "Al was training guys that had no ability." That was at least in part, Drummond and others say, because Tomko never wavered from his long-held position that wrestlers shouldn't be paid to appear on the promotion's television program, which Tomko viewed as a service to the wrestlers since—at least when audiences tuned in—it gave the wrestlers exposure to the viewing masses, who, Tomko reasoned, would then pay to see the TV wrestlers in person at their local arenas. But unfortunately, there were few opportunities to make any money on the road during Tomko's final years as a promoter, and few wrestlers who had other options seemed to regard appearing for free on *All-Star Wrestling* as a good career move.

Asked whether the wrestlers on Tomko's roster in the late 1980s had an inkling of where the promotion was headed, Verne Siebert, who wrestled for All-Star/UWA during most of the 1980s before getting out in late 1988, says, "We knew." While some former wrestlers hold to the view that Tomko did what he could to save his promotion and was simply the victim of changing times and an inability to adapt or a reluctance to listen to suggestions that might have pumped new life into the promotion, Moretti—whose offer to help Tomko book matches and programs was declined in the mid–1980s— has a different perspective. "I could never figure it out," he says. "We'd have a hot angle, and he'd just pull the rug out. I always wondered if Al actually tried to sabotage the territory for tax reasons."

In any event, the deathblow to Tomko's UWA came when CHAN-TV (branded as BCTV) announced it would stop producing and televising *All-Star Wrestling* in mid–1989. While some former wrestlers and observers blame the demise of Tomko's promotion largely on BCTV producer Ross Sullivan— who they say despised wrestling and, especially as ratings dropped, was eager for BCTV to pull the plug on *All-Star Wrestling*—the fact, regardless of Sullivan's views on wrestling, was that interest in the UWA had fallen to such a point that the promotion, with or without TV, seemed unlikely to survive much longer.

After the UWA folded in mid–1989, Tomko resurfaced from time to time in Vancouver independent wrestling but focused primarily on establishing and running a family pet-treat business from his adopted town of Blaine, Washington, the same town in which Kiniski lived for over four decades until his death. Tomko passed away in August of 2009, eight months before Kiniski.

13

Portland Wrestling's
Last Hurrah

While All-Star Wrestling underwent a change in ownership in the late 1970s before declining significantly by the early 1980s, Owen's Pacific Northwest Wrestling held steady and showed few signs of slowing down during the period. A degree of continuity was evident, with veterans such as Savage—who continued to double as the Washington promoter—Stasiak, Boyd, Ramos, and Tony Borne performing in much the manner they had done for years. Other proven wrestlers such as Anson, Adrian Adonis, Snuka, and Ventura appeared throughout the territory in the late 1970s. Ed Wiskoski, a solid 270-pound Missourian trained by all-time wrestling legend Harley Race, arrived in Portland in 1977 and wasted little time in capturing the NWA Pacific Northwest Heavyweight title from Savage. Other impressive newcomers included future AWA World Champion Rick Martel; Jay Youngblood, who held a share of the most widely recognized version of the NWA World Tag Team championship both before and after enjoying four Pacific Northwest Heavyweight title reigns; and the Kiwi Sheepherders, future WWF Bushwhackers Butch and Luke.

Other key figures arriving in the territory in the late 1970s included rugged Arkansan Sam Oliver Bass, who would go on to WWF fame as Cowboy Ron Bass; "Killer" Tim Brooks, a tough Texan who had wrestled in numerous territories and been most successful in the Midwest and Texas; Ron Starr, a championship-level wrestler in several territories; and Matt Borne, son of Tony, who teamed with his father during his Dec. 6, 1978, career debut in Portland and went on to wrestle for many promotions—including the WWF and WCW—over the course of a long career.

There were other wrestlers of note in Pacific Northwest Wrestling during the late 1970s—including all-time area legend Lonnie Mayne, who spent most of 1977 in the Northwest before passing away in his native California the following year. But as far as the late 1970s/early 1980s period in Pacific Northwest Wrestling is concerned, two wrestlers clearly stood out from the pack.

Roddy Piper was a Scottish Canadian native of Saskatchewan who grew up in Winnipeg, Manitoba, during that city's rich wrestling-club era. Expelled from school and estranged from his family, Piper worked at gyms and became familiar with the wrestling business before making his wrestling debut while in his late teens. From 1973 to 1975 he had a close association with Al Tomko, appearing regularly with Tomko's Manitoba-based Central Canadian Championship Wrestling and on AWA cards in and near Manitoba. Piper also began wrestling in Missouri and surrounding states in the fall of 1974, sharing ring time with a variety of veterans including Pat O'Connor and Bulldog Bog Brown. In early 1975 Piper ventured to Texas, where, over the course of several months, he faced many new opponents, including Mad Dog Vachon and John Tolos. After returning to Manitoba's Central Canadian Championship Wrestling briefly in the spring of 1975, Piper spent most of the remainder of that year in Canada's Maritime provinces, gaining more valuable experience in the ring with the likes of Bob Brown and Leo Burke; established U.S. territorial grapplers such as Johnny Weaver and Alfred Hayes; Bobby Bass (no relation to Sam Oliver Bass), who would go on to hold a share of the NWA Canadian Tag Team championship five times during the early part of the Tomko era in Vancouver; and eastern Canada headliners Mike Dubois and Gilles Poisson.

In late 1975 Piper set off for the U.S. West Coast—though well south of the Pacific Northwest. Touching down in Southern California near the end of the year, he kicked off his three-year stay in the Golden State with moderate success, trading victories with other wrestlers on the undercard as more established names such as John Tolos, Chavo Guerrero, and Black Gordman held down higher positions on NWA Hollywood Wrestling cards promoted by the LeBell brothers, Gene and Mike, in Los Angeles, San Diego, and other cities in Southern California. Piper soon caught the attention—and raised the ire—of California fans, however, and quickly moved into the spotlight. Showcasing his impressive ring presence and cutting-edge interview skills, Piper was rewarded with a share of the NWA Americas Tag Team championship—the first title of his career—within two months of his debut in California. Two weeks later he defeated Chavo Guerrero for the NWA Americas Heavyweight title, formerly held by such all-time greats as Édouard Carpentier, Ernie Ladd, Terry Funk, Killer Kowalski, Bobo Brazil, The Sheik, and Fred Blassie and a variety of wrestlers well known to Northwest fans, including Tolos, Don Muraco, Kinji Shibuya, 1964 NWA Pacific Northwest Heavyweight champion Pampero Firpo, three-time early 1970s Pacific Northwest Tag Team champion Frankie Laine, and Seattle native Greg Valentine.

While Piper was a dominant wrestler and personality in Southern California from 1976 through 1978, he was in great demand elsewhere as it became apparent he was an emerging superstar in professional wrestling. The Mid-

Atlantic Gateway website (www.midatlanticgateway.com) shows records of Piper appearances in Texas and Mexico during the height of his successful run in Southern California, along with month-long tours with New Japan Pro Wrestling in 1977 and 1978—the second of those tours "undercover" as the Masked Canadian, a character he also played at times in the NWA Hollywood territory.

Piper also made appearances in Roy Shire's San Francisco territory and became a top attraction at one of the most renowned wrestling venues at the time—the Cow Palace in Daly City, on the edge of San Francisco (not to be confused with a smaller "Cow Palace," at the Lane County Fairgrounds in Eugene, Oregon, which hosted many Pacific Northwest Wrestling shows beginning in 1960). Piper divided much of 1978 between the Southern California and Northern California territories, and on June 24, while still headlining cards from the Los Angeles area to San Diego, Piper won the San Francisco territory's NWA United States Heavyweight title—a title formerly held by Pacific Northwest standouts Pepper Gomez, Shibuya, Bearcat Wright, Pat Patterson, Rocky Johnson, The Brute, Mr. Fuji, Dean Ho, Muraco, and the wrestler Piper defeated on June 24 at California's Cow Palace, Lonnie Mayne. Mayne would win the title back from Piper three weeks later and continue to hold it, along with the Southern California NWA Americas Heavyweight title, until his death in August of 1978.

Roddy Piper's rise in wrestling accelerated when he was given a chance to show off his verbal and ring skills in California. After making an impact in both the Southern California and Northern California territories from 1976 to 1978, Piper debuted in Don Owen's Portland territory, where he would have tremendous success en route to becoming a national star.

It was in California from 1976 to 1978 that Piper became a star—making his mark as a loudmouthed manager and having 14 title reigns during his run in the Golden State. While in California, he faced off against a long list of successful wrestlers with ties to the Northwest, including Mayne, Johnson, Gomez, Patterson, John Tolos, Butcher Vachon, André the Giant, Haystack Calhoun, Larry Zbyszko, Dean Ho, and Jimmy Snuka. Piper also had opportunities in California to wrestle Gory Guerrero, Chavo's father and the grandfather of early 21st-century WWF notables Eddie Guerrero and Chavo Guerrero, Jr. Gory Guerrero, who was a star wrestler in Mexico early in his career, had his own connection with the Northwest, having headlined in Pacific Northwest Wrestling in 1955 while holding a share of the promotion's tag team championship that summer. In California, Piper also had the opportunity to face one of Japan's top wrestlers, Tatsumi Fujinami, who a decade later, in 1988, would hold the Pacific Northwest Heavyweight title for two months during a period in which he was shuttling between Japan—where he was a featured performer with New Japan Pro Wrestling—and several U.S. territories, including Pacific Northwest Wrestling.

In California, Piper also had opportunities to wrestle Keith Franks— the future Adrian Adonis—and Ron "Sam Oliver" Bass. Piper also teamed with both Franks and Bass in California, holding the NWA Americas Tag Team championship with each, and formed a successful team in California with future Pacific Northwest Wrestling opponent Bull Ramos. But it was another wrestler whose path crossed Piper's in California who is credited with convincing Piper to move up the West Coast to Oregon.

Like Piper, Buddy Rose held the San Francisco territory's NWA United States Heavyweight title in 1978 and was noted for frenetic matches and his ability to deliver entertaining promos, or interviews. Both were still in their mid-twenties, already had plenty of championship experience, and had been trained, at least in part, by Al Tomko prior to Tomko's departure from Manitoba for British Columbia. Piper had begun his career in Manitoba, and Rose, from neighboring Minnesota, had received his training and begun his career in the AWA, making regular tours to Manitoba under the promotion of AWA Manitoba agent Tomko.

While Piper and Rose obviously had much in common, a key difference is that Rose was already an established wrestler in the Pacific Northwest when he suggested Piper come to Oregon. Prior to winning his first San Francisco-territory heavyweight title, Rose was a four-time NWA Pacific Northwest Tag Team titleholder, twice with Jesse Ventura and twice with Ed Wiskoski. Whether Rose simply convinced Piper it was time for a change or whether Piper was also drawn for other reasons to Oregon may not be certain—though the fact that Piper put down lasting roots in Oregon strongly suggests he saw more than business opportunities in the Beaver State.

On Oct. 7, 1978, barely a week after winning the NWA Americas Heavyweight title for the fifth time, Piper made his debut, in a mid-card match at the Portland Sports Arena, with Pacific Northwest Wrestling. After reeling off a series of impressive performances in cities such as Portland, Seattle, Eugene, and Salem—including a victory over Snuka and draws with Savage and Boyd—and making a brief visit north to test the waters in British Columbia, Piper won his first title in Pacific Northwest Wrestling by the end of the year when he and Killer Tim Brooks took the promotion's tag team title from Savage and Boyd.

In January of 1979 Piper returned to California, as he did regularly during the first half of that year. In 1979 Piper also appeared in Hawaii; competed regularly in Vancouver—often sharing the ring with wrestlers such as Savage, Jonathan, Steinke, Jaggers, and Rose; and appeared in several preliminary or television matches in the eastern U.S. for the WWWF/WWF, including a few matches at Madison Square Garden. But despite his many absences from Pacific Northwest Wrestling in 1979, Piper held the promotion's singles title for over four months that year and a share of the territory's tag title for over three months.

It was clear at the time that Piper's ability to engage and rile fans had not lost a step in his move up the coast from California. Though Piper had always been gifted in his ability to deliver strong interviews, in his book *In the Pit with Piper*, he said it was during his time in the Portland territory that "I became an innovator of the concise and educated wrestling interview, which I was now treating as a kind of art form" (71). Explaining further, Piper said, "Your interview must be in sync with your match. In other words, you must carry through into your match what you said beforehand. Otherwise your interview means nothing" (73).

While Piper had long been an engaging performer on the microphone, over the course of his stay in Portland he became a more refined, focused deliverer of promos. Since early in his wrestling career, Piper had shown the ability to antagonize or insult audiences and present himself as a wrestler to hate. But in the Northwest, he delivered promos that were highly effective in drawing fans to arenas to see his matches. And he usually delivered in the ring as well, putting on serious but entertaining matches and engaging fans in a way that few wrestlers in the territory ever had.

While Piper had some fan support in the Northwest from the start, he was clearly a heel during the early part of his stay in Oregon and aligned at times with fellow heel Buddy Rose, who played a key role in turning Piper into the hottest babyface in the territory. During an April 1979 four-vs.-four match at the Portland Sports Arena, disagreement among teammates led to disintegration of the Piper-Rose alliance, and a series of Rose–Piper matches in weeks that followed established Piper as a clear fan favorite.

Piper was a complete package in Pacific Northwest Wrestling: a showman who played bagpipes and—even while yelling—often delivered nuanced and compelling state-of-the-art interviews; a wrestler with such ring presence that he could stir a crowd with almost any wrestling move he chose to use; and a professional who took his matches seriously. In 1979–1980 he held the NWA Pacific Northwest Heavyweight title as both an effective heel and a babyface who was perhaps the most popular ever in Portland, and he was a frequent tag team champion, most prominently with Rick Martel. The Piper-Martel combo held the promotion's tag team title three times in 1980 and was hugely popular. Piper and Martel also took their tandem to Vancouver, holding the Canadian Tag Team championship in mid–1980—and, interestingly, both would leave Pacific Northwest Wrestling later in 1980 after losing "loser leave town" matches to Buddy Rose.

Of course, it was opportunity elsewhere and not the loss of a match that determined Piper's departure from the Pacific Northwest in the fall of 1980. But before moving on to the national stage, Piper engaged in a series of heated battles against the likes of Wiskoski, the Kiwi Sheepherders, Igor Volkoff, Sam Oliver Bass, and especially Rose. Piper also had the opportunity to wrestle NWA Heavyweight champion Harley Race in both major Northwest wrestling territories in early 1980.

Piper's success following his departure from Pacific Northwest Wrestling in 1980 is well known to many people who follow professional wrestling. His first stop after leaving the Northwest was Jim Crockett's NWA Mid-Atlantic territory, where Piper soon earned a series of victories over fellow Pacific Northwest Wrestling alumnus Matt Borne and, just a few weeks after arriving in the territory, won the NWA Mid-Atlantic Television title, defeating Paul Jones in a tournament final. Jones, about 15 years earlier, had enjoyed a successful mid–1960s run in Pacific Northwest Wrestling, winning the territory's tag team championship with Pepper Martin and holding the NWA Pacific Northwest Heavyweight title twice. Jones was also a popular and fairly successful wrestler in British Columbia in the mid–1960s.

Over the course of a run lasting just over three years, Piper, while never winning the NWA World title, held several titles in the Crockett promotion and was a key player throughout the territory, centered in the Carolinas but, at the time, reaching all the way from the southern United States to southern Ontario. Also during his years with NWA Mid-Atlantic—highlighted by matches against Ric Flair, Ricky Steamboat, Jack Brisco, Greg Valentine, former Pacific Northwest Heavyweight champion Jay Youngblood, Wahoo McDaniel, and many other leading wrestlers of the era—Piper appeared in Florida; Puerto Rico; the Kansas City territory, where he teamed with Bulldog Bob Brown; St. Louis, facing off against Brown among others; and Japan.

During his mid–1983 tour of Japan, Piper had several matches with Tomomi "Jumbo" Tsuruta, who was a national amateur wrestling champion in Japan and an Olympic competitor before debuting as a pro wrestler in 1973 and spending most of that year wrestling in Texas and Japan. In 1974 Tsuruta wrestled briefly in Oregon and British Columbia, demonstrating that he was clearly one of the most skilled young wrestlers in the world, and over the course of his long career, Tsuruta emerged as an all-time legend of Japanese wrestling and, for a time in 1984, holder of the AWA World Heavyweight title. When his wrestling days were over, Tsuruta renewed his connection to the Northwest by moving to Oregon to take a researching post at the University of Portland, but sadly, his return to the Northwest was short-lived, as cancer ended his life, at age 49, in 2000.

In 1982 and 1983 Piper appeared regularly in the NWA Georgia territory, making appearances on *Georgia Championship Wrestling*, which could be seen nationally via satellite on Ted Turner's WTBS. Piper also appeared occasionally on Pacific Northwest Wrestling cards, participating in main events in mid–1983 against the likes of Flair—then NWA Heavyweight champion—and Rose. By this time Piper had made a transition in the Mid-Atlantic and Georgia territories similar to the one he had made during his initial run in Pacific Northwest Wrestling, as he was now firmly established as a huge fan favorite in both eastern NWA territories.

Piper's impressive ring presence, his ability to draw and engage fans, his almost unparalleled wit and interview skills, and his growing national popularity via WTBS made him one of the leading wrestlers in the United Sates in the early 1980s. It was hardly a surprise, then, when the World Wrestling Federation—with Vince McMahon's national expansion in its early stages—added Piper to its roster in January of 1984. Piper's first appearance with the WWF was on Jan. 24, the day after Hulk Hogan won the WWF Heavyweight championship for the first time.

McMahon, who had purchased the former World Wide Wrestling Federation (WWWF) from his father two years earlier, had chosen Hogan as the babyface hero to help carry his promotion—whose name had been shortened to the World Wrestling Federation (WWF) in 1979—to national status. And while he would proceed to steamroll many of his competitors out of business, McMahon clearly shared the common promoters' wisdom that getting the most out of a babyface depended on matching him against first-class heels.

McMahon, who had been a WWWF/WWF promoter and television announcer when his father owned the promotion and when Piper appeared at a few WWWF/WWF events and television tapings in 1979, was familiar with Piper's work and had no doubt watched Piper's rise to the upper echelon of the wrestling business while in the employ of the McMahons' competitors. In McMahon's estimation, Piper had the makings of a lead heel who could help take the WWF nationwide and beyond.

Given Piper's success in the WWF—and the WWF's success when Piper took center stage—McMahon's judgment in this instance would be hard to argue with. Whether by putting on hard-fought, realistic-looking matches; insulting and enraging his audience; or belittling and abusing fellow wrestlers in the "Piper's Pit" television interview segment he hosted, Piper quickly gained recognition as one of the top heels of his generation. He wrestled regularly for the WWF until 1992, and while he once held the promotion's Intercontinental Heavyweight title—at the time, the WWF's second most prestigious singles championship—Piper is probably better remembered for being a headliner at the first WrestleMania event in 1985 and for hosting a "Piper's Pit" segment the previous year in which he attacked fellow Pacific Northwest Wrestling legend Jimmy Snuka with a coconut. And in keeping with the pattern of his career, Piper is also remembered for making a successful transition from being the most hated heel in the WWF to becoming one of its most popular wrestlers.

In the latter years of his career, Piper had a successful run in WCW before returning as a part-time performer for the WWF/WWE—in the process, appearing in Seattle's 2003 WrestleMania 19—and making appearances with several small wrestling promotions. Besides enjoying a long and successful wrestling career, Piper also appeared in films, games, and a variety of television programs. Living west of Portland, Oregon, following his wrestling career, Piper survived a 2006 cancer scare and went on to host the modern-day version of "Piper's Pit" via Internet podcast before passing away, as a result of a heart attack, on July 31, 2015.

Along with Piper, Buddy Rose was a dominant wrestler in the U.S. Northwest during the late 1970s, but unlike Piper, Rose achieved most of his career success in Pacific Northwest Wrestling. While he had success in other territories—including main-eventing in the WWF and holding a share of the AWA World Tag Team championship—from 1976, the year of his arrival in Oregon, until 1989, Rose held a championship in Pacific Northwest Wrestling 20 times.

That probably would have seemed unlikely given Paul Perschmann's introduction to pro wrestling in the early 1970s and his reported reaction upon arriving, as Buddy Rose, at the Portland Sports Arena for the first time. Though Perschmann reportedly grew up as a wrestling fan in Minneapolis and, according to Brian Hoops at the *Pro Wrestling Torch* website (www.pwtorch.com), "broke into wrestling in 1971 as a referee in the AWA," his first attempt at graduating from Verne Gagne's wrestling camp in 1972 was not a success, as Perschmann dropped out. Fellow trainee Ric Flair did likewise, although Flair reports, in *Ric Flair: To Be the Man* (Greenberg et al., ch. 2), that Gagne insisted he continue and that he, Flair, made it through the camp—noted for its spartan conditions—before debuting as a pro wrestler later in 1972. Perschmann, meanwhile, returned to the camp the following year, graduated, and went on to spend about two years wrestling in the AWA, broken up by visits to Missouri; Texas; and the WWWF, where he appeared as the masked Executioner. While Rose put in plenty of miles during his first few years as a wrestler, he was never billed as a main eventer until he arrived in Oregon in the spring of 1976. And while Rose quickly reached new heights as a wrestler after arriving in the Northwest, it appears he had some hesitation about the situation he was in. As *Wrestling Observer Newsletter* editor Dave Meltzer reports in the May 13, 2009, *Observer*, "[Rose] pulled into the Portland Sports Arena and immediately wondered what he had gotten himself into." Particularly during his time in the AWA, Rose had wrestled in major arenas, and apparently the idea of headlining cards in Don Owen's converted bowling alley had to grow on him.

While he had wrestled mainly under his own name before arriving in the Northwest, Perschmann was billed as Buddy Rose upon his arrival in Pacific Northwest Wrestling. According to Mike Rodgers, Terry Funk—NWA champion at the time, who was defending his title on a tour of Texas while Perschmann wrestled there in early 1976—played a key role in the name change. Perschmann, says Rodgers, "was in Amarillo right before he came to Portland. He was trying to figure out a name, and Terry Funk came up with Buddy Rose—'Rose' because Portland is known as the 'Rose City.'"

His early matches in the Northwest saw Rose main-eventing against the likes of Savage, Snuka, Youngblood, and Matt Borne and teaming with the likes of Ramos and Ventura. Rose was a so-called "heat magnet" from the start, angering fans with his loudmouthed, arrogant, bleached-blond, underhanded character, but Meltzer credits Terry Funk—in Portland on Oct. 15, 1976, to defend his NWA Heavyweight title against Snuka on a card on which Rose also appeared—with offering suggestions leading to the further development of the "Playboy" Buddy Rose character that would make such an impact on wrestling audiences in the Northwest.

Ten days later, on Oct. 25, 1976, Rose won the first wrestling championship of his career, teaming with the equally flamboyant Jesse Ventura to wrest the NWA Pacific Northwest Tag Team title from multi-time champions Savage and Snuka. Each of those teams would have another turn holding the title in the next several months. By mid-1977, after the Rose-Ventura combo's second and final championship reign ended at the hands of Lonnie Mayne and British veteran Les Thornton, the blond team split up and Rose and Ventura engaged in a series of matches, with Ventura recast as a babyface and Rose continuing to play a heel. As David Cohen reports in *Jesse Ventura: The Body, the Mouth, and the Mind*, "a feud between the two [was] hyped and wound up in a 'Loser Leaves Town' match" (50), which Rose won, although wrestlingdata.com indicates Ventura wrestled again in Portland later in 1977. Ventura also had dozens of matches in Pacific Northwest

Wrestling—including further meetings with Buddy Rose—over the course of 1978 and 1979.

Besides feuding with Ventura during his early years in the Northwest, Rose is well-remembered for his late–1970s matches against Savage, Snuka, Boyd, Thornton, Youngblood, Mayne, Sam Oliver Bass, Adrian Adonis, Red Bastien, Stasiak, and especially Piper. Rose also had the opportunity in 1977 to wrestle Harley Race and Gene Kiniski in Portland and Seattle. The late 1970s also saw the introduction of Rose's long-lived tag team with Wiskoski, with the pair winning their first NWA Pacific Northwest Tag Team championship in December of 1977—over a decade before they would win the last of their four tag team titles in Pacific Northwest Wrestling.

Rose's dominance in late–1970s and early–1980s Pacific Northwest Wrestling—including seven heavyweight title reigns before 1982—was all the more impressive given that he was also headlining cards and winning championships in Northern California and British Columbia during the same period. Rose's list of regional heavyweight and tag team championships from 1976 until the early 1980s is probably as impressive as any wrestler's in the United States or Canada.

In mid–1982 Rose left the West Coast and headed for the WWF on the East Coast, where over the next two years he often appeared in main events or semi-main events and mounted repeated challenges to WWF Heavyweight champion Bob Backlund. From 1982 to 1984 in the WWF, Rose was cast as a lead heel and was often accompanied by his manager the Grand Wizard, aka Ernie Roth, who as Abdullah "the Weasel" Farouk had managed the Sheik for many years in Detroit and Toronto. With or without his manager at ringside, Rose was promoted as a legitimate threat to Backlund's WWF Heavyweight title and the WWF Intercontinental title, held by former WWWF World Heavyweight champion Pedro Morales, who had appeared briefly in Pacific Northwest Wrestling in the late 1960s while headlining in California.

From 1982 through 1984—the peak of his run in the WWF—Rose returned to the Pacific Northwest frequently enough to win the NWA Pacific Northwest Heavyweight title for the eighth time and to win a share of the promotion's tag team championship with three different partners. He also made tours of Japan, and he wrestled in Vancouver—where he was well established after holding both singles and tag team titles in All-Star Wrestling earlier in the decade—for Stampede Wrestling in May of 1984.

While 1984 was a strong year for Rose in the WWF, he had limited success there in 1985, perhaps because, as was the case with Adrian Adonis, Rose was experiencing weight-gain problems that likely did not bode well for his future with the WWF, given the company's emphasis on wrestlers with sculpted physiques as the promotion continued to expand nationally and internationally. As it turned out, Rose was gone from the company by April;

and though Paul Perschmann had the opportunity to participate in the inaugural WrestleMania on March 31, 1985, at Madison Square Garden just before leaving the WWF, it was not as the flamboyant Buddy Rose but back under a mask as The Executioner—and in a brief losing effort that clearly signaled his departure.

The following year, Rose, though physically past his prime, was back in a prominent position in the wrestling business, kicking off an eight-month AWA Tag Team championship run at a May 17, 1986, television taping with fellow bleached blond "Pretty Boy" Doug Somers, who had been a mid-carder in Pacific Northwest Wrestling during most of 1984. Also appearing at the May 17, 1986, series of AWA television tapings at the Hammond, Indiana, Civic Center were several notable alumni of the major wrestling promotions in the Pacific Northwest—among them, Nick Bockwinkel, Larry Zbyszko, Curt Hennig, and Ed Wiskoski, who was now appearing in the AWA as the arrogant and bigoted Colonel DeBeers.

Rose and Somers had a good run as seemingly overmatched, crowd-riling, up-to-no-good champions who seemed to squeak by with their tag team title match after match for eight months. While the AWA schedule was less taxing than the WWF's or even Pacific Northwest Wrestling's, which did not usually involve long trips but kept top wrestlers active most nights, the Rose-Somers duo—backed by manager Sherry Martel (no relation to Rick Martel), one of the leading female wrestlers of her day in the U.S.—clearly was one of the top American tag teams of the mid–1980s. The Rose-Somers reign was noted especially for a series of outstanding encounters with the Midnight Rockers, Marty Jannetty and Shawn Michaels—the latter widely considered one of the best wrestlers in the world during the 1990s—culminating in Rose and Somers' loss of the AWA championship to the Rockers in early 1987.

In the AWA, Rose's expanding waistline played into his ring persona. Though he was nowhere near as large as he would eventually become, Rose's shtick involved his objecting vehemently whenever a ring announcer called his weight as 271 pounds—all of which Rose appeared to be. Rose would correct the announcer, telling him the correct weight was 217 pounds, not 271, and the crowd and TV announcers ate it up.

Back in Pacific Northwest Wrestling in 1988 and 1989, Rose was booked as a competitive singles wrestler, though he was clearly not the serious presence in the ring that he used to be and would never hold a singles title again. He won the Pacific Northwest Tag Team championship twice in 1988 and 1989, once with longtime partner Wiskoski, who was back in the Northwest in 1988 and '89 as Colonel DeBeers.

Rose's return to the WWF in 1990 saw him cast primarily as an obese, comedic buffoon, though, even at well over 300 pounds, he could display some unexpected skills in the ring. As reported in *USA Today* on April 30, 2009, "Rose described himself as 'heavy in the seat, light on the feet.'" But this time around, he was booked to lose the vast majority of his matches and now, in his late thirties, had little hope of recovering his reputation as a serious wrestler—even in the Northwest—after his year in the WWF was over. Though Rose made limited wrestling appearances for years after his last WWF run ended in early 1991, by that time he was clearly living off his reputation. When his ring appearances were few, Rose ran a wrestling school with Wiskoski for a time in Portland. Rose was also known to keep in close contact with the wrestling business once he was out of the ring altogether.

Reports indicate Rose's life was not easy from the time his wrestling career declined. Meltzer, in the May 13, 2009, *Wrestling Observer*, reports that Rose "lived a checkered life. He had problems with drugs, [in particular,] cocaine and somas, the latter until his death on April 28 at his home in Vancouver, Washington." Meltzer also reports that Rose had a couple of brushes with the law—once, 20 years before his death, relating to tax evasion, for which Rose reportedly spent some time in jail; and once in relation to marriage-related domestic violence and unlawful imprisonment charges. According to Meltzer's May 13, 2009, report, Rose was also listed by Washington State in 1999 as a deadbeat dad. In his last years, Rose, at a dangerously heavy weight, reportedly had diabetes-related problems that are widely believed to have contributed to his April 2009 death by natural causes.

While Rose's career had its ups and downs, at his best he was an engaging, creative performer committed to making the most of his abilities and drawing fans to arenas. In his Rose obituary, Meltzer describes Rose's character as a rich boy who tended to get his way, who scored well with women, who received his share of beatings, and who usually slipped by on flukes or by making excuses. Kevin Eck of the *Baltimore Sun*, in his April 29, 2009, pro wrestling blog entry, adds, "During his heyday in the 1970s and '80s, the rotund Rose was the ultimate example of not judging a book by its cover. Despite his flabby physique, Rose was actually a gifted worker. He could deliver a nice dropkick, was a proficient bump-taker and cut good promos." Eck might have added that Rose, along with Roddy Piper, was largely responsible for taking Pacific Northwest Wrestling to perhaps its greatest heights in the late 1970s; that Rose, like Piper, continued to make his home in the Pacific Northwest when his wrestling days were over; and that Rose, given the level of his performances and the reactions he evoked—both as a heel and a babyface—from Northwest fans over a long period of time, clearly warrants a place at or near the top of any short list of the best-remembered, most impactful, and most successful wrestlers in the history of pro wrestling in the Pacific Northwest.

While Rose and Piper often saved their most intense ring encounters for each other, they had a strong supporting cast during the late–1970s/early–1980s heyday of Pacific Northwest Wrestling. Top hands in the territory among the new guard included Wiskoski, Martel, Bass, Jerry Oates, Young-blood, Matt Borne, Steve Regal, Curt Hennig, and brothers Brett and Buzz Sawyer—all of whom were titleholders in Pacific Northwest Wrestling and all of whom had prominent places on major U.S. promotions' rosters at some point in the 1980s. Two from that group—Martel and Hennig—would go on to hold the AWA Heavyweight title and achieve major success in the WWF.

Also prominent in late–1970s/early–1980s Pacific Northwest Wrestling were two wrestlers who would later become national stars. Iranian native Khosrow Vaziri had a strong background in amateur wrestling before begin-ning his transition to the professional ranks at Verne Gagne's training camp in 1972. In the late 1970s, Vaziri—as the Iron Sheik—was a tag team champion in both All-Star Wrestling and Pacific Northwest Wrestling, and several years later he would be the WWF World Heavyweight champion Hulk Hogan would defeat to kick off his first WWF championship reign in 1984. Mean-while, Nova Scotia native Wade "Rocky Johnson" Bowles, who had held a share of the Vancouver territory's tag team title with Don Leo Jonathan in 1967 before winning numerous U.S. regional titles over the next decade and a half, enjoyed major success in Pacific Northwest Wrestling in 1981 and 1982 before moving on and holding a share of the WWF World Tag Team title from 1983 to 1984 and, eventually, watching his son Dwayne "The Rock" Johnson achieve stardom in both the wrestling and Hollywood entertainment worlds.

While the old guard—proven attractions such as Stasiak, Kiniski, Boyd, and Tony Borne—continued to play prominently on Pacific Northwest Wrestling cards well into the 1980s (in Boyd's case, as late as 1989, after nearly an eight-year absence from the Northwest), the hottest action and reactions in the territory most often seemed to center on Rose. Rose's real-life, though short-lived, marriage in 1981 to Borne's daughter Toni Rae added a layer of tension to storylines and to the real-life conflict involving the Perschmann and Borne families. An even more memorable situation involved Rose's threat earlier that same year to throw the NWA Pacific Northwest Heavyweight title belt—which he had "stolen" from champion Jay Youngblood—off the Fremont Bridge in Portland. As Meltzer reports in the May 13, 2009, *Wrestling Observer*, "Rose went on television on a Saturday night and said that the next afternoon at 1 p.m., he would be throwing the belt into the [Willamette] River. Rose rented a limo and came out with announcer Frank Bonnema…. A huge crowd came out, stopping traffic in both directions."

While every indication was that Rose's tossing of the championship belt was pure "angle" or storyline and that Don Owen had already made arrange-

Bull Ramos and the Iron Sheik were a wild pair who guaranteed hard-hitting matches during their Pacific Northwest Tag Team title reign in 1978. The Iron Sheik's stay in both the Portland and Vancouver territories was relatively brief, as he would move on to greater exposure in the AWA and the WWF the following year. The highlight of his career would come a few years later, when he would hold the WWF World Heavyweight title from late 1983 to early 1984.

ments to replace his promotion's old, tattered title belt with a new one, Rose did have some history of going off the storyline during his career. In San Francisco, following a late–1970s falling-out with promoter Roy Shire, Rose addressed the crowd at a Cow Palace show and spoke his mind about Shire.

Indeed, the Rose persona—whether he was cast as a heel or a babyface—was based largely on a flamboyant athlete's penchant for speaking his mind.

But with Rose concentrating largely on making his name elsewhere beginning in 1982—and with Piper back in the territory only for occasional appearances—the early to mid-1980s saw Pacific Northwest Wrestling undergo changes, some planned and others driven by necessity.

In October of 1982, *Portland Wrestling* lost its popular longtime voice when Frank Bonnema, who had hosted the program since 1967, passed away at age 49 after suffering a heart attack a few weeks earlier. Bonnema, who had worked for KPTV as a news announcer and movie host before *Portland Wrestling* returned to KPTV in 1967 after a dozen years on rival station KOIN-TV, had been a constant when *Portland Wrestling* weathered a few changes during his tenure as commentator—the obvious ones being the change in setting when the show moved its shooting location to the Portland Sports Arena in 1968 and a few TV scheduling changes over the years.

Portland Wrestling switched from Friday broadcasts to live Saturday night broadcasts early during Bonnema's tenure as the program's announcer. In 1970 KPTV moved *Portland Wrestling* forward an hour, from 9:30–11:00 to 8:30–10:00, with the show normally ending as the main event was about to get underway. That formula—presenting a heated undercard while teasing fans to come to the arena to see next week's main event—worked well for nearly a decade until, as Meltzer reports, the head of KPTV saw a bloody match and decided the show would be better kept out of prime time. In 1979 Bonnema's familiar voice—along with Tom Peterson's live arena commercials and Don Owen's outraged reactions to some of the villains on his cards—helped smooth what could have been a difficult transition from prime time to a slot more associated with bedtime.

As it turned out, the tape-delayed programs airing from 11 p.m.–12:30 a.m. did very well, as Pacific Northwest Wrestling had built a large and dedicated audience over the years. And while the move to later hours on KPTV may not have been a welcome change to Owen or his wrestlers, overall, the station continued to support the program, including covering production costs.

Portland Wrestling weathered the loss of Bonnema in 1982, replacing him with Don Coss, who had been the fill-in announcer on the show and, earlier, the regular wrestling announcer on Salem's KVDO-TV for local promoter Elton Owen. Joining Coss as a host of *Portland Wrestling* was Dutch Savage, who had retired as a wrestler the year before. But Savage soon had his differences with Don Owen, sold back his share of Pacific Northwest Wrestling, gave up his promotional activities in Washington, and ended up turning over his share of *Portland Wrestling* announcing duties to Stan Stasiak.

Pacific Northwest Wrestling suffered another loss in 1982 when Elton

Owen retired. This time, the void was largely filled by Don's son Barry Owen, who had been active in the promotion most of his life and was well equipped to take over promotion of shows in places such as Eugene, Washington State, and spot show locations throughout the circuit. Elton Owen passed away in 1993.

Probably the greatest challenge facing Pacific Northwest Wrestling in the 1980s was the same one plaguing All-Star Wrestling in Vancouver and numerous regional promotions throughout the United States and Canada. With so much wrestling available on cable television, local fans often expected their local promotions to pull out all the stops and present a wrestling product that measured up to what could be seen on cable. Local promotions in the 1980s found it difficult to maintain the status quo and simply make the case that they knew best what their fans wanted, as promoters who refused to change with the times were usually among the first to go out of business.

The problem, from a local promoter's standpoint, was that resources simply were not available to duplicate what promotions such as Fritz von Erich's Texas-based World Class Championship Wrestling, Bill Watts' New Orleans-based Universal Wrestling Federation, and Jim Crockett Promotions were able to present on television. Even more daunting was the prospect of competing with the World Wrestling Federation, which by 1984 was often presenting two or three house shows nightly in different cities from coast to coast to go with hours of weekly television programming available to wrestling fans nationwide.

Promoters who, like Al Tomko, tried to put on a low-end, "WWF-lite" type of product generally were not successful in pulling the wool over local fans' eyes. Though WWF wrestlers were recognized by fans as the real deal, there is little evidence that fans in the Northwest or elsewhere were interested in seeing imitations of the major leaguers on their local wrestling shows. To their credit, Don and Barry Owen seemed to recognize that fans of Pacific Northwest Wrestling still wanted action-packed, relatively believable arena and television shows, new wrestlers to get behind, and more of the unique, homegrown flavor of Pacific Northwest Wrestling.

Working agreements with the Crockett and von Erich promotions brought wrestlers such as Iceman King Parsons, Brett and Buzz Sawyer, Chris Adams, Gino Hernandez, Ricky "Lance Von Erich" Vaughn, the Road Warriors, Magnum T.A., and Nikita and Ivan Koloff into the territory to complement one of the better local-talent corps available to regional promotions in the U.S. during the 1980s. Among standouts in Pacific Northwest Wrestling during the years when local promotions seemed to be facing the threat of extinction were the Dynamite Kid, a cutting-edge wrestler who achieved stardom in the United Kingdom, Japan, Stampede Wrestling, and, eventually, the WWF; and Curt Hennig, future AWA Heavyweight champion and, later,

WWF headliner "Mr. Perfect," who in 2003 would become one more prominent wrestler of his generation to die a premature, drug-related death. Tough
veterans such as Mike Miller and Bobby Jaggers—both mid–1980s NWA
Pacific Northwest Heavyweight titleholders—were key wrestlers, as were
three-time Pacific Northwest Tag Team champion and future WWF Tag Team
champion Tom Prichard and Portland natives Larry "Rip" Oliver and William
"Billy Jack" Haynes.

Based on his Pacific Northwest Wrestling title history alone, Oliver has
to be considered one of the most successful wrestlers in the promotion's history. In all, from 1980–1991, Oliver amassed a total of 28 title reigns in the
territory—12 as the heavyweight champion. Though not a major star elsewhere, he had a solid career that took him to several U.S. promotions; to
Vancouver, where he twice held a share of the NWA Canadian Tag Team title,
once with Buddy Rose; and to Japan. Among Oliver's opponents in Japan was
Seattle-born Japanese wrestler Masahiro Chono, who from the 1980s well
into the 21st century had an extremely successful career in Japan, where at
times he faced opponents with ties to Northwest wrestling, including Matt
Borne, Buzz Sawyer, Scott Norton, Tatsumi Fujinami, and Mr. Saito.

In the Northwest, Oliver excelled as both a partner and an adversary of
Rose. He became the lead heel in Pacific Northwest Wrestling when Rose left
to start his successful WWF run in 1982, and Oliver has to be credited with
playing a major role in keeping Pacific Northwest Wrestling relatively strong
during a period in which other regional promotions of similar size were
becoming insignificant or shutting their doors.

William Haynes was a powerful man in his late twenties who reportedly
had spent time in prison for armed robbery prior to traveling to Calgary to
train under Stu Hart. After a brief stay in Stampede Wrestling, often appearing
on cards featuring a young Bret Hart and a young Dynamite Kid, Haynes
returned—as "Billy Jack"—to his native Oregon and almost immediately got
involved in a series of heated matches against Oliver. Reportedly after a threat
of legal action by Tom Laughlin, writer and star of the movie *Billy Jack*,
Haynes lengthened his ring name to Billy Jack Haynes, but the name change
in no way slowed his success in Pacific Northwest Wrestling, as the rugged
hometown hero was a huge favorite in Portland and throughout the territory
from 1982 to 1986. During those years Haynes had a total of seven singles
and tag team championship runs in the Northwest to go along with title runs
in Florida and Texas and successful tours of Japan.

While not the most polished wrestler in the Northwest, Haynes was a
muscular, charismatic wrestler of the sort Vince McMahon liked to have on
his shows when the WWF was getting established as a national brand in the
1980s. As a result, Haynes joined the WWF roster in 1986, staying there for
two semi-successful years before leaving on terms generally described as bad.

Playboy Buddy Rose is flanked by Billy Jack Haynes (left) and Curt Hennig. All three were active figures in the Northwest in the 1980s while also making names in the major national promotions. While Hennig had the greatest impact on a national scale, Rose is the wrestler many fans would most readily identify with Pacific Northwest Wrestling during its strong period in the late 1970s and 1980s.

According to Everton Bailey, Jr., at www.oregonlive.com (*The Oregonian*), in 2014 Haynes filed a lawsuit in federal court claiming that the WWF/WWE "both hid and denied medical research and evidence of traumatic brain injuries sustained by its wrestlers, including the possibility of chronic traumatic encephalopathy." Bailey adds that Haynes "claimed in the lawsuit that he suffered at least 15 concussions and that his time working for [the WWF] left him with depression and symptoms of dementia." In a somewhat similar case, as reported by Chris Dolmetsch in a July 18, 2016, Bloomberg report, other wrestlers with ties to the Northwest—Snuka, Oliver, Ron Bass, Butch Reed, Don Leo Jonathan, Jesse Barr, and Ken Patera—are among over 50 plaintiffs in a 2016 federal lawsuit claiming their well-being was compromised when WWE hid from wrestlers "the long-term effects of neurological injuries from years of being pounded in and out of the ring."

Back in Oregon in the late 1980s, Haynes promoted some shows in opposition to Don Owen, using established Pacific Northwest Wrestling talent including Oliver, Miller, and Ed Moretti. But Haynes soon took a break from promoting, and he was back in Pacific Northwest Wrestling—winning the promotion's tag team title with former rival Oliver—before the decade was over.

While Haynes' stay in the WWF may have been relatively brief and is usually characterized as disappointing, it far exceeded the level of success achieved by another muscular newcomer from the same era who was recruited by the WWF. Tom Magee was a native of Winnipeg who migrated to Port Coquitlam, BC, won numerous national and international powerlifting championships as a superheavyweight in the early 1980s, and captured the 1984 Mr. British Columbia bodybuilding title. In 1985 Magee kicked off his pro wrestling career with Stampede Wrestling, which was back in business from 1985 through 1989 under the leadership of Bruce Hart, who had been a key creative force in early–1980s Stampede Wrestling before taking back the reins of the company after McMahon apparently had a case of buyer's remorse and released the Harts from terms of their 1984 agreement shutting down Stampede Wrestling.

Though he won no championships in Stampede Wrestling during his stay there from October 1985 to March 1986, Magee, usually positioned near the middle of the card, had a strong winning record while performing on Stampede shows in Alberta and in Vancouver, Surrey, Victoria, Nanaimo, and several towns in the interior of British Columbia. He also toured with All Japan Pro Wrestling in early 1986—which was unusual for a North America-based wrestler so early in his career—and was booked to win most of his matches in Japan.

Magee caught the attention of the WWF, which, Nevada says via email, saw major potential in the former World's Strongest Man runner-up, "feeling that with his look, he could be the 'next Hulk Hogan.'" Following a tryout match at an Oct. 7, 1986, WWF television taping in Rochester, New York, against Bret Hart, Magee was snapped up by the WWF and put on the road in January of 1987. But, as Nevada says, "they soon realized that he didn't have the charisma or ring talent for the role they proposed." Many observers credit Hart—regarded as a first-class worker—with having made Magee look like a far better wrestler than he actually was during the tryout. "Not long after the Magee experiment," Nevada notes, "McMahon did find two guys of a similar prototype that did hit the mark—Rick Rude and Ultimate Warrior." Meanwhile, Magee, while remaining with the WWF until 1990, wrestled relatively few matches for the company after mid–1987 and, though considered an excellent athlete, was never a main eventer. In 1988, with only a small number of WWF commitments on his schedule, Magee returned for another tour with All Japan Pro Wrestling, this time losing nearly all his matches, including a few encounters with pro wrestling freshman John Tenta. Magee also did some competitive powerlifting during his tenure with the WWF, and after retiring from wrestling he earned acting roles in several movies.

Many of the highlights in Pacific Northwest Wrestling in the 1980s revolved around the return of Piper—for an occasional appearance—or Rose, who, despite his declining condition and extensive travels with the WWF and AWA, often headlined Pacific Northwest Wrestling shows throughout the decade. On May 21, 1985, Piper and Rose wrestled each other on a sellout show at the Portland Memorial Coliseum commemorating the 60th anniversary of the Owen family's debut in wrestling promotion. According to Meltzer, Piper defied his boss at the time, Vince McMahon, in order to work the show. Meltzer, in the May 13, 2009, *Wrestling Observer*, describes the loyalty Piper felt toward Don Owen and Jim Crockett, Jr., the promoter Piper worked for after leaving Pacific Northwest Wrestling in 1980. Meltzer says Piper, during his early years in the WWF, "refused to work any [WWF] shows in Oregon or the Carolinas because he felt Owen and Jim Crockett had treated him so well and he didn't want to work against them." It was his loyalty and his respect for Owen and Pacific Northwest Wrestling that drove Piper to defy his powerful boss in order to contribute to making the Owen anniversary show a big success. While other wrestlers likely would have paid for such impudence with their jobs, Piper, one of the hottest wrestlers in the world on the heels of WrestleMania 1, probably did not have much to worry about.

Other key wrestlers participating on the Owen family anniversary show included former 1980s NWA Pacific Northwest Heavyweight champions Wiskoski, Karl Steiner (Montreal native Bob Della Serra, older brother of Rocky Della Serra), Jaggers, Ricky Vaughn, Miller, and Hennig. Wrestlers on the show who had left the territory and already become major names in wrestling included, besides Piper and Rose, Sergeant Slaughter and Rick

Martel, who defended his AWA Heavyweight championship on the show against Miller.

The main event pitted local favorite Billy Jack Haynes against NWA World Heavyweight champion Ric Flair. While Flair's contribution to Pacific Northwest Wrestling's success in the 1980s may not be as obvious as the contributions of Rose, Oliver, Haynes, and others who wrestled primarily in the Pacific Northwest for extended periods, it should not be overlooked. As an excellent wrestler, an outstanding talker, a flamboyant personality, and a credible world champion, Flair headlined cards throughout the territory during the early to mid–1980s, exciting fans with competitive matches against the likes of Rose, Rocky Johnson, Brett and Buzz Sawyer, Piper, Oliver, Jaggers, Hennig, Steiner, Haynes, and Dusty Rhodes, a major wrestling star of the 1970s and 1980s who held the NWA World Heavyweight title both before and after making several appearances with Pacific Northwest Wrestling in 1986. More important from a business standpoint, Flair's appearance on a Pacific Northwest Wrestling show often spiked attendance. As Barry Owen put it in a Sept. 24, 1999, *SLAM! Wrestling* article by John Molinaro, "From Lou Thesz to Ric Flair, we had every NWA champ come through here. They all defended against whoever was our top guy at the time. Of all the champs, Ric Flair was the best draw for us. Every time he came in, it was a sellout."

But despite continued strong local television ratings, some well-attended shows, a fairly well-stocked roster, and decades of tradition, Pacific Northwest Wrestling clearly was facing an uphill battle by the mid–1980s. Part of the reason had to do with the changing nature of the Northwest itself. Wrestlers in the territory were no longer performing for "an audience full of loggers and lumberjacks," as Barry Owen, in the same *SLAM!* article, described Pacific Northwest Wrestling's live show patrons in earlier years. While the promotion had thousands of aging diehard fans, its continued success also depended in part on drawing new, younger fans—who now had numerous other entertainment options in every city or town of significant size in the Northwest. As far as the major cities of Portland, Seattle, and Tacoma were concerned, there seemed no limit to the entertainment options available to an emerging class of young professionals and minors who were on the lookout for major league attractions.

Sports-wise, there were NBA options available in Portland and Seattle, and the Mariners and Seahawks were hot tickets in Seattle throughout the 1980s. But as far as wrestling went, the World Wrestling Federation was setting the bar with regard to what fans should expect of major league wrestling throughout the United States and Canada—even if WWF ring action itself left much to be desired, as far as many serious fans of pro wrestling were concerned. To newer, more casual fans of wrestling—drawn to glitz, glamor, and state-of-the-art production—the WWF, whether on television or at an arena show, was major league wrestling, and a locally produced show, featuring wrestlers the WWF deemed unworthy of luring away, was not.

WWF tours through the Northwest in 1986 and 1987 drew fairly strong crowds overall, although a May 1987 WWF house show in Eugene attracted far fewer fans than a joint Pacific Northwest Wrestling/AWA show that same month in the same city featuring a Curt Hennig challenge for Nick Bockwinkel's AWA World Heavyweight title, which Hennig would win the following night at California's Cow Palace; an AWA World Tag Team title challenge by Rip Oliver and Mike Miller; and a matchup between Jimmy Snuka and Larry Zbyszko. A dozen WWF shows in Portland in 1986 and 1987 averaged about 5,000 fans—not outstanding, perhaps, but a fair turnout for shows featuring the usual brief Hulk Hogan WWF title defense and some undercard matches highlighting wrestlers familiar to Oregon fans, such as Adrian Adonis, Dynamite Kid, Matt Borne, George Wells, and Billy Jack Haynes. In Washington the WWF drew some impressive crowds in Tacoma, exceeding 20,000 for a Tacoma Dome show in 1986 and topping 20,000 again for a show at the same venue in 1987. Attendance at several other WWF Tacoma shows during the late 1980s topped 10,000. A 1987 WWF television taping at Seattle Center Coliseum, meanwhile, drew about 16,000 fans. At the television taping, one match saw Rip Oliver—who had held both major Pacific Northwest Wrestling titles a few months earlier—lose to WWF star Don Muraco. For several months in 1987, Oliver wrestled on the undercard of WWF shows,

Nick Bockwinkel, who dropped the AWA World Heavyweight championship to former Pacific Northwest Heavyweight champion Curt Hennig in May of 1987, was himself a former holder of the Pacific Northwest Heavyweight title. In 1963 and 1964 a much younger Bockwinkel had been an impactful presence in the Northwest, enjoying two heavyweight title runs to go with three tag team title reigns in Pacific Northwest Wrestling.

in the process making appearances in Tacoma and Portland as well as Seattle.

Also appearing on some 1980s WWF shows in the Pacific Northwest were two wrestlers who were clearly among the best of their era to come out of the region.

Ken Patera, younger brother of late 1970s/early 1980s Seattle Seahawks coach Jack Patera, was a Portland native who excelled in multiple sports while attending Portland's Cleveland High School. While attending Brigham Young University in the mid–1960s, Patera focused primarily on shot-putting, and in 1967 he was a gold medalist in the shot-put at the Pan-American Games. In the late 1960s he focused on weightlifting, and his efforts paid off in four consecutive U.S. national weightlifting championships as a superheavyweight from 1969 to 1972 and a gold medal at the 1971 Pan-American Games. Battling injuries a year later, Patera—one of the favorites going in—competed in weightlifting at the 1972 Olympics in Munich but failed to win a medal.

According to Andrew Lutzke at culturecrossfire.com, Ken's brother "Jack Patera was the Minnesota Vikings defensive coach and he hooked Ken up with Verne Gagne." As a result, Patera joined Gagne's 1972 bumper crop of trainees and made his pro wrestling debut, as a babyface, in the AWA that same year en route to achieving major success—as an outstanding performer in the ring and one of the top heels of his era—in the AWA, various NWA territories, and the WWWF/WWF, where he was a headliner and top heel challenger for the promotion's heavyweight title during parts of the 1970s and 1980s. After serving most of a two-year prison sentence following an altercation, alongside mid–1970s Northwest wrestling star Mr. Saito, with police officers in Wisconsin, Patera returned with his spinning full nelson finishing hold to the WWF, wrestling as a babyface and teaming at times with new WWF recruit and fellow Oregonian powerhouse Billy Jack Haynes.

Greg Valentine, son of all-time wrestling legend Johnny Valentine, was born in Seattle and spent the early years of his life there. According to his website at www.gregthehammervalentine.com, the younger Valentine—born John Wisniski, Jr.—accompanied his father on his wrestling travels while a teen and then, while still a teen, "decided to drop out of college and became a wrestler," training under Stu Hart and the Sheik.

Appearing in Stampede Wrestling as Johnny Valentine, Jr.—as the elder Johnny Valentine was remembered as a former headliner in the territory—Wisniski, Jr., lost the majority of his matches over a three-month period in 1970 before leaving Alberta and spending most of the next two years in the U.S. Midwest, competing at times as Baby Face Nelson; teaming with his father on occasion as Greg Valentine; and forming a successful "brother" tag team, as Johnny Fargo, with 1963 NWA Pacific Northwest Tag Team title-holder Don "Fargo" Kalt, who worked briefly, as the American Dream, for

Super Star Championship Wrestling in the 1970s. In 1973, with five tag team title runs in other territories under his belt, Greg Valentine competed for several months in Pacific Northwest Wrestling, sometimes as a headliner.

Valentine had significant success in the 1970s, winning nearly half of his 40-plus career titles during that decade. During the 1970s he was a headliner in numerous territories, a serious contender for world titles, half of a red-hot tag team with Ric Flair, a no-nonsense bruiser noted for his leg-breaking figure-four leglock and his powerful elbow smash, one of the top heels in wrestling, and a key player in the WWWF/WWF.

The 1980s saw Valentine achieve major success in Jim Crockett's NWA Mid-Atlantic territory—where Valentine engaged in a heated feud with Roddy Piper—and, again, the WWF, where he held the promotion's number two singles title, the Intercontinental championship, as Patera had done a few years earlier. Valentine was also a WWF World Tag Team champion in the mid–1980s and a key figure as the company expanded during that period, raising the stakes for numerous regional wrestling promotions, many of which would not be able to stay in the game much longer.

Pacific Northwest Wrestling faced a big challenge in the late 1980s when the Oregon Boxing and Wrestling Commission was formed to oversee ring-related activities and events throughout the state. Prior to that time, wrestling in Oregon had been overseen by smaller town or county commissions which often seemed to have minimal interest in what took place in wrestling rings. The new commission, however, headed by Executive Director Bruce Anderson, seemed to take its role seriously and imposed new regulations on wrestling promotions in the state. In 1988 the commission issued a ban on "juicing," or cutting of a wrestler's skin—usually by using a concealed razor blade tip—during matches. As Pacific Northwest Wrestling events were sometimes noted for bloody matches, this caused some concern among wrestlers, who were unlikely to support any measures that could tame their product and reduce attendance in Portland and around the territory. According to Wilson and Weldon in *Chokehold* (451), Matt Borne, in a KPTV interview, promised there would be blood at an upcoming show in Portland and dared the commission to do anything about it. On Nov. 12, 1988, Borne bled as promised, Anderson and the commission took note of it, and from that point on, Pacific Northwest Wrestling probably had an even stronger force than the WWF to worry about. As far as the immediate aftermath of Borne's "juicing" on the Nov. 12 show was concerned, Mike Rodgers reports that the commission shut down the promotion for two weeks "until Owen promised to follow the rules."

Owen and associates continued promoting events in Portland, Salem, Eugene, and other stops throughout the territory during the late 1980s and early 1990s, combining established names such as Oliver, Rose, Borne,

Haynes, Moretti, Wiskoski/DeBeers, and Miller with key newcomers including Scott Levy, aka Scotty the Body, who wrestled and doubled as Coss' quick-witted broadcast partner for a time in the late 1980s; Japanese star Tatsumi Fujinami; Len Denton, who doubled as booker while wrestling as "The Grappler"; strongman Scott Norton; Brian Adams; "Bruise Brothers" Ron and Don Harris; "Southern Rockers" Steve Doll and Rex King; and Ferrin Barr, Jr., aka Jesse Barr and son of longtime Pacific Northwest Wrestling preliminary wrestler and referee Ferrin "Sandy" Barr.

While Pacific Northwest Wrestling by this stage had neither the roster depth nor the local or regional impact it had enjoyed a decade or two earlier, it still had its share of talented grapplers in the late 1980s and early 1990s—some of whom went on to wrestle for the larger promotions that, as the territorial period of North American wrestling was drawing to a close, were commanding a bigger and bigger piece of the wrestling pie.

Matt Borne gained national exposure in the 1990s as Doink the Clown in the WWF and Big Josh in World Championship Wrestling (WCW), the Ted Turner-owned version of what had previously been Jim Crockett Promotions. Adams, the Harris Brothers, and the Southern Rockers were recruited to the WWF, where, respectively, they became Crush, the Blu Brothers, and the tag team of Well-Dunn. Levy eventually became a star as Raven in Philadelphia-based Extreme Championship Wrestling before successfully taking that character to WCW and the WWF. Norton, meanwhile, went on to enjoy success in WCW and major stardom in Japan.

Perhaps the most promising wrestler of the late 1980s/early 1990s era in Pacific Northwest Wrestling was another son of Sandy Barr, Art Barr. After achieving success as an amateur wrestler, Art Barr left Oregon State University and began training to be a pro wrestler with his father, his brother Jesse, and Matt Borne. Though on the small side at well under 200 pounds, Art Barr debuted as a pro wrestler at age 20 on a New Year's Day 1987 Pacific Northwest Wrestling show in Salem, and over the course of the next two years—generally situated near the middle of the card—he showed good skill and movement while performing generally entertaining matches against opponents including Moretti, Chris Colt, Cocoa Samoa, C.W. Bergstrom, Scott Peterson, Joey Jackson, Oliver, The Grappler, Mike Golden, Rose, and DeBeers—all of whom at some point held a title in Pacific Northwest Wrestling. Barr himself became a champion in late 1987, briefly holding the new NWA Pacific Northwest Television title toward the end of his rookie year.

Barr's career took a major step forward—and backward—in 1989. Early that year, on the heels of the popular movie *Beetlejuice*, Art Barr, as John Molinaro reports in a Nov. 29, 1999, *SLAM! Wrestling* article, "was christened as Beetlejuice by [Pacific Northwest Wrestling] alum Roddy Piper in a memorable TV angle."

Molinaro describes Barr in the role of his wrestling character, Beetle-juice: "Dressed in ripped jeans, face paint and flour in his hair, the Beetlejuice character was based on the Michael Keaton movie of the same name. Before each match, Art would sing and dance down to ringside, leading a trail of children to the ring like a pied piper. It was a character marketed directly at young children."

While Barr, a legitimately skilled wrestler, was not portrayed as a serious grappler as Beetlejuice, the character transformation—along with his quick, high-flying style—led to his becoming a featured wrestler and personality. But just a few months after his introduction as Beetlejuice, Barr ran into legal problems when an encounter with a 19-year-woman after a wrestling show in Pendleton, Oregon, led to charges of rape. As prowrestling.wikia.com reports, "In late 1989 Barr pleaded guilty to first-degree sexual abuse, was fined, sentenced to community service and put on probation." While that may not sound like much of a penalty for sexual abuse, Barr now had the burden of a criminal record. But even so, he continued wrestling for Pacific Northwest Wrestling in 1990, winning the promotion's tag team title twice with partner Jeff "Big Juice" Warner.

Barr's luck in Oregon ran out, reports Molinaro, when "his wrestling license [there was not] renewed, not because of the [sexual assault] case, but because he lied on his application about a drug charge as a teenager." Because of Barr's small size, Molinaro continues, it seemed "there was no way that Art would ever progress in the steroid-big wrestler era of the late 80s/early 90s." Yet Barr was offered a job with WCW, the second-largest promotion in the United States. Recast as "The Juicer," a more lawsuit-safe version of Beetlejuice, Barr continued in much the same manner in which he had left off in the Northwest, wowing fans with his innovative moves and appealing largely to children. But after Oregon newspaper reports and columns discussing Barr's past started being sent to newspapers in cities where Barr was scheduled to appear with WCW, the promotion decided to cut ties with Barr, who, despite his abundant talent, seemed to have few job prospects in the United States.

In 1991 he began wrestling for the Mexican EMLL promotion (now CMLL), one of the world's top promotions at the time. As the "Love Machine," Barr made an excellent living and sold out arenas as a top heel singles and tag-team wrestler—most notably, with future WWE champion Eddie Guerrero as his partner—for the next three years in both the popular Mexican EMLL/CMLL and AAA promotions. As Molinaro reports, "Barr was largely responsible for advancing the style of wrestling in Mexico. He was a true pioneer, combining the acrobatic, ballet-like grace of Lucha Libre, the stiffness of Japanese Puroresu and the big bumps and heel charisma of American wrestling into a revolutionary working style. More than anybody else, he helped change the landscape of wrestling in Mexico forever."

But, Molinaro continues, "Despite all the success he had achieved there, Art hated Mexico. He was far from his son Dexter and his wife back in Oregon. He missed his mom terribly. He was homesick.

"As a way to deal with the pressure of being far from home, Art turned to alcohol and prescription drugs. For Art, drugs and alcohol was an escape from the reality of being so far from his family."

Even after achieving major success in Mexico, Barr—despite his earlier difficulty getting his license renewed—wrestled occasionally in Oregon. In early 1992 he won the Pacific Northwest Tag Team title with brother Jesse during a visit home. But Art Barr, according to Molinaro, "was on a dangerous path of self-destruction." While he had two more highly successful years in Mexico, during a Thanksgiving visit home to Oregon in November of 1994, Barr—reportedly with alcohol and prescription drugs in his bloodstream, though the exact cause of death is unclear—passed away at his home in Springfield, Oregon.

As fate had it, Pacific Northwest Wrestling—the *remnant* of Pacific Northwest Wrestling—was in the Barr family's hands at the time of Art's death in 1994. For several years prior to that, it was decidedly difficult for almost any regional wrestling territory in the United States to withstand the advances of the WWF and WCW as national promotions, the evolving expectations of wrestling fans, and the changing reality with regard to television. Because the larger promotions—committed to building fan bases nationwide for their traveling arena shows and pay-per-view television events—were willing to pay local television stations to air their syndicated weekly television programs, it became increasingly difficult for smaller promotions to compete for television exposure, long considered the lifeblood of any successful wrestling promotion. Even Verne Gagne's AWA—for three decades, one of the most successful wrestling promotions in the world—was out of business by 1991. As far as *Portland Wrestling* was concerned, KPTV made the decision in late 1991 to cancel the 38-year-old program, even though it was still the highest-rated local show in its market. According to Barry Owen, his father was offered a contract by KPTV to continue airing *Portland Wrestling*, but Don Owen—now in a world in which wrestling promotions were expected to buy airtime—declined. Soon after, airing in *Portland Wrestling*'s former time slot on KPTV was the WWF *Superstars of Wrestling* syndicated program. The best Don Owen could do, meanwhile, was buy ad time on WWF TV programs for his upcoming live wrestling shows.

Kayfabememories.com reports that Owen was offered a broadcast deal on Fox Sports in the early 1990s. While regional exposure on Fox Sports could perhaps have helped keep Pacific Northwest Wrestling afloat for a time, it also would have raised the stakes considerably. Owen's longtime deal with KPTV had put the financial burden of producing the *Portland Wrestling* show on the station's shoulders. Without a similar commitment from Fox Sports, the financial burden on a now-struggling promotion would have been overwhelming, and Owen declined the Fox Sports offer.

The early 1990s was an era in which top-of-the-line wrestlers were hard to come by for regional promotions, as the WWF, in Barry Owen's words, was "going after everybody." Getting television exposure was often an impossible challenge, and presenting a product in arenas that measured up to fans' changing perception of what constituted major league wrestling was a financial impossibility for smaller promotions. Sponsorship deals were hard to come by—or to maintain, as reflected in Pacific Northwest Wrestling's longtime association with Tom Peterson coming to an end as the curtain was falling on the promotion. Added to all the other challenges Don Owen and Pacific Northwest Wrestling were facing in the early 1990s were the regulations and obligations the Oregon Boxing and Wrestling Commission imposed on a regional wrestling company fighting for its life and the fact that the National Wrestling Alliance—formerly committed to backing up its member promotions—had all but run its course. All of those hurdles resulted in fewer and fewer fans coming out to the arenas to support Pacific Northwest Wrestling when it was at its most vulnerable.

In mid–1992, deciding enough was enough, Owen sold what remained of his promotion to Sandy Barr. While the Portland Sports Arena was not part of the deal, during the early going of his new promotion Barr was able to continue holding shows there.

Although Barr had gained considerable experience behind the scenes during his years of association with Don Owen—particularly in Salem, where Barr took over as the local promoter after Elton Owen retired—it is possible he did not fully understand the challenges he would face at the helm of a small wrestling promotion in the 1990s. Repackaging his new purchase as Championship Wrestling USA (CWUSA), Barr scaled the promotion down to one essentially serving the Portland area alone and not the much larger territory Pacific Northwest Wrestling had served for decades. Continuing to use many wrestlers familiar to Pacific Northwest Wrestling fans during that promotion's latter years—including Al Madril, John Rambo, C.W. Bergstrom, Bruiser Brian Cox, Mike Winner, Brickhouse Brown, Steve Doll, and Jesse Barr—along with proven regional stars—among them, Wiskoski/DeBeers; and booker Billy Jack, the latter sometimes appearing as the villainous Black Bart—Barr scrapped the old Pacific Northwest Wrestling titles and created new titles for his promotion, establishing Bart Sawyer as CWUSA's first singles champion as holder of the promotion's Television title, which would remain the top CWUSA singles title until the spring of 1997 while being a local showcase for champions including Winner, Rambo, Cox, three-time champion Sawyer, five-time champion DeBeers, and five-time champion Buddy Wayne.

A "World" Heavyweight title, held by Matt Borne, was established during the final months of CWUSA's existence in 1997.

With television exposure for his CWUSA product limited at first to community access cable, Barr managed to secure a slot on local broadcast television, although he had to pay for it. According to www.kayfabememories. com, the slot Barr secured on KOIN-TV was not particularly advantageous, as it was "early in the morning, and the time [changed] weekly by 15 minutes or so depending on what infomercials [were] on before it." Paying for the production of his television show—usually hosted by Don Coss and Al Madril—and paying for television time on top of that seemed a losing proposition for a promoter running mainly weekly shows in a limited local market, even when that promoter occasionally had access to major wrestling stars such as the returning "Love Machine" Art Barr and "Superfly" Jimmy Snuka. With no shortage of entertainment options for the ticket-buying public in the 1990s, Barr was in a tough financial situation as far as wrestling was concerned, and drawing small crowds to weekly shows in Portland and sporadic events in Washington did not bode well for the future of Championship Wrestling USA.

Don Owen's sale of the Portland Sports Arena to a church and continued regulatory pressures from the Oregon Boxing and Wrestling Commission contributed to Barr's decision, in 1994, to move his weekly wrestling shows out of Oregon to the Bagley Center in nearby Vancouver, Washington. But in mid-year, Barr took his chances by promoting a stadium show in Portland that made a few national headlines—though it fell far short of living up to them.

Although the June 24, 1994, Portland card featured some capable wrestlers, the highlight of the show was supposed to have been an appearance by controversial figure skater and Portland native Tonya Harding, who presumably was going to get involved in the action. But, as Greg Oliver reports in a June 4, 2007, SLAM! Wrestling article following Sandy Barr's death, "It all went awry when the athletic commission insisted that Harding was not a licensed manager and could not remain at ringside." As things played out, Harding accompanied Art Barr, Eddie Guerrero, and Bruiser Brian Cox to the ring for a three-on-three match before taking her place on an elevated seat in the audience and proceeding to watch the match quietly. The result, from Sandy Barr's perspective, probably could not have been more disappointing.

In his new setting of Vancouver, Washington, Barr, using his familiar set of wrestlers based in the U.S. Northwest along with British Columbia-based wrestlers including Michelle Starr and amateur standout Mike Roselli, often attracted crowds exceeding 500. Occasionally, he would bring in big-name wrestlers from the Mexican AAA promotion in which his son the "Love Machine" had become such a prominent player. Among such Mexico-based wrestlers—who, despite their fame in Mexico, were not well known to Northwest fans and, presumably, were not the best investment Barr could have made if his intent was to spike attendance—were Konnan and Perro Aguayo, two legends of Mexican wrestling, along with Guerrero and Rey Mysterio, two young and extremely talented wrestlers who, despite their small size, would go on to success in WCW and, eventually, superstardom and heavyweight title runs in WWE. Sandy Barr's association with Mexican wrestling ended with the passing of son Art in late 1994.

Although 1995 was a relatively quiet year for Barr's promotion, one highlight was an appearance in February by Roddy Piper to pay tribute to an appreciative Don Owen, who was known to hold Piper in the same high regard that Piper had for him.

While Owen to this day has many backers who share Piper's view and laud Owen's business acumen and his ability to run a successful regional wrestling promotion for half a century, there are others who advise taking a more critical look at Owen in assessing his contributions to wrestling in the Northwest. Despite the perception that Owen was one of the fairer promoters of his day in terms of how he paid his wrestlers, Silverstone says Owen was far less than fair when it came to his view of members of the Jewish faith. Others suggest Owen could hold a grudge or be unpleasant and sometimes hard to work with. Moretti, who appeared on Owen shows from 1978 right to the final months of Owen's tenure as a promoter, goes further: "He was a cattleman, and he treated his wrestlers like cattle.... I think he liked his cattle better than us."

Barr, meanwhile, while never achieving a level of success to rival Owen's, is generally remembered in positive terms. Roselli recalls, "Sandy Barr was the nicest guy I met in wrestling. He was honest and respectable."

Matt Borne took over as Barr's booker in 1996, and the wrestling action that year often centered on DeBeers, Bart Sawyer, Buddy Wayne, and Borne himself. But though the promotion had a small but loyal audience in southern Washington and northern Oregon, Barr's promotional activities do not appear to have been profitable. According to www.kayfabememories.com, "the shows didn't draw much money" and were "mostly funded by Sandy Barr's financially successful Flea Market." Yet Barr continued promoting in Vancouver, Washington, until June 1997, with KOIN airing his shows until a month or two later. After that, as reported in www.kayfabememories.com, "the remnants of Portland Wrestling that had been hanging by a thread broke off."

14

British Columbia, 1989–2017

Since the demise of Tomko's UWA in 1989, there have been numerous attempts at wrestling promotion in British Columbia, some undertaken by wrestlers formerly employed by Tomko or Sandor Kovacs and others by relative newcomers to the wrestling business. The success of British Columbia wrestling promotions in the 1990s and into the 21st century has varied widely, with some promotions dying off before the majority of fans in their areas even knew they existed and, at the other end of the spectrum, another promotion adapting to the times, holding the interest of a small but loyal audience, and passing an impressive 20 years in business in 2016.

Among the early promoters in the post–Tomko era were four wrestlers who had worked for Tomko in the 1980s. Two—Rocky Della Serra and Timothy Flowers—had wrestled in British Columbia for years and also made some appearances with Pacific Northwest Wrestling in the 1980s. The other two—both young relative newcomers to professional wrestling who had joined Tomko's UWA roster as that promotion neared the end in the late 1980s—were native British Columbian Mike Roselli and Californian Mark Vellios, better known in the BC wrestling world as "Gorgeous" Michelle Starr.

In mid-1989 Della Serra and partner Fred Roselli—the father of Mike Roselli—established Pacific Coast Championship Wrestling (PCCW), which held weekly cards in Cloverdale (Surrey), BC, and sporadic spot shows for most of a year, featuring performers including Tomko alumni Della Serra, Flowers, Starr, Verne Siebert, Mike Roselli, Oly Olsen, Randy Tyler, and—several times—Tomko himself, appearing as "Robotron," a character Tomko had briefly tried out while he was still promoting. About 10 months after his promotion's debut card, Della Serra returned to Montreal for a year and PCCW went on hiatus, Nevada reports in *Wrestling in the Canadian West* (95).

Returning to British Columbia in the summer of 1991, Della Serra reopened PCCW, this time with Mike Roselli—barely out of his teens, despite already having wrestled professionally for a few years—as his partner. But, according to Nevada, "the duo soon had a falling out, and split the company down the middle" (95). Both groups, using local wrestlers, proceeded to run shows on alternate weeks at the Cloverdale Fairgrounds and also held shows in other locations in southern BC. But both groups also took a hit from the emergence of a newer promotion, Michelle Starr's West Coast Championship Wrestling (WCCW), which by 1992 took over the Cloverdale Fairgrounds base—a coveted wrestling venue in British Columbia—and employed the promoters it had exiled, Della Serra and Roselli, as wrestlers. While WCCW held the majority of its shows in Surrey/Cloverdale, WCCW shows also took place in a variety of other southern British Columbia cities, including Hope, Chilliwack, Abbotsford, and New Westminster.

WCCW employed numerous locally and regionally established wrestlers, including Starr himself, Della Serra, Roselli, Moretti, Morowski, Olsen, Flowers, Wayne, Tyler, and Terry "The Frog" Tomko. WCCW also introduced a popular newcomer to wrestling, John "Johnny Canuck" Collins, who was already in his thirties when he trained to be a wrestler under Starr, who in Greg Oliver's July 19, 2014, *SLAM! Wrestling* report shortly after Collins' death from a heart attack called the 300-pound-plus Johnny Canuck—named after a classic Canadian comic book hero—"the biggest local [British Columbia] wrestling drawing card ever without TV exposure." Asked to comment further, Mark "Michelle Starr" Vellios adds by telephone, "He was definitely a larger-than-life person." Referring to Canuck's help getting him into longshoreman work, Vellios says, "He's taken care of my family. He left the world too early."

Among major wrestling names brought in to appear on WCCW shows were Rick Martel, Tito Santana, Bad News Allen, the Sheepherders, Hercules Hernandez, and Surrey's John Tenta. Cooperation was usually good between Starr's WCCW and Sandy Barr's Championship Wrestling USA, and wrestlers connected to the U.S. Northwest—including Rose, DeBeers, Snuka, Matt Borne, Jesse Barr, and C.W. Bergstrom—made appearances with WCCW. Yet it was a constant struggle for almost any small regional wrestling promotion in the 1990s to eke out a profit, and Starr, rather than continuing to fight an uphill battle, shut down WCCW in August of 1995.

Besides wrestling on PCCW and WCCW shows from 1989 to 1995, Timothy Flowers was active as a promoter in British Columbia before, during, and after that period. Flowers first ventured into promoting in 1988 when his concern over the direction in which Tomko's UWA was heading caused him to leave that promotion and to put his own promotional vision to the test. Flowers formed International Championship Wrestling (ICW) and, in the early going, according to *Wrestling in the Canadian Northwest*, promoted cards most Friday and Saturday nights in a small territory stretching from New Westminster to Hope (90).

Flowers put his promotion and his differences with Tomko aside in 1989, briefly rejoining the UWA until that ship sank in mid-year. For the next six years, Flowers appeared regularly with PCCW and WCCW and left the Northwest occasionally to wrestle in other parts of Canada and in Europe. He also promoted shows occasionally in the Vancouver area and on Vancouver Island, using a core of established British Columbia grapplers and bringing in some name outsiders, including Bad News Allen, Martel, the Sheepherders, DeBeers, Valentine, Jim Neidhart, and Matt Borne as Doink the Clown, as well as Tenta.

Seeing an opening after Starr's WCCW shut

Early in his career, Jimmy "Superfly" Snuka was a popular performer up and down the West Coast. After earning a national reputation in the WWF and retiring as a full-time wrestler in the early 1990s, Snuka continued to turn up on occasion on independent wrestling shows in the Northwest.

down, Flowers established a base in Cloverdale and set out to establish himself as a leading wrestling promoter in the Northwest. His main rivalry—often heated and sometimes nasty—was with the newly formed Extreme Canadian Championship Wrestling (ECCW) promotion, based in New Westminster, which featured edgy or outlandish characters and a more over-the-top form of simulated violence. Another promotion—Della Serra's follow-up to PCCW, called Pro Wrestling Canada (not to be confused with another short-lived Vancouver-area promotion of the same name about a decade later)—had been active in Cloverdale during part of 1995 and 1996 but had made little impact and was already out of business when Flowers' ICW moved into Cloverdale.

Flowers had some success as a promoter from 1996 to 2001, running shows mainly in Surrey/Cloverdale—typically, drawing crowds of a few hundred—but also holding shows in Abbotsford and smaller towns around southern BC and establishing a small presence in Washington. Flowers mainly employed local or lesser-known wrestlers but also used regionally known wrestlers such as Wayne, Moretti, Della Serra, and Gerry Morrow and sometimes brought in name wrestlers such as Rose, Martel, Santana, Neidhart, Miller, Allen, the Sheepherders, Borne, Valentine, and DeBeers. After several years of relative success, however, Flowers' ICW had already exceeded the expected lifespan of a small, independent wrestling promotion without television exposure in an age when wrestling promotion was falling more and more beyond the reach of all but a well-to-do few. While Flowers continued to wrestle occasionally and promote events from time to time for some years afterward, ICW as a regular promotion in British Columbia closed down in the fall of 2001.

ECCW, originally Extreme Canadian Championship Wrestling, was modeled largely on the Philadelphia-based Extreme Championship Wrestling promotion popularized in the early 1990s by independent promoter and future WWE personality Paul Heyman. Like the Philadelphia-based promotion, Extreme Canadian Championship Wrestling branded itself as an alternative to the more conventional, mainstream wrestling promotions of the day—in particular, WCW and the WWF, which dominated the North American wrestling landscape in the 1990s. Both ECW and ECCW positioned themselves as racier, sometimes adult-themed, often ultra-violent alternatives to the more sanitized, child-friendly, cartoonish major promotions of the day. But the fact was, WCW and the WWF were engaged in a heated battle during much of the 1990s and shed much of their family-friendly image in favor of a more "extreme" approach at least partway along the lines of ECW's and ECCW's in order to one-up the competition, and ultra-violent simulations—often bordering on the real thing—and sexual themes were common especially in the WWF during much of the 1990s.

Extreme Canadian Championship Wrestling was established in 1996 by John Parlett, who had worked in a supporting role for Starr's WCCW. Under Parlett's ownership, ECCW shows were held throughout Vancouver Island during the first half of 1996, featuring a cast of wrestlers including Starr, Canuck, Roselli, Olsen, and Bart Sawyer and appearances by Jimmy Snuka. In July of 1996, ECCW debuted on the British Columbia mainland with a show at Eagles Hall in New Westminster, which served as the promotion's home base for several years. On that show were the Starr-Canuck tandem, a pair of violent heavyweights known as the Glamour Order of Discipline; Matt Borne as Doink; and a hard-hitting women's match between Iron Maiden, who had wrestled around British Columbia dating back to the late Tomko era, and British Columbian Velvet McIntyre, a Sandy Barr trainee and Pacific Northwest Wrestling/All-Star Wrestling alumna who had gone on to hold a share of the WWF Women's Tag Team title in 1984 and the WWF Women's championship for six days in 1986. It was almost immediately clear that Eagles Hall suited the ECCW adult-oriented style well, as Nevada reports that "the layout was … conducive to taking action into the crowd and, frequently, onto the busy Columbia Avenue outside. These factors combined with the fact that the hall was downstairs from a business with a liquor license made the site ideal for an edgy, adult-focused program" (126). Toward the end of 1996, Starr became part-owner of the promotion.

Holding most of its 1997 shows at Eagles Hall, ECCW used mainly the same core of wrestlers, with Starr and Canuck the dominant tag team through most of the year. The promotion's Heavyweight title, meanwhile, was traded among familiar names such as Canuck, Starr, Roselli, and Randy Tyler and high-flying New Zealander Adam Dykes, a relatively small grappler known as El Antorcha/The Torch.

The following year, 1998, featured a series of violent battles between members of the newly disbanded (and later-reunited) Starr-Canuck team, with Canuck becoming the hottest babyface in British Columbia; generally strong cards featuring a growing roster; and the addition of Dave Teixeira to ECCW management and ownership. Teixeira adopted the name Dave Republic for his work as a manager and spokesman/performer, and he was widely recognized as a strong addition to ECCW's live product.

In August of 1998 ECCW faced a challenge from Flowers' ICW promotion, which ran a show in New Westminster in direct competition with a regular ECCW event a few blocks away, constituting what many viewed as a serious breach of wrestling etiquette. Nevada says, via email, "When Flowers ran head to head against ECCW, he did so with former ECCW headliner [Dr.] Luther atop of the card. This is reflective of the bad blood between the organizations at that time." ICW failed to establish a lasting presence on ECCW's home turf, however, and Luther, who led a heel faction called the "Army of Darkness," later returned to ECCW as a headliner.

While the National Wrestling Alliance (NWA) was a shell of its former self by this time, ECCW—presenting a wrestling product largely at odds with wrestling tradition—was openly a member of the NWA. Although the anticipation and atmosphere hardly approached the level of earlier times when NWA champions such as Kiniski, Thesz, and Watson would defend the title in British Columbia, ECCW's standing in the NWA helped bring late–1990s/early–2000s NWA World Heavyweight champion and big-name Mixed Martial Arts (MMA) competitor Dan Severn to British Columbia twice in 1998 to defend the title that had been considered the holy grail among wrestlers during and before the All-Star Wrestling era.

By 1999 ECCW ownership was firmly in the hands of Starr and Teixeira, "moving John Parlett effectively out of the equation," as Nevada reports in *Wrestling in the Canadian West* (127). With a newly established training school called the House of Pain, the promotion held generally successful shows throughout British Columbia, featuring the old core along with various supporting players and newcomers—the most prominent, perhaps, 400-pound BC native Juggernaut, who would go on to become a six-time ECCW Heavyweight champion.

The next year, 2000, saw ECCW depart from its home base in New Westminster when the sale of Eagles Hall forced a change of venues. The promotion landed in Surrey and held its main shows at Bridgeview Hall beginning in late 2000. Also in 2000, ECCW increased its cross-border presence and held cards in a variety of Washington cities, including Bellingham, Mt. Vernon, Auburn, Olympia, Everson, Vancouver, Everett, Longview, Shelton, and Ellensburg. The expansion to Washington was not smooth, however. In a situation somewhat reflecting difficulties promoters Owen and Barr had faced in Oregon, "Washington State," as Nevada reports in *Wrestling in the Canadian Northwest*, "provided its own unique challenges for [ECCW]." Specifically, the state required an ambulance to be present at wrestling events, which, Nevada says, "made the card economically unfeasible to run." The ambulance-on-hand requirement caused the Washington Athletic Commission to cancel a show in Bellingham in November of 2000, Nevada says, "just moments before the scheduled opening bell" (129). Matt Farmer, who wrestled for ECCW in 2000 and 2001, adds, "They had a city code [in Bellingham] that you could not rent the city ambulances, and even though the Elks Lodge we were running [had] a fire department with ambulances very close by, we were not allowed to hold the event."

Further conflict with the Washington Athletic Commission greatly reduced ECCW's presence in the United States by mid–2001. While ECCW did for a time continue to run some shows in Washington—and even as far south as Portland, Oregon—after its skirmishes with the Washington Athletic Commission, its promotional efforts centered squarely on British Columbia, where it held shows all over the southern part of the province—primarily at ECCW's new home base of Bridgeview Hall and at Vancouver's Russian Community Center—and occasionally in the north.

Challenges from athletic commissions were not limited to Washington. As Nevada reports, the Vancouver (BC) Athletic Commission required ECCW, in order to hold its shows in the city, to pay fees which were "designed with a grand production in mind, comparable to WWE level" (130). Nevada reports that ECCW met with the commission in 2002, made the case that commission regulations were hurting independent wrestling promoters, and went on to draft and present a proposal "that would stagger the fees based on the size of the venue ... and the Commission accepted it." Nevada continues, "The Commission relented, perhaps with the recognition that the revenue being generated from independent wrestling cards wasn't significant enough to warrant taxation. After only a short time, the Commission stopped paying attention to professional wrestling altogether" (131).

In 2001 ECCW featured name outsiders including Terry "Sabu" Brunk, real-life nephew of the Sheik and an ex–ECW champion who was perhaps the North American wrestler most associated with the "extreme" style ECW and ECCW sought to present; "Fallen Angel" Christopher Daniels, recognized as one of the best technical wrestlers of his era; and Bryan Danielson, who has to be considered one of the top wrestlers ever to emerge from the Pacific Northwest.

Danielson's story, well known to hardcore wrestling fans for over a decade, has become more familiar to millions of newer, perhaps more casual, wrestling fans in recent years. It's the story of an Aberdeen, Washington, native whose only dream of further education after high school involved learning to be a professional wrestler. With no particular background as a wrestler, Danielson set his sights on attending a wrestling school and, at 18, ended up training with 1990s/2000s WWF/WWE superstar Shawn Michaels, who established the Texas Wrestling Academy (TWA) in San Antonio when he was on a lengthy hiatus from wrestling due to injury. Danielson was a standout student and got his early experience as a wrestling performer in the Frontier Martial Arts promotion in Japan—a company whose style was often similar to ECW's and ECCW's—and Michaels' small TWA promotion in 1999 and 2000.

Best known at the time as American Dragon, Danielson toiled briefly in the WWF developmental training ground before setting out as a globe-trotter in search of matches, further knowledge of his craft, and any tricks or techniques he could use to give fans entertaining and innovative yet believable matches night after night. Though he weighed well under 200 pounds and didn't have movie star features or the chiseled, muscled-up look some promoters and casual wrestling fans were looking for, Danielson never seemed to have any trouble finding work.

From 2001 to 2009 Danielson wrestled for numerous promotions worldwide, both as American Dragon and under his real name. He held numerous smaller-promotion titles during that period as well as a share of a major promotion's Junior Heavyweight Tag Team title when he wrestled for New Japan Pro Wrestling in 2004. He also held the emerging Ring of Honor promotion's World Heavyweight title for over a year in 2005/2006. Prior to that, American Dragon held ECCW's Canadian Junior Heavyweight title in 2001, the first year Danielson appeared on ECCW shows. He would continue to make ECCW appearances during most of the next six years.

In 2009 Danielson—a seasoned veteran widely considered among the most skilled pro wrestlers in the world—had another shot at the WWE developmental leagues, and he debuted early the next year on WWE's NXT television competition for aspiring wrestlers vying for spots on the WWE roster. Programmed to lose the majority of his matches on NXT, Danielson—recast as Daniel Bryan—was given some opportunities to shine but was generally positioned as a weak, bland competitor who looked a bit out of his league in seeking a spot on the WWE main roster.

After being eliminated from NXT, Bryan continued wrestling, with only middling success, in WWE's Florida developmental promotion. In mid–2010 he was part of an angle in which NXT competitors invaded WWE shows, but when the action got a little too heated—with Bryan "choking" a ring announcer with the announcer's necktie—WWE, concerned about sponsors' reaction to Bryan's action, fired him. Two weeks later, Bryan Danielson was back to wowing fans on the independent circuit, but then, when the heat was off for his "strangling" a defenseless announcer, Danielson was invited back to WWE.

"Daniel Bryan" returned to WWE in a much stronger position than the one in which he had left. Returning at the August 2010 SummerSlam pay-per-view event, Bryan was a key part of the winning team's victory over his old NXT cohort. He continued to win his share of matches over the next several weeks before capturing his first WWE title—the United States championship—at the Sept. 19, 2010, WWE Night of Champions event in St. Louis.

Gradually becoming one of WWE's more entertaining characters—cast at times as an overachieving underdog and at other times as an easily angered, borderline psychotic—Bryan won his first WWE World Heavyweight title in late 2011 and enjoyed a lengthy run as co-holder of the WWE Tag Team title in 2012/2013. On the rise as a huge fan favorite, Bryan held the WWE Title twice, though both times briefly, in 2013.

The WWE storyline in late 2013 was centered largely on Bryan's look and attributes, with WWE executive vice president Stephanie McMahon, in storyline, declaring Bryan a "B-plus player," suggesting he was not an "A player" of the sort that WWE management wanted as the face and champion of the promotion. The storyline involved WWE management putting every obstacle in Bryan's path and Bryan—with fans at almost every arena chanting "*Yes! Yes! Yes!*" in unison with one of the unlikeliest of big-time wrestling heroes—persevering and capturing the WWE World Heavyweight title one more time in the main event of the April 6, 2014, WrestleMania 30 event held before a sold-out audience of about 75,000—many of them *Yes!*-chanting—fans in New Orleans.

Barely a month after the pinnacle of his career, however, Bryan underwent serious neck surgery, and his ability to return to the ring was in question.

But he managed to return in January of 2015, and following an angle and a series of matches that teased the possibility of his challenging once more for the WWE Heavyweight title at WrestleMania 31, Bryan instead captured the promotion's Intercontinental title in the opening match of the televised portion of WrestleMania 31, with 75,000-plus fans again in attendance.

Then, for the second straight year, Bryan found himself on the injured list just weeks after tasting victory at WrestleMania—the second time, as a result of accumulated concussions stemming from years of hard-hitting matches. This time there would be no returning to the ring for Danielson, who announced his retirement in February of 2016, cutting short a remarkable career and path to the top of his profession. Since retiring, he has remained a popular on-camera presence on WWE television broadcasts.

Another Pacific Northwest native who combined bookings in ECCW with matches for various other wrestling promotions before gaining some fame as a pro wrestler is Delta, BC, native Kyle Greenwood, best known professionally as Kyle O'Reilly. O'Reilly, a student at ECCW's House of Pain wrestling school, made his ECCW debut in 2005 at age 18 and spent stretches during the early years of his career in ECCW, where he held the NWA Canadian Junior Heavyweight title three times in 2007 and 2008. O'Reilly has made his name in wrestling by performing at a high level in matches with numerous promotions in several countries. To North American wrestling fans, he gained attention over several years as a performer for the Ring of Honor promotion, which has a syndicated television program and promotes shows in much of the United States and occasionally holds events in Canada. In the summer of 2017 O'Reilly earned a spot on WWE's NXT roster, and among the matches that helped set him on a course to get there were several Ring of Honor encounters with one of the wrestlers who trained O'Reilly for his ring career: Othello, Washington, native Wesley "Davey" Richards.

Davey Richards also wrestled for ECCW during the early years of his career. With a smallish frame and excellent technical skills, Richards followed an early career path similar to Bryan Danielson's by wrestling for numerous promotions in North America and overseas; adopting techniques designed to elevate the quality and believability of his matches; holding a share—twice, in Richards' case—of the Junior Heavyweight Tag Team championship in New Japan Pro Wrestling; and enjoying a lengthy reign as the Ring of Honor World Heavyweight champion.

While Richards wrestled nearly all of his ECCW matches during the first few years of his career, from 2004 to 2007, he returned briefly to ECCW in 2013. In 2014 he joined the Nashville-based Total Nonstop Action (TNA) promotion, which has some minor national and international TV penetration, and proceeded to win the promotion's World Tag Team championship several times in 2014 and 2015 with former Ring of Honor partner Eddie Edwards.

Shortly after Richards and Edwards ended their fifth TNA World Tag Team title reign in early 2016, Richards suffered an ACL injury. He returned to the ring later in the year but suffered further injury in 2017.

While established British Columbia ring veterans such as Moretti, Della Serra, Wayne, and Roselli and hundreds of lesser-known wrestlers have appeared on ECCW cards over the years—many hailing from British Columbia and the neighboring U.S. Northwest—the promotion has also attracted many well-known wrestlers who have come for a few matches or made more regular visits. Name wrestlers brought into the promotion over the years—besides those already mentioned—have included Buddy Rose, Kia "Awesome Kong" Stevens, Honky Tonk Man, the Sheepherders, Colonel DeBeers, Matt Borne, Brutus Beefcake, Koko B. Ware, Tito Santana, Salofa "Rikishi" Fatu, Robert "Kurrgan" Maillet, Colt Cabana, Jim Neidhart, Nattie "Natalya" Neidhart, Greg Valentine, Sean "Val Venis" Morley, T.J. "Tyson Kidd" Wilson, and Eric Young.

Nevada—a top ECCW competitor himself from 2003 to 2006, with a lengthy ECCW Heavyweight title run in 2003–2004—reports, in *Wrestling in the Canadian Northwest*, that ECCW briefly had a television contract in 2005–2006, but shortly after the contract with KVOS-TV of Bellingham, Washington, was canceled in September of 2006, Michelle Starr turned his stake in the promotion over to ECCW wrestler Nathan "Disco Fury" Burke, who had been a featured wrestler with the promotion since 1998 (132). Burke, who became a key behind-the-scenes player for ECCW, recalls the period in which he had a share of ECCW ownership as "amazing…. [That's where] I learned to book a show." While with ECCW, Burke also had a hand in training talented newcomers such as O'Reilly, Harv Sihra, and Nicole Matthews.

Nevada, who had wrestled for nearly a decade and logged over two dozen title reigns mainly in his native Manitoba prior to joining ECCW in early 2002, was also a key trainer of up-and-coming wrestlers after his arrival on the West Coast. Among wrestlers Nevada helped train are Matthews, who has gone on to earn some recognition in the United States and overseas while frequently returning to wrestle in British Columbia, and BC brothers Harv and Gurv Sihra—formerly the Bollywood Boyz—who, in late 2011/early 2012, made a few high-profile wrestling appearances in India; in 2015, won a tag team title tournament with Global Force Wrestling, a U.S. promotion established in 2014 by TNA cofounder Jeff Jarrett; and, in 2017, are better known as the Singh Brothers in WWE.

Nevada also trained BC native Marty Sugar, who made appearances for a few years with ECCW before establishing Kelowna-based Big West Wrestling in 2011. In 2017 Sugar remains a featured wrestler as well as the promoter for Big West Wrestling, one of three wrestling promotions vying for attention and enjoying some success in British Columbia's Okanagan Valley.

After taking a brief breather from wrestling following his departure from ECCW, Starr established the newest version of All-Star Wrestling, which used some wrestlers who had appeared on ECCW cards. Since 2007, Starr's All-Star Wrestling—still in operation in 2017—has usually held about 10 to 20 shows per year in a variety of southern British Columbia locations including North Vancouver, Squamish, Kelowna, Vernon, Abbotsford, Chilliwack, and Cloverdale. Shortly after establishing his version of All-Star Wrestling, Starr was joined at the helm by Burke, who remains involved in All-Star Wrestling and describes the company's product as "family-friendly." Burke also notes that many of the fans who turn out for All-Star Wrestling shows in the present day are the same fans who supported All-Star Wrestling in the 1980s.

Starr's was actually the second attempt to resurrect the All-Star Wrestling name during the post–Tomko era, as two other ECCW veterans—Mike Roselli and Randy Tyler—established an All-Star Wrestling promotion in Vancouver in 2000. For Roselli this was his second go at wrestling promotion, following his brief run as a promoter of Pacific Coast Championship Wrestling (PCCW) in the early 1990s. Roselli and Tyler's All-Star Wrestling promotion, using predominantly local grapplers trained at the All-Star-affiliated "Wrestle Plex" school and holding events on BC's Lower Mainland and on Vancouver Island, was soon passed on to other promoters before fading away in 2004.

That version of All-Star Wrestling's Heavyweight champion at the time the promotion closed, Layne Fontaine, established a new promotion, Top Ranked Wrestling, based in Abbotsford, in partnership with Clint Istace, another wrestler on the BC independent circuit. Featuring wrestlers such as Tyler, Karl "Jason the Terrible" Moffat, Vid Vain, and Sweet Daddy Devastation, Top Ranked Wrestling was able to do what no other British Columbia wrestling promotion had managed to do since the Tomko era—that is, secure a television deal ensuring penetration into much of BC's Lower Mainland and northern Washington. That was the deal that brought ECCW to the air on Bellingham's KVOS-TV, which was available over the airwaves and via cable in southern British Columbia. In December of 2005, just a few months after Top Ranked Wrestling's deal with KVOS was struck, ECCW purchased Top Ranked Wrestling, along with its television deal, and that led to ECCW's only weekly television show—*NWA Top Ranked Wrestling*, hosted by Mauro Ranallo and, later, Scotty Sweatervest—which lasted less than a year. Ranallo, a native of Abbotsford, has since gone on to achieve his dream of being a WWE television commentator.

Though ECCW's path has not always been smooth, that probably makes its record as a long-lasting independent wrestling promotion in the WWE era all the more impressive. Over the years ECCW has attracted some negative publicity for its sometimes ultraviolent style and for occasional storyline violence by men against women, and its fans have been noted for getting too rowdy at times. As a result, the promotion has been denied access to some venues and had the occasional commissioner or politician speaking out against it.

A further challenge came in 2010, when Teixeira left ECCW after providing considerable direction and financial backing to the promotion for a dozen years. But despite all challenges, over two decades after its debut, ECCW—renamed Elite Canadian Championship Wrestling in 2012—remains a key force in independent wrestling and shows few signs of slowing down.

ECCW's main driving force during the 2010s has been Scott "Scotty Mac" Schnurr, a native of Kelowna who first wrestled for ECCW in 2000. While bringing in name outsiders for some shows, Scotty Mac as a promoter has ended ECCW's association with the NWA and focused on developing young wrestlers and giving them an opportunity to shine. He says, "We're building up our fan base with our own talent." Among the homegrown talent featured on ECCW shows during Mac's watch are Matthews, the Bollywood Boyz, Nelson Creed, Artemis Spencer, and Mac himself, who has had at least 20 title runs in the Northwest during his career in the ring.

Firmly believing ECCW is British Columbia's leading promotion in the present era, Mac says, regarding Starr's All-Star Wrestling—generally seen as ECCW's strongest competitor in recent years—"We do things much differently. We have a different set of ideas, and we're appealing to a different audience." Yet, looking back on his early days in ECCW, Mac says, regarding Starr, "I'll always be grateful to him. He broke me in."

Mac has done his share of traveling over the course of his career, including a brief stint in 2015 as a featured performer with the Luchando promotion, established in Paraguay in 2014 by then Vancouver-based writer and energy and investment adviser Joel Chury.

Chury, who had been a wrestling fan in his native Calgary in earlier years, says he had fallen out of touch with wrestling until several years after he relocated to Vancouver in 2007. In 2011 a friend invited him to an ECCW show, and Chury says, "The sights, the sounds, the smells … it all came back to me. I was loving every minute of it and decided that I was going to become a regular." In the process, Chury says, "I offered my services to Scotty and ECCW to help dress up their website."

Chury's interest in ECCW led to a friendship with Scotty Mac, and in 2012, as Chury was preparing for a move to Paraguay, Mac wrote him into ECCW's storyline as what Chury recalls as "an overzealous babyface fan who was tired of Scotty Mac's heelish ways." As Chury describes it, his three-month-long program with Mac resulted in "getting my ass kicked into the corner and out of the ring … getting superkicked to the back of the head, and receiving an elbow from the top rope." He adds, "It was glorious."

During an earlier visit to Paraguay, Chury says, "I figured that I would look into the local entertainment scene, and one of the things I noticed was a glaring lack of wrestling. I asked around, and found out that wrestling used to be incredibly popular back in the '90s. The show was called Supercatch … with really silly gimmicks and costumes, and really backyard looking wrestling. It was pretty awful, but many Paraguayans remembered it fondly."

Back in Paraguay after playing "Joel the Fan" in ECCW, Chury looked into the details of setting up a wrestling promotion in the South American nation and determined there was no reason he couldn't do it. While encountering "a few false starts, including lawyers that didn't register trademarks when they said they would, and 'partners' that tried to siphon money out of the operation before any money was really made," Chury soon established Luchando; prepared to bring in Mac as a babyface and Jason "J-SIN" Sullivan—then based in Oregon—as a superheavyweight "monster heel" to lead the wrestling end of his promotion; found a television network eager to secure programming aimed at young audiences in exchange for a flat fee allowing Luchando to retain other earnings, including those from advertisers; and assembled "a solid team of Paraguayans … chomping at the bit to be trained and get in the ring." Along with a hungry core of Paraguayan wrestlers led by veteran wrestler and trainer Blas Benitez, Luchando in 2015 featured a core of talent based in the Northwest, including Mac, who made many of the company's creative decisions until it became apparent his vision for Luchando did not mesh well with Chury's; Sullivan, described by Chury as "one of the most underrated wrestling minds I've ever encountered"; Oregon-based Derek Drexl, who, like Sullivan, trained under Buddy Rose; KC Spinelli, a female grappler who has appeared on numerous wrestling shows in the Northwest since debuting as a wrestler in 2009; and Chury, who on camera played rich, loudmouthed foreign expatriate manager Don Chaco.

According to Sullivan, Luchando enjoyed a successful run as a Saturday night feature on Paraguay's Red Guarani television network during part of 2015. In 2016 Luchando returned to the air on Tigo Sports, a popular network in Paraguay, Bolivia, and other areas of Latin America. And while Luchando appears to be under new ownership in 2017, founder Joel Chury can be credited with resurrecting some interest in home-based professional wrestling in the heart of South America, giving some hard-to-come-by opportunities to wrestling hopefuls on that continent, and providing an unforgettable experience—"life-changing," according to Sullivan—to a small core of wrestlers with ties to the Pacific Northwest.

Back in British Columbia, meanwhile, while ECCW and All-Star Wrestling are seen as competitors for the same wrestling audience—with ECCW sometimes running shows in All-Star Wrestling's home base of Cloverdale—it has not been unusual to see wrestlers on one promotion's roster appearing on the other promotion's shows, as Mac himself has done on several occasions. Perhaps the best example of a wrestling performer who has successfully managed to balance work with both promotions is Sweatervest—Bellingham, Washington, radio personality Scott "Scotty VanDryver" Kuipers—who started out as an ECCW ring announcer while Starr was there and later followed Starr to All-Star Wrestling. In 2017, Sweatervest remains a popular ring announcer for both All-Star Wrestling and ECCW. Since 2016 he has also been the storyline commissioner for Wise Pro Wrestling, a small start-up affiliated with All-Star Wrestling and based in East Vancouver.

With all the challenges associated with running a viable wrestling promotion or trying to make a name as an independent wrestler in the current era, it is common to see many of the same wrestlers appearing on shows run by various promotions in the Northwest. Promotions in British Columbia that have provided opportunities to Northwest wrestlers in recent years include Vancouver Island-based Victoria City Wrestling, the Vancouver Island Wrestling Federation, and, more recently, the Pure Wrestling Association (PWA) and Vancouver Island Pro Wrestling (VIPW), the latter two running shows on Vancouver Island since 2013 and still active in 2017; the Prince George, BC-based Maniac Wrestling Alliance, promoted by BC native and wrestler Stuart "Mauler" Brown; Surrey-based New Attitude Wrestling, a short-lived follow-up effort by ECCW founder John Parlett; New Canada Pro Wrestling, promoted by ex–ECCW wrestler Seth "Taj Johnson" Knight; and a trio of promotions based in the Okanagan Valley and all operating in 2017: Thrash Wrestling, established by Nick Szalanski and active primarily around Vernon and Enderby; Invasion Championship Wrestling, a charity fundraising promotion, established by Kelowna residents Mike Chisolm and Mike Rizzo, that has brought in major names such as Mick Foley and Jeff Jarrett; and Sugar's Big West Wrestling. The three Okanagan promotions, while presenting their own distinct brands, have worked together in promoting some events. Thrash has also promoted events in the Okanagan in partnership with Starr's All-Star Wrestling, while Invasion Championship Wrestling and Big West Wrestling have presented Okanagan shows in cooperation with ECCW.

The future of independent wrestling promotions is never easy to predict, but probably the biggest story about wrestling in British Columbia during the past quarter-century has been the remarkable staying power of Extreme Canadian Championship Wrestling/Elite Canadian Championship Wrestling. While ECCW crowds have never been huge, semiannual shows in recent years at Vancouver's Commodore Ballroom have drawn a buzz and excellent attendance; and, most impressively, over the course of over 20 years of operation, British Columbia-based ECCW has outlasted countless small wrestling companies trying to make a mark in an increasingly difficult business—and it has outlasted plenty of larger wrestling companies as well, including the prototype on which it was at least partly modeled: the Philadelphia-based Extreme Championship Wrestling, which, despite having TV penetration in much of the United States, a long-distance touring schedule, and regular pay-per-view events, went out of business in 2001 before being repurposed for a few years as a WWE brand and then dying for a second time.

15

Washington and Oregon
The Last Two Decades

After Sandy Barr's CWUSA in Vancouver, Washington, died a quiet death in 1997, wrestling fans in the Evergreen State had to depend largely on television when it came to getting their fill of action in the ring. During that period, Vince McMahon's WWF and Ted Turner-Time Warner's WCW were in the midst of a heated battle, with both promotions setting their sights on increasing their nationwide audience mainly through their Monday night head-to-head cable TV battle—WWF RAW vs. WCW Nitro, with the latter holding the lead through most of 1996 and 1997 before RAW stormed back in 1998—and by taking their traveling shows around the country.

During the height of the WWF–WCW battle in the latter half of the 1990s, Washington State boasted little in the way of homegrown wrestling action. That period saw the final act of Barr's CWUSA and a few shows promoted by a group calling itself the American Wrestling Federation (AWF) at the Lucky Eagle Casino in Rochester, Washington, a short distance south of Olympia. Those AWF casino shows, held in the summer of 1996, were loaded with ex–WWF wrestlers, including Sergeant Slaughter, Tito Santana, Honky Tonk Man, Bob Orton, Jr., and the Northwest's Buddy Rose and Greg Valentine. Also on the cards were Northwest grapplers Ed Moretti, Buddy Wayne, Sumito, and Billy Two Eagles.

In 1997 WCW joined the WWF in running shows in Washington State. From 1997 to 2000 both companies held successful house shows, RAW or Nitro tapings, and major pay-per-view events in cities such as Seattle, Tacoma, Yakima, and Spokane. But by 2001, WCW—held back by a lack of creativity and a tendency to continue featuring older, perhaps too-familiar wrestlers rather than promoting and highlighting new wrestlers—was out of business as a separate entity, as documented in Washington writer Bryan Alvarez' book *The Death of WCW* (cowritten by R. D. Reynolds). Since the demise of WCW and the fire-sale purchase of its assets by the WWF, the WWF/WWE has continued to bring its road show to Washington State on occasion, though attendance at those shows has generally declined since the 1990s—with WrestleMania 19 at Safeco Field in 2003 an obvious exception.

Meanwhile, with WCW out of the picture, the closest thing to a "major league" wrestling competitor that WWE has faced in Washington has been the TNA promotion, which ran some shows in smaller cities such as Kennewick, Kent, and Wenatchee in 2009 and 2011. At the time, TNA was a distant second to WWE among U.S. wrestling promotions, though in 2017—renamed Global Force Wrestling—it has perhaps fallen to third place, behind Baltimore-based Ring of Honor.

British Columbia's ECCW was active in Washington, particularly from 2000 to 2002 and again in 2006 after taking over Top Ranked Wrestling's broadcast deal with KVOS-TV. While the TV agreement and ECCW's presence as an active wrestling promotion in Washington ended at about the same time in 2006, ECCW briefly maintained a foothold in the state through its association with the new NWA Washington promotion, in existence from late 2007 through 2008.

Tim Flowers' International Championship Wrestling (ICW)—which stopped holding regular events in British Columbia in 2001—ran occasional shows primarily in the Tacoma area, in association with wrestler-promoter Mark Ferguson, from 2002 to 2006, with Flowers holding the promotion's heavyweight championship during most of that period.

Washington's Pinnacle Professional Wrestling promotion, which began operation in 2005, had an unlikely association, on the surface, with the Minnesota-based American Wrestling Association (AWA), the promotion closely associated with Verne Gagne. The original AWA went out of business in 1991, however, and the resurrection of its name by Dale "Gagne" Gagner (no relation to Verne) meant little or nothing to newer wrestling fans in the Northwest. Yet, over the course of about two years, from late 2005 to late 2007, Pinnacle Professional Wrestling/AWA Washington held mainly monthly shows in such cities as Auburn, Everett, Pacific, and Tacoma, often featuring rising wrestlers including Washington native Davey Richards, Harry Smith (D.H. Smith/British Bulldog, Jr.), and T.J. "Tyson Kidd" Wilson, along with ECCW headliners Disco Fury, Juggernaut, and Sumito. In April of 2007— five years after the former World Wrestling Federation changed its name to World Wrestling Entertainment following its legal skirmish with the World Wide Fund for Nature over use of the initials WWF—WWE, which reportedly had purchased the right to the original AWA's name along with its videotape library, filed suit against Dale Gagner to prevent the resurrected "AWA" from operating as such and selling franchise rights to the AWA name to wrestling companies such as Pinnacle. In 2008 the United States District Court of Minnesota ruled in WWE's favor.

A few other Washington-based promotions since the turn of the century are worth noting. One is Tulalip Championship Wrestling (TCW), which during most of its first two years in operation from 2008 to 2009, ran mainly monthly shows at the Tulalip, Washington, Boys and Girls Club. From 2010 until closing down in 2012, TCW held most of its shows at the Pacific Rim Ballroom and Supper Club in Marysville, Washington. Over the course of its existence, TCW featured notable wrestlers including former WWF/WWE personalities Honky Tonk Man, David "Gangrel" Heath, and Nick "Eugene" Dinsmore, along with female grappler Malia Hosaka. Among Northwest-based wrestlers appearing with TCW were J-SIN; Buddy Wayne; Aaron Bolo; Wade Hess; Matt Farmer; and author, newsletter editor, and part-time wrestler Bryan Alvarez.

New Generation Wrestling (NGW) is a small promotion that had some activity in Tacoma, Puyallup, and other locations in west-central Washington until late 2015. Established in 2009, NGW featured performers such as founder Coach Mike Jones, Bolo, Kellen Raeth, Christopher Ryseck, and former WCW star Kevin Sullivan. While inactive as a stand-alone promotion since 2015, NGW has maintained some visibility on shows promoted by Suquamish Championship Wrestling (SCW) in Bremerton and Suquamish.

SCW has been a small but resilient presence for over a decade, holding mainly monthly shows—many at the Suquamish, Washington, Tribal Center—since 2006. Featured performers for SCW have included Raeth, Exile, and female grappler Andrea the Giant.

Compared to many other states, Washington has had a limited amount of wrestling action in recent years. Independent wrestling action in Washington in recent times has mainly been limited to SCW and, since 2013, North West Pro Wrestling (NWP) shows within access of the Seattle-Tacoma-Olympia corridor; occasional events run in Seattle by the 3–2–1 Battle, Project 42, Combat Pro Wrestling, and Lucha Volcanica promotions; Inland Pro Wrestling, formerly Spokane Anarchy Wrestling, which in 2015 moved indoors after eight years as a mainly backyard promotion; DEFY Wrestling around Seattle and Tacoma; and scattered shows that take place in usually small venues throughout the state. While WWE continues to cruise through Washington for several shows every year, the Evergreen State can hardly be considered a hotbed of live wrestling action at present.

Many observers attribute that to onerous regulations put on wrestling promotions by the Washington Athletic Commission. Required at every professional wrestling event in the state are safety barriers and security staff to protect spectators and an ambulance, presumably to protect wrestlers. Promoters are required to hold licenses costing about $500 and to turn over six percent of gross receipts and $1 per ticket sold. Wrestling events in Washington are also required to be held in venues that have been approved and passed state inspection. There are exceptions to the state regulations, however, for wrestling events held on sovereign land, such as Native American reservations. As Farmer notes, "The licensing board has no jurisdiction over these areas."

While a national promotion such as WWE can easily bear the cost of state regulations, smaller promotions and would-be promoters have long argued that Washington's restrictions make it virtually impossible to run events in the state profitably—or at all. In 2014 Washington State House Bill 2573 was introduced as a means of possibly lifting the burden off small, home-grown wrestling promotions. According to the public testimony,

> Current law makes theatrical wrestling events very expensive, and the regulations are possibly not necessary.... It can be very difficult or impossible for a wrestling promoter to put on a small show because of all the regulations imposed. The DOL [Department of Licensing] requires some substantial fees and revenue sharing in addition to expenditures such as ambulances on standby and metal barricades.... This is part of the reason Washington has among the least active pro-wrestling communities in the nation.

Though the bill, as Farmer suggests, "really lacked a focus, nor did it offer suggestions," it did aim to establish the groundwork for the DOL to consult experts familiar with the wrestling business, examine wrestling regulation practices in other states, and put together a report by Nov. 1, 2014, addressing, as House Bill 2573 states, "the extent to which organizations that infrequently sponsor or host a noncompetitive theatrical wrestling event require regulation" and "the extent to which wrestling events that do not involve competition require regulation." The bill appeared headed for passage into law in early 2014, but after overwhelming passage by the Washington House of Representatives, House Bill 2573 never made it through the Senate, and the investigation and report by the Department of Licensing never materialized.

A second attempt at possibly easing regulations on wrestling promotions in Washington was initiated when a follow-up bill, House Bill 2388, was introduced to the legislature in 2016. While HB 2388 differed only slightly from HB 2573, Washington Rep. Zack Hudgins, who sponsored the legislation he describes as "good for small businesses ... good for our arts community [and] Latino community," reports that a touch of humor was added to the revised bill. "The last line," he says, "is something like 'Washington State is ready to rumble.'"

While HB 2388 also failed to make it through the Senate after overwhelming passage by the House, Hudgins—reelected to an eighth term in November of 2016—co-sponsored a third bill in 2017, which quickly passed both houses and was signed into law. While the new legislation stemming from 2017 House Bill 1420 does not alter the landscape for professional wrestling companies per se, it does allow "theatrical wrestling" schools to hold shows "for training purposes," using mainly "amateur" wrestlers, without having to bear much of the burden Washington–based wrestling promotions have found so onerous in recent times.

An effort aimed at educating people about the challenges independent wrestling promoters face in Washington State is *Lucha Ilimitado vs. The State of Washington*, a film released in 2017 which draws its inspiration from interaction between the promoters of an Oct. 12, 2016, independent wrestling show in Yakima, Washington, and the Washington Department of Licensing. A blurb for the film says, "When a group of wrestlers come together to help a children's charity, a state bureaucracy tries to shut down the event." According to a Facebook post by Richard O'Sullivan, president of the New York–based Lucha Ilimitado venture and director of the film, Lucha Ilimitado provided required medical information for all of its wrestlers to the Department of Licensing only to find that the DOL "couldn't (or wouldn't) accept physicals done in certain places." O'Sullivan continues, "We could either cancel wrestler bookings or we could get them to Washington prior to the show and have their physicals and [blood work] done ourselves. We chose the second option."

According to O'Sullivan, wrestlers who needed blood work were brought to Seattle the day before the show in order to ensure all wrestlers on the card would meet state licensing requirements, but when a computer glitch prevented Lucha Ilimitado from meeting the deadline for furnishing medical information, further negotiation with the DOL ensued. When problems were not yet ironed out as showtime loomed, O'Sullivan writes, "I put wrestlers who were unlicensed in the ring and I ordered the referee to ring the bell."

While reports indicate the show—featuring an impressive roster of name wrestlers including Rey Mysterio, Jeff Hardy, Juventud Guerrera, El Hijo del Santo, Konnan, and MVP—was a crowd-pleasing event that met its goal of raising some money for the Nora Sandigo Children Foundation, O'Sullivan concludes, "If we ever go back to Washington, it'll be on an Indian reservation."

It was a somewhat similar situation in Oregon—with wrestling essentially being held to the regulatory standards of legitimately contested combat sports—that had precipitated Don Owen's departure from the wrestling business after over 60 years' involvement in promotion; hastened Sandy Barr's decision to move his CWUSA promotion to Vancouver, Washington, after the sale of the Portland Sports Arena; and even dissuaded Vince McMahon from holding any WWF/WWE events in Oregon for a full decade, from early 1993 to mid–2003. WCW also avoided running shows in Oregon as long as WCW remained in operation during that period. While the cost of meeting Oregon Boxing and Wrestling Commission requirements was not onerous for the large promotions, it is widely believed that the WWF/WWE and

WCW were unwilling to accept a requirement calling for the commission's drug testing of wrestlers.

Serving on the Oregon Boxing and Wrestling Commission for about two years in the 1990s was Ed Giovannetti, better known to Northwest wrestling fans as Ed "Moondog" Moretti. According to Moretti, he was impressed by the Oregon commission's Executive Director Bruce Anderson, who, Moretti says, "proved to me he was concerned about wrestlers' welfare. He banned blood … he tried to get guys on drugs some help, and he would hold promoters to task." On Anderson's recommendation, Moretti was appointed to the commission, where, he says, "I was persona non grata" among promoters and some wrestlers, who saw him as "the enemy" working in collusion with a government body some perceived as having it in for the wrestling industry.

But Moretti is proud of what he helped accomplish during his years on the commission. "We cleaned up a lot of the bad things in the business," he says, pointing at drug testing and physical examination requirements that came about while he served on the commission as key accomplishments. Moretti also cites a regulation requiring regular cleaning of wrestling rings in Oregon—aimed at minimizing the risk of dangerous staph infection—as an accomplishment he's proud of.

After the Oregon commission took a small step back from regulating wrestling events in 2002, WWE resumed running occasional shows in the Beaver State, with the company's first show back in Oregon taking place on Saturday night, May 31, 2003—two months after Seattle's highly successful WrestleMania 19—at Portland's Rose Garden arena (now Moda Center). Since that time, Oregon has stood alongside Washington and British Columbia as a regular, though relatively infrequent, stop on the WWE circuit. Oregon has also hosted a few other out-of-state promotions' shows in recent years—specifically, visits by TNA and the much smaller, Michigan-based Juggalo Championship Wrestling.

Like British Columbia and Washington, Oregon has been home to a variety of small, independent wrestling companies since 1994, when Sandy Barr moved his struggling promotion out of the state. In fact, Barr himself, after shutting down his CWUSA promotion in Vancouver, Washington, in 1997, later got back into promoting shows in Oregon, although they were sparsely attended, and perhaps for good reason: The venue was Barr's Portland flea market, which Barr had continued to operate during his three years of running wrestling shows at the Bagley Center in nearby Vancouver. Though Barr bought some airtime on KOIN-TV to televise his flea market shows, interest never picked up significantly. Yet Barr continued to run the weekly shows until his death. As Susan Gage reports in a June 5, 2007, oregonlive.com (*Oregonian*) blog post, "Barr, a towering figure in a faded sport, died Saturday evening at the flea market in Portland's St. Johns neighborhood, where he held wrestling matches on Tuesday nights amid the mattresses, dinette sets and other detritus." After Barr's death, his son, part-time wrestler Josh (J.R.) Barr, continued running the events, under the banner of PDX Wrestling, for a short time before the Barr promotion closed down permanently.

Since the 1990s, a few small Oregon wrestling companies have linked their activities to Don Owen's promotion—at least in name. The first was spearheaded by Matt Borne along with Jeff and Ivan Kafoury, the latter a radio station owner, in 1997. Dubbed Portland Wrestling, the promotion held shows at Portland's Aladdin and Roseland Theaters and, as Barr did in his final years, at a Portland flea market. Featured on some Kafoury shows from the late 1990s to early 2000s were Bruiser Brian Cox; Josh Wilcox, a former University of Oregon football star who debuted as a wrestler in 1997 when his NFL dream did not pan out; and British Columbians Mike Roselli, Randy Tyler, and "Mad Bomber" Nelson Creed. Meanwhile, the promotion's *Portland Wrestling: Total Chaos* television show on Salem-Portland's KWBP-TV (now KRCW-TV) was cohosted for a time by Don Coss.

In 2003 a newer version of *Portland Wrestling* hit the airwaves on KWBP-TV, hosted by the station's ad salesman Frank Culbertson, who had done some television and ring announcing for local wrestling shows. Serving as color commentator alongside Culbertson on the new *Portland Wrestling* was Mike Rodgers, longtime editor of *Ring around the Northwest,* a newsletter covering events and personalities in Northwest wrestling. Joining Culbertson and Rodgers as an architect of the new incarnation of *Portland Wrestling* was Ed "Moondog" Moretti.

In the final issue of *Ring around the Northwest* in 2013, Moretti writes,

> In the early 2000's, I was living and working in Donald, Oregon, and we had a café there everybody from around the area seemed to love to eat at. Mike, Frank, and I would meet there every once in a while to talk about wrestling, past and present. Frank was one of the only guys in those days besides Mike that accepted that I had been on the Boxing and Wrestling Commission and seemed to understand that I really wanted to help wrestling, not hurt it. I remember that one of the topics we'd always discuss was if the three of us had some kind of opportunity to open Portland Wrestling back up, how we would do it. We all felt very similar about what mistakes had been made and what kind of things we'd do to avoid the pitfalls. The main thing to me was we all trusted each other and all vowed to keep each other in check and watch each other's back.

According to Moretti, Culbertson announced in 2003 that financing and a television spot on KWBP for the new *Portland Wrestling* seemed to be in the works. "I loved to tell Mike and Frank that we were the new Gold Dust Trio," Moretti writes.

Moretti continues, "Frank, Mike, and I met at the TV station that Frank worked at in Portland to finalize our plans and meet all the TV crew that would film and produce the show. I could not believe my eyes when [Roddy] Piper and [Len 'The Grappler'] Denton walked in the room Mike and I were sitting in. They walked in with Frank."

Moretti says he had advised Culbertson against using Denton and Piper, whom Moretti saw as not always operating in the best interests of the company they were working for. "I had explained many times during our phone conversations and meetings at the diner how Piper and Denton had swerved and worked Don and Barry to get things the way they wanted them in Portland Wrestling," he writes.

When Culbertson explained that KWBP-TV wanted Piper to be involved with the new program and that Denton was there to assist Piper, writes Moretti, "I left the station that day with a feeling of dread to say the least, but decided to trust that Frank knew what he was doing and we had a TV show to get ready for."

Culbertson's *Portland Wrestling* had what is generally recalled as an impressive roster and television presence from its inception in 2003 until 2005. Rodgers says, "The actual promotion had booking ideas from Frank, Grappler, Moretti, and myself. There was some great talent—Dr. Luther, Bryan Danielson, Black Dragon (Bret Como), Scotty Mac, Tony Kozina, Bryan Alvarez, Grappler, and Moretti. Roddy Piper was in and out." Vance Nevada, who appeared on *Portland Wrestling* from 2003 through 2004, says the promotion had "all the tools and television to make things roll."

Yet, from a management standpoint, things were unraveling, as Moretti describes ongoing friction resulting from his unhappiness with Denton's and Piper's growing influence in the company. Rodgers, meanwhile, expresses frustration over questionable booking decisions that left audiences flat and that he would have handled differently. Moretti returned to his native California in mid–2005 to attend to his ailing mother, and while he intended to return to Oregon to help with monthly *Portland Wrestling* tapings, he says Culbertson never returned his phone calls and Denton informed him he wouldn't be needed for further tapings. The promotion was facing other problems in 2005. Rodgers says that, while the Oregon Boxing and Wrestling Commission had earlier informed Culbertson that his TV-only promotion would not be required to get a license, "The commission came back and said they would need a license.... Right at that time of the license problems, the station changed hands and the new owners were not interested in wrestling." Culbertson eventually got his promoter's license, and the *Portland Wrestling* tapings—now aimed at a small audience on local cable access channel 14— moved to the Kliever Armory in Northeast Portland.

But the promotion was shut down in 2007 after Culbertson was arrested on embezzlement charges unrelated to wrestling and subsequently sentenced to 30 days in jail, given five years' probation, and ordered to pay restitution. In 2013 Culbertson faced newer, more serious charges relating to major theft and computer crimes. That same year, he was sentenced to eight years in prison.

With Culbertson out of the picture, Don Coss—who had taken over Rodgers' spot as cohost of Culbertson's *Portland Wrestling*—moved in and bought the rights to Portland Wrestling. In October of 2012 Coss and Roddy Piper launched a new Saturday night television show, *Portland Wrestling Uncut*, on KPTV, with Coss announcing and Piper directing as well as serving as a fill-in color commentator for Josh Wilcox. After two months on KPTV, *Portland Wrestling Uncut*—taped at KPTV's studio in Beaverton, Oregon—was moved to the Saturday night schedule of sister station KPDX-TV. Featuring such performers as The Grappler, Exile, Big Ugly, and Roddy Piper's son Colt Toombs, *Portland Wrestling Uncut* provided an energetic television program to help plug house shows in outlying cities such as Pendleton and The Dalles during the promotion's year or so of operation under Coss and promoter Pete Schweitzer, who had been involved in the Kafoury promotion and gone on to promote shows of his own before fading from the scene and resurfacing several years later with *Portland Wrestling Uncut*.

Another effort to shine the spotlight on Portland wrestling was spearheaded by Matthew "Matt Legit" Merz, who was also one of the creative forces behind *Portland Wrestling Uncut*. Several years earlier, in 2005, Merz began featuring some of the surviving classic *Portland Wrestling* footage on cable access TV stations. From there, Merz offered free access to original *Portland Wrestling* footage at www.youtube.com/LegitProWrestling, where a selection of classic *Portland Wrestling* footage can still be seen in 2017, along with footage from several small and short-lived independent wrestling organizations in Oregon during the post–Owen era, including J.R. Barr's PDX Wrestling in 1997–1998, Johnny Fairplay's New Dimension Wrestling in 2000, and Skag Rollins' New Revolution Wrestling in 2006–2007. Merz, a leading historian of professional wrestling in the Pacific Northwest, has also written and produced documentaries investigating and preserving the history of wrestling in Oregon and elsewhere.

Numerous other small promotions have been based in Oregon since the demise of Pacific Northwest Wrestling—and, in the case of Billy Jack Haynes' Oregon Pro Wrestling Federation (OPWF), even before Don Owen shut down his promotion. After running shows in opposition to Pacific Northwest Wrestling in the late 1980s, Haynes and OPWF owner Ron Barber continued to promote occasional shows around Portland until 1995. Then, around the time OPWF's operations ended, Pacific Coast Wrestling, a small promotion about which little information is recorded, began running shows before fading quietly in the mid–1990s.

Independent promotions in Oregon since the start of the 21st century have included Pacific Northwest Championship Wrestling (PNCW), run by Schweitzer from 2004 to 2006 and using local and regional wrestlers in cities such as Portland, Eugene, Salem, and Milwaukie, Oregon, just south of Portland. Milwaukie, besides being the site of PNCW shows, was also the home base of Championship Pro Wrestling Oregon (CPW), which ran shows from 2005 to 2007 in association with British Columbia's Extreme Canadian Championship Wrestling. A few years later, Oregon had a home-based "extreme" promotion of its own, as Portland Xtreme Wrestling (PXW) ran small shows, using local wrestlers such as the Widowmaker and Buddy Highway, for about three years, starting in 2009. Also appearing with PXW was C.W. Bergstrom, a Portland native who had debuted in Pacific Northwest Wrestling in 1987 and who was the NWA Pacific Northwest Heavyweight champion when Don Owen's promotion folded in 1992. Bergstrom later became a two-time CPW champion, and he also wrestled for the Northwest Wrestling Alliance (NWWA), which ran shows in the Portland-Milwaukie area from 2007 to 2012. According to Merz, the NWWA was composed partly of wrestlers who had performed for New Revolution Wrestling (NRW) until that promotion shut down in 2007. Among those NRW alumni was Jason Sullivan, who, Merz reports, ended up leaving the NWWA over creative differences, taking much of the promotion's roster with him. Terry Farness, who had been a partner in the NWWA, also left with Sullivan.

Around the time the NWWA folded, Power Pit Pro Wrestling brought the action—supplied by Northwest wrestlers such as Erik Hanson, Ike Van Dyke, Moose Morrow, Badd Blood, and Buddy Highway—to Roseburg, Oregon, where the Power Pit promotion ran small shows until mid–2015.

Oregon promotions established in recent times and operating in 2017 include WrestleSport, which since 2014 has run shows once or twice a year in Portland; Pacific Northwest Pro Wrestling, which plays to a loyal crowd in northwest Oregon; and Prestige Championship Wrestling, which has been entertaining fans in eastern Oregon. Meanwhile, Blue Collar Wrestling (BCW) has operated since 2010 and featured founders-wrestlers Tommy Celcious, Tex Thompson, and Badd Blood; British Columbia's Michelle Starr and Scotty Mac; Gregor Petrov; Pacific Northwest Wrestling alumni Mike Miller and Bart Sawyer; and former BCW wrestling school head trainer Donovan "Buddy Highway" Etzel. BCW shows generally take place Sunday nights at the North Portland Eagles Hall.

"We're the only promotion that holds weekly shows in the Northwest," says BCW co-owner Tom "Tex Thompson" Machen, who helped set up rings for the Owen, Barr, Kafoury, and Culbertson promotions and, with Blue Collar Wrestling, has been active as a co-owner, wrestler, and trainer. In early

2015 BCW joined the National Wrestling Alliance, and in 2017, it is the only current NWA member based in the Pacific Northwest.

Don't Own Anyone Pro Wrestling—better known as DOA Pro Wrestling—has run small shows around Portland and in Salem, Eugene, Oregon City, and other locations since its inception in 2008. Using Northwest wrestlers such as Jeremy Blanchard, Ryseck, Exile, Bergstrom, Kellen Raeth, Davey Richards, the Amerikan Gunz, and Derek Drexl, DOA has entertained fans in the Portland area with high-energy shows for over nine years and has also played a role in training up-and-coming wrestlers at its DOA Asylum Training Academy.

Cofounded by Jason "J-SIN" Sullivan, DOA has been booked and directed since 2016 by Drexl, who works closely with DOA cofounder and promoter Terry Farness. In 2015 DOA scaled down slightly, holding shows at its training academy in Troutdale, Oregon, after losing access to its former venue of East Portland's Moose Lodge earlier in the year. But in 2016, reports Drexl, "We found a new full-time home at Wattles Boys and Girls Club in Southeast Portland, and attendance is definitely picking up."

West Coast Wrestling Connection (WCWC), established in 2005, is the oldest pro wrestling promotion still operating in Oregon in 2017. In a dozen years of promoting shows mainly in Portland, Salem, and across western Oregon, WCWC founder Jeff Manning—along with his management team, which included Len "The Grappler" Denton and ex-WWF star D'Lo Brown—has hit on an effective combination of training up-and-comers at the WCWC wrestling school, presenting a mix of newcomers and seasoned wrestlers on WCWC shows, and keeping core fans' interest high via WCWC's weekly television program, most recently taped at the Clackamas Armory southeast of Portland and broadcast Saturday nights at 11 p.m. on KPDX-TV, which can be seen in most of Oregon.

WCWC has featured many Northwest-based wrestlers, including Jeremy Blanchard, Caleb Konley, Wade Hess, Mike Santiago, Aaron Bolo, Kellen Raeth, Tommy Celcious, Kenny Lush, Michelle Starr, and the WCWC wrestling school's head trainer Erik Baeden. Wrestlers brought in from outside the Northwest to fill out or headline shows have included Ring of Honor wrestler Jimmy Jacobs, former NWA World Heavyweight champion Adam Pearce, ex–WCW wrestler Michael Modest, and former WWF/WWE wrestler Gangrel. With its relatively solid television base, a dozen years of delivering spirited entertainment to Oregon wrestling fans, and what appear to be a proven business plan and a capable leadership team, WCWC probably has to be considered the leading wrestling promotion based in the American Northwest heading into 2017.

While committed to presenting strong wrestling shows for his core audience in Oregon, West Coast Wrestling Connection owner Jeff Manning has also taken his vision outside the Northwest. In 2015 Manning established Paragon Pro Wrestling—featuring a strong core of wrestlers, including WCWC competitors Konley, Santiago, Gangrel, Alexander Hammerstone, Tyshaun Prince, and Eric Right—and ran a series of monthly television tapings at Sam's Town Hotel and Gambling Hall in Las Vegas that scored airtime on Pop-TV, the Madison Square Garden (MSG) Network, Detroit's WADL-TV, and Canada's Fight Network.

16

Another 130 Years?

In an era dominated by WWE and colored by fans' perception of what constitutes major league wrestling in the 21st century, it is difficult for any regionally based promotion in the Pacific Northwest or elsewhere to build and maintain significant fan support while exercising the sort of financial discipline required to stay above water. The fact that several promotions currently operating in the Pacific Northwest appear to have found a niche and a winning formula is a testament to the vision and devotion of numerous people committed to keeping alive the rich tradition, dating back to 1883, of pro wrestling in the Pacific Northwest.

While regional wrestling in the Northwest may no longer have the presence or audience that it used to—especially during the height of the Owen, Kovacs, or Elliott promotions—there are people with strong Northwest ties who are committed to keeping the region's wrestling tradition alive and who are looking out for the best interests of wrestling as a whole. For over 30 years until 2013, Oregon's Mike Rodgers published a newsletter, *Ring around the Northwest*, chronicling events in Northwest wrestling for readers in the region and those looking in from the outside. Dean Silverstone, 1970s promoter of Super Star Championship Wrestling and author of his life-in-wrestling memoir *"I Ain't No Pig Farmer!,"* has hosted many reunions of ex–Northwest wrestlers and been a key figure in the Cauliflower Alley Club, a national nonprofit organization, open to fans, promoting knowledge of pro wrestling and its history and the best interests of ex-wrestlers. Vance Nevada and Matt Farmer, besides being active for years in Northwest wrestling rings, have been key figures in preserving memories of Northwest wrestling in the 20th century, and Nevada's *Wrestling in the Canadian West* was an invaluable resource in the preparation for writing this book. Farmer, meanwhile, hosts a podcast, Indyriffic, that gives a platform to participants in the world of independent wrestling in the Pacific Northwest and elsewhere, and he has been involved in promotion of independent wrestling shows in Washington. J Michael Kenyon, who passed away in April of 2017, was a storehouse of little-known details and facts about Northwest wrestling lost to nearly everyone else. And Washington's Bryan Alvarez, editor of the *Figure Four Weekly* newsletter as well as a wrestling radio show host, has been a prominent voice in American wrestling in recent years.

Numerous wrestling trainers associated with a variety of wrestling promotions and academies in the Northwest eagerly work with trainees hoping to take up their places in the Northwest's rich wrestling tradition. Meanwhile, wrestling promoters in the region, facing modern-day challenges that often seem impossible to surmount, display rare determination as they continue the Northwest tradition of presenting live wrestling entertainment to fans who value professional wrestling not simply as a television event but as a homegrown, interactive experience. Without a doubt, the most resilient promoter in the recent era of Northwest wrestling has been Mark "Michelle Starr" Vellios, described by Mike Roselli as "the one real old-school wrestling promoter" left in the Northwest. According to Nevada, Starr "is single-handedly responsible for more than 900 live events" in an era with few television opportunities and limited mainstream attention. Echoing many other observers of wrestling, particularly in British Columbia, over the past quarter-century, Nevada says, "Starr is the reason for a generation of wrestling in the Northwest."

Finally, the current crop of Northwest natives and transplants in the wrestling business—from newcomers at tiny venues on up to those regularly appearing on television and moving up the ladder of their profession—overwhelmingly seem to make no secret of their Northwest roots and their devotion to the region.

Any way you look at it, 2003's WrestleMania 19 event at Safeco Field, dollar-wise and attendance-wise, far surpasses any other event in the history of professional wrestling in the Pacific Northwest. Numerous other WWF/WWE shows in British Columbia, Washington, and Oregon likewise stand among the highest-grossing, best-attended shows in Northwest wrestling history. Yet many older fans retain cherished memories of a Northwest wrestling tradition predating the current era in which relatively few fans get their fill of wrestling through any means other than cable or satellite television—and, now, the Internet—or by purchasing pricey tickets when the WWE traveling show comes to the nearest major city once or twice a year.

Wrestling in the Northwest has always reflected its locale and its era, and the Pacific Northwest in 2017—even in small communities—offers seemingly endless entertainment options and, through the miracle of technology, the opportunity for faraway events to find an audience of some sort in almost any locality. In some cases, events emanating from outside the Northwest can be made to seem almost "local." Yet the immediacy and the lasting impact or relevance of "outsider" wrestling shows to local fans and communities seems mainly lost in the present day. Reactions of fans in arenas at wrestling shows in British Columbia, Washington, and Oregon during the days of wrestling territories were more heated than just about anything seen at a WWE show today. Fans were not "in on" the show or privy to the secrets of wrestling, as so many are today. In the territorial days, the wrestlers—the skilled ones—engaged the fans, and the fans seldom responded with indifference. Today, some of that heated interaction is on display at shows put on by promotions like ECCW, All-Star Wrestling, DOA, and WCWC.

Whether regional wrestling will make a mainstream comeback in the Northwest remains to be seen. But whether it does or not, there can be no denying its place in the history of the Pacific Northwest dating back over 130 years or the passion of those seeking to return the art and spectacle of regionally based professional wrestling to a prominent place in the consciousness and identity of the Northwest for another 130 years.

Bibliography

Alvarez, Bryan, ed. *Figure Four Weekly.* Weekly newsletter covering the pro wrestling industry. Current and archived issues are available to subscribers at www.f4wonline.com. Last accessed 20 Oct. 2016.

Bailey, Everton, Jr. "WWE requests ex-Portland wrestler Billy Jack Haynes' concussion lawsuit be dismissed." *The Oregonian* website (2 April 2015), www.oregonlive.com/portland/index.ssf/2015/04/wwe_requests_ex-portland_wrest.html. Last accessed 31 Oct. 2016.

Beekman, Scott M. *Ringside: A History of Professional Wrestling in America.* Westport, CT: Praeger, 2006.

brewerygems.com. Website of Washington State brewery historian Gary Flynn. Information about the Heidelberg Brewing Co. is at www.brewerygems.com/columbia.htm. Last accessed 27 Oct. 2016.

Burke, Nathan. Phone interview. October 26, 2015.

cagesideseats.com. A four-part post going into detail on Gorgeous George begins at www.cagesideseats.com/2014/6/19/5823666/i-am-the-gorgeous-one-the-story-of-gorgeous-george-part-1. Information about Wilbur "Lord Patrick Lansdowne" Finran can be found on the same page. Reference to George's money-throwing stunt in Hollywood is in part 3 of the series, found at www.cagesideseats.com/2014/6/26/5846620/i-am-the-gorgeous-one-the-story-of-gorgeous-george-part-3. Last accessed 26 Oct. 2016.

California Digital Newspaper Collection. Website at cdnc.ucr.edu/cgi-bin/cdnc. The *Sausalito News* reference to the 1913 Berg–Grimm match in Seattle is at cdnc.ucr.edu/cgi-bin/cdnc?a=d&d=SN19130524.2.38. Last accessed 18 Oct. 2016.

Capouya, John. *Gorgeous George: The Outrageous Bad-Boy Wrestler Who Created American Pop Culture.* Kindle ed. New York: HarperCollins, 2008.

Chury, Joel. Email consultation and phone interview. November 18–29, 2015.

classicwrestlingarticles.wordpress.com. Links to a wide selection of mainstream news articles on professional wrestling from various regions dating back to the 1800s. The March 7, 1940, *Seattle Times* article on the in-ring death of referee John Stevens is found at classicwrestlingarticles.wordpress.com/2013/09/02/wrestlers-warned-as-death-probe-ends/#more-2462. Last accessed 19 Oct. 2016.

Cohen, Daniel. *Jesse Ventura: The Body, the Mouth, and the Mind.* Brookfield, CT: Twenty-First Century Books, 2001.

Condello, Tony. Phone interview, October 3, 2016.

Dolmetsch, Chris. "WWE Sued by 'Superfly' Snuka and Others over Brain Injuries." Bloomberg report (18 July 2016), www.bloomberg.com/news/articles/2016-07-18/wwe-sued-by-superfly-snuka-and-others-over-brain-injuries. Last accessed 18 Oct. 2016.

Drexl, Derek. Email consultations. November–December 2015; October 6–8, 2016.

Drummond, Neil. Phone interviews. November 23, 2015; October 20, 2016.

Eck, Kevin. "Remembering Playboy Buddy Rose." Online *Baltimore Sun* blog entry (29 April

2009), www.baltimoresun.com/bs-mtblog-2009-04-remembering_playboy_buddy_rose-story.html. Last accessed 31 Oct. 2016.

Farmer, Matt. Email consultations. September–December 2015; October 30–31, 2016.

Fussman, Cal, and Killer Kowalski. "What I've Learned: Killer Kowalski." Online edition of *Esquire* (31 Aug. 2008), www.esquire.com/sports/interviews/a3195/kowalski0807/. Last accessed 21 Oct. 2016.

Gage, Susan. "Portland wrestler, promoter Sandy Barr dies at 69." *The Oregonian*/Oregon Live blog post (5 June 2007), blog.oregonlive.com/breakingnews/2007/06/portland_wrestler_promoter_san.html. Last accessed 3 Nov. 2016.

Garner, Dwight. "Perfumed, Coiffed and Grappling with Demons." *The New York Times* (19 Sept. 2008), www.nytimes.com/2008/09/19/books/19book.html?_r=0. Last accessed 26 Oct. 2016.

Goldstein, Richard. "Killer Kowalski, Wrestler, Dies at 81." *New York Times* obituary (31 Aug. 2008), www.nytimes.com/2008/09/01/sports/01kowalski.html. Last accessed 21 Oct. 2016.

Greenberg, Keith E., Mark Madden, Richard Oriolo, and Ric Flair. *Ric Flair: To Be the Man.* Kindle ed. New York: Pocket Books, 2004.

gregthehammervalentine.com. Official website of Seattle-born wrestler Greg "The Hammer" Valentine. Last accessed 31 Oct. 2016.

Hoops, Brian. "HOOPS BLOG: Remembering 'Playboy' Buddy Rose." *Pro Wrestling Torch* website (30 Aug. 2009), www.pwtorch.com/artman2/publish/The_Specialists_34/article_31744.shtml#.WCwV_vkrK00. Last accessed 16 Nov. 2016.

Hornbaker, Tim. *National Wrestling Alliance: The Untold Story of the Monopoly That Strangled Pro Wrestling.* Toronto: ECW Press, 2007.

Hudgins, Zack. Phone interview. October 29, 2016.

InYo: The Journal of Alternative Perspectives on the Martial Arts and Sciences. Website at www.ejmas.com/jalt/. Reference to the *Tacoma Daily Ledger* report on the September 1907 Klank-Roller match in West Seattle can be found in Joseph R. Svinth's article, "A Day to Rest and Wrestle: Benjamin Franklin Roller, Master of Angles and Feuds" (2000), at www.ejmas.com/jalt/jaltart_svinth_0700.htm. Last accessed 18 Oct. 2016.

Johnson, Steven. "'Ho! Ho! Ho!' cries still ring out for Dean Higuchi." *SLAM! Wrestling* website (slam.canoe.com/Slam/Wrestling) article (19 April 2010), slam.canoe.com/Slam/Wrestling/2010/04/08/13511026.html. Last accessed 29 Oct. 2016.

_____. "John Hill, man of many faces, dies at 68." *SLAM! Wrestling* website article (12 Mar. 2010), slam.canoe.com/Slam/Wrestling/2010/03/12/13215206.html. Last accessed 29 Oct. 2016.

Jonathan, Don Leo. Phone interview. October 11, 2015.

kayfabememories.com. Information about Herb Owen's takeover of the Portland wrestling promotion is posted by Mike Rodgers at www.kayfabememories.com/Regions/pnw/pnw31.htm. Information about the Justice Department's investigation of the NWA and about Kurt von Poppenheim's attempt to get a promoter's license in Oregon (and quoting Dean Silverstone) is at www.kayfabememories.com/Regions/pnw/pnw31-2.htm. Information about the Owen endgame and Sandy Barr's promotional effort is also at www.kayfabememories.com/Regions/pnw/pnw31-2.htm as well as www.kayfabememories.com/Regions/pnw/pnwintro-2.htm. John Baumer's post describing the Portland Sports Arena's atmosphere and commenting on *Portland Wrestling* and *Big Time Wrestling* is at www.kayfabememories.com/Regions/pnw/pnwintro.htm. Reference to the 1983 All-Star Wrestling tour of Jordan is at www.kayfabememories.com/Regions/allstar/allstar4-2.htm. Last accessed 15 Nov. 2016.

Kenyon, J. Michael. Email consultations. December 29–30, 2015.

"Korean to the Core." *Newsweek* article on Rikidozan (16 Jan. 2005), www.newsweek.com/korean-core-117247. Last accessed 27 Oct. 2016.

legacyofwrestling.com. An informative survey of Washington State's wrestling promotions and wrestling highlights, particularly from the 1930s–1950s, based on research by wrestling historian and author Tim Hornbaker, can be found at www.legacyofwrestling. com/WashingtonTerritory.html. Information about Bob Murray and the 1955 sale of the Seattle wrestling promotion to Whipper Billy Watson, also based on Hornbaker's research, is at www.legacyofwrestling.com/SeattleOffice.html; Hornbaker-researched information on Johnny Doyle is at www.legacyofwrestling.com/Doyle.html; information about Ted Thye and the Justice Department's 1958 inquiry into the practices of Don Owen, based on Hornbaker's research, is at www.legacyofwrestling.com/TedThye.html; information about Rikidozan, also researched by Hornbaker, is at www.legacyof wrestling.com/Rikidozan.html; and information about the Kennedy promotion in Pendleton, OR, researched by Hornbaker and J Michael Kenyon, is at www.legacy ofwrestling.com/PortlandTerritory.html. Last accessed 21 Nov. 2016.

Lutzke, Andrew. "Kayfabe, Lies and Alibis: Ken Patera Shoot Interview." Culturecrossfire. com summary (21 Nov. 2013) of a Ring of Honor "shoot interview" (20 Nov. 2004) with Patera, culturecrossfire.com/wrestling/ken-patera-shoot/. Last accessed 17 Nov. 2016.

Mac, Scotty. Phone interview. October 29, 2015. Email interview. November 21–25, 2015.

Machen, Tom. Phone interview. December 7, 2015.

Manning, Jeff. Phone interviews. November 11, 2015; October 19, 2016.

McCoy, Heath. *Pain and Passion: The History of Stampede Wrestling.* Kindle ed. Toronto: ECW Press, 2007.

Meltzer, Dave, ed. *Wrestling Observer Newsletter.* Weekly newsletter covering the pro wrestling industry. Current and archived issues are available to subscribers at www.f4wonline. com. Last accessed 31 Oct. 2016.

Merz, Matt. Phone interviews. September 18, 2016; October 20, 2016.

_____. "Portland Wrestling" site at www.youtube.com/user/LegitProWrestling. Website contains video footage highlighting many wrestlers and promotions from the Northwest. Last accessed 19 Nov. 2016.

midatlanticgateway.com. Website devoted to honoring the heritage of wrestling in the Mid-Atlantic region. Career record of Northwest wrestling legend Roddy Piper is at www. midatlanticwrestling.net/resourcecenter/results/pages/results_piper.htm. Last accessed 14 Nov. 2016.

Molinaro, John. "Art Barr: What could have been." *SLAM! Wrestling website article* (29 Nov. 1999), www.canoe.ca/WrestlingStarBios/barr_art.html. Last accessed 17 Nov. 2016.

_____. "Owen Legacy Strong in Pacific Northwest." *SLAM! Wrestling* website article (23 Sept. 1999), www.canoe.com/SlamWrestlingNWA51/sep23_owen.html. Last accessed 29 Oct. 2016.

_____. "Remembering the Great Portland Territory." *SLAM! Wrestling* website article (24 Sept. 1999), www.canoe.com/SlamWrestlingNWA51/sep24_portland.html. Last accessed 31 Oct. 2016.

Mooneyham, Mike. "Lewin a Mystical Figure in Wrestling Business." *The Post and Courier* (2 Feb. 2014), www.postandcourier.com/staff/mike_mooneyham/lewin-a-mystical-figure-in-wrestling-business/article_c316944b-de97-5111-b1a6-31762ff84551.html. Last accessed 29 Oct. 2016.

Moretti, Ed (Moondog). Phone interviews. September 28, 2015; October 31, 2015; November 17, 2015.

Murray, David. "Wrestling Champ Dean Higuchi—the *Today* Interview." *Langley Today* (24 Dec. 2010), www.langleytoday.ca/sports-feature-wrestling-champ-dean-higuchi-the-today-interview/. Last accessed 29 Oct. 2016.

Nevada, Vance. Email consultations. September–December 2015.

_____. *Wrestling in the Canadian West.* Gallatin, TN: Crowbar Press, 2009.

Noland, Claire. "John Tolos dies at 78; notorious wrestling villain known as the Golden Greek." *Los Angeles Times* (1 June 2009), www.latimes.com/local/obituaries/la-me-john-tolos1-2009jun01-story.html. Last accessed 29 Oct. 2016.

Oliver, Greg. "Al Tomko—a true original—dies." *SLAM! Wrestling* website article (6 Aug.

2009), slam.canoe.com/Slam/Wrestling/2009/08/06/10379921.html. Last accessed 30 Oct. 2016.

_____. "'Apache' Bull Ramos still battling." *SLAM! Wrestling* website article (13 Oct. 2004), slam.canoe.com/Slam/Wrestling/2004/09/26/644878.html. Last accessed 29 Oct. 2016.

_____. "Gene Kiniski dead at 81." *SLAM! Wrestling* website article (14 April 2010), slam.canoe.com/Slam/Wrestling/2010/04/04/13464196.html. Last accessed 30 Oct. 2016.

_____. "Promoter Sandy Barr loved the business." *SLAM! Wrestling* website article (4 June 2007), slam.canoe.com/Slam/Wrestling/2007/06/03/pf-4231164.html. Last accessed 31 Oct. 2016.

_____. "Remembering Johnny Canuck, a Lumberjack and a Loverboy." *SLAM! Wrestling* website article (19 July 2014), slam.canoe.com/Slam/Wrestling/2014/07/19/21818211.html. Last accessed 1 Nov. 2016.

_____. "Sandor Kovacs felled by Alzheimer's." *SLAM! Wrestling* website article (2 July 2004), slam.canoe.com/Slam/Wrestling/2004/07/02/522831.html. *SLAM! Wrestling* has a record of matches from Kovacs' in-ring career at slam.canoe.com/Slam/Wrestling/ResultsArchive/Wrestlers/kovacs.html. Last accessed 20 Oct. 2016.

_____. "Seattle promoter Harry Elliott dead at 101." *SLAM! Wrestling* website article (26 June 2006), slam.canoe.com/Slam/Wrestling/2006/06/26/1654927.html. Last accessed 27 Oct. 2016.

Oliver, Greg, and Steven Johnson. *The Pro Wrestling Hall of Fame: The Heels.* Toronto: ECW Press, 2007.

_____, and _____. *The Pro Wrestling Hall of Fame: The Tag Teams.* Toronto: ECW Press, 2005.

Olsen, Todd (Oly). In-person interview. October 10, 2015.

1wrestlinglegends.com. Website created and maintained by Scott Teal as an extension of Crowbar Press. Dean Silverstone's "The History of the Seattle Promotion," including comments on Tex Porter, Harry Elliott, and Silverstone's Super Star Championship Wrestling, is at www.1wrestlinglegends.com/column/dean-00.html. Last accessed 27 Oct. 2016.

onlineworldofwrestling.com. The Tony Borne page, including Dave Meltzer's assessment of Borne's place among Northwest wrestling greats, is at www.onlineworldofwrestling.com/bios/t/tony-borne/. The Shag Thomas page is at www.onlineworldofwrestling.com/bios/s/shag-thomas/. Last accessed 11 Nov. 2015.

originalpeople.org. Information about Viro Small, Reginald Siki, Luther Lindsay, Shag Thomas, Sweet Daddy Siki, Bobo Brazil, Bearcat Wright, and other African American pioneers in pro wrestling can be found in Denny Burkholder's article, "Pro Wrestling's Black Stars" (Feb. 2002), at www.originalpeople.org/history-black-americans-sport-pro-wrestling. Last accessed 21 Nov. 2016.

Owen, Barry. Phone interview. December 14, 2015.

Patterson, Rick. Phone interview. October 1, 2016.

Piper, "Rowdy" Roddy, with Robert Picarello. *In the Pit with Piper.* New York: Berkley, 2002.

portlandoregon.gov. Official website of the city of Portland, OR. Historical information cited or summarized in ch. 5 ("Golden Age and Connections to the Northwest") providing background to Luther Lindsay's 1953 arrival in Portland is at www.portlandoregon.gov/bps/article/412697 (pp. 12–18). Last accessed 26 Oct. 2016.

"Pro wrestler 'Playboy' Buddy Rose dies." *USA Today.* Associated Press article (30 April 2009), usatoday30.usatoday.com/news/nation/2009–04–30-buddyrose-obit_N.htm. Last accessed 31 Oct. 2016.

Pro Wrestling Illustrated. Website at www.pwi-online.com. Historical survey dating back to the 1700s is accessible at www.pwi-online.com/pages/wrestlingframe.html. Last accessed 18 Oct. 2016.

Professional Wrestling Hall of Fame and Museum. Website at www.pwhf.org. Individual pages are devoted to over 40 inductees who had some connection to the Pacific Northwest during their careers. The Gorgeous George, Verne Gagne, and Don Leo Jonathan pages can be seen at 0362dc8.netsolhost.com/halloffamers/bios/george.asp, 0362dc8. netsolhost.com/halloffamers/bios/gagne.asp, and 0362dc8.netsolhost.com/halloffamers/bios/jonathan.asp, respectively. Last accessed 29 Oct. 2016.

Professional Wrestling Historical Society. Website at www.prowrestlinghistoricalsociety. Joe Acton biography is at www.prowrestlinghistoricalsociety.com/acton-joel.html. Last accessed 18 Oct. 2016.

prowrestling.net. A partial transcript of Joe "Road Warrior Animal" Laurinaitis' radio interview discussing the death of Michael "Road Warrior Hawk" Hegstrand (18 April 2011) is at www.prowrestling.net/artman/publish/miscnews/article10018019.shtml. Last accessed 13 Nov. 2016.

prowrestling.wikia.com. A fan-created website along the lines of Wikipedia. The Al Tomko page is at prowrestling.wikia.com/wiki/Al_Tomko. The Art Barr page is at prowrestling. wikia.com/wiki/Art_Barr. Last accessed 31 Oct. 2016.

Reynolds, R.D., and Bryan Alvarez. *The Death of WCW*. Toronto: ECW Press, 2004.

Rippel, Joel A. *Minnesota Sports Almanac: 125 Glorious Years*. St. Paul: Minnesota Historical Society Press, 2006. Rippel's "Wrestling" section in chapter 8 mentions—along with Verne Gagne—Ted Thye, Jesse Ventura, and Ric Flair, three significant figures in Northwest wrestling.

Rodgers, Mike. Email consultations. September–November 2015.

Roselli, Mike. Phone interview. November 3, 2015. Email consultations. November 5–16, 2015.

Russo, Ric. "[Whatever] Happened to … Bugsy McGraw?" *Orlando Sentinel* (22 Dec. 2000) article on Mike "The Brute" Davis, articles.orlandosentinel.com/2000–12–22/entertainment/0012210530_1_bugsy-mcgraw-vince-mcmahon-professional-wrestling. Last accessed 29 Oct. 2016.

Shoemaker, David. *The Squared Circle: Life, Death, and Professional Wrestling*. New York: Gotham, 2013.

Siebert, Verne. Phone interview. October 12, 2015.

Silverstone, Dean. In-person interviews. October 4, 2015, and October 10, 2015.

_____, with Scott Teal. *"I Ain't No Pig Farmer!"* Gallatin, TN: Crowbar Press, 2014. www.crowbarpress.com/cbp-books/19-ds.html

Slagle, Steve. "Haystacks Calhoun." [Haystack Calhoun was often referred to as "Haystacks" Calhoun.] Professional Wrestling Online Museum website, www.wrestlingmuseum.com/homeie.html. Last accessed 29 Oct. 2016.

Solomon, Brian. *WWE Legends*. New York: Pocket Books, 2006.

Starr, "Gorgeous" Michelle. Phone interview. October 18, 2015.

Sullivan, Jason. Phone interview and email consultation. November 17–23, 2015.

Sweatervest, Scotty. Phone interview. October 11, 2015. Email consultation. November 6–12, 2016.

Terry, John. "Portland Professional Wrestling." *The Oregon Encyclopedia*, a project of the Oregon Historical Society, oregonencyclopedia.org/articles/portland_professional_wrestling/#.WAQc2eArK0l. Last accessed 27 Oct. 2016.

_____. "'Portland Wrestling' lit up early TV screens and NW fans." *The Oregonian* website (25 Sept. 2010), www.oregonlive.com/O/index.ssf/2010/09/portland_wrestling_lit_up_earl.html. Last accessed 29 Oct. 2016.

Thesz, Lou, with Kit Bauman. *Hooker*. Kindle ed. Gallatin, TN: Crowbar Press, 2014 (based on 1995 bound manuscript edition). www.crowbarpress.com/cbp-books/13-lt.html.

Thompson, Lee. "The professional wrestler Rikidozan as a site of memory." *Sport, Memory and Nationhood in Japan: Remembering the Glory Days*, edited by Andreas Niehaus and Christian Tagsold. Kindle ed. London: Routledge, 2013, ch. 11.

Tillman, Jodie. "From pro wrestler to Bible teacher, he helps Tampa shelter residents grapple with life." *Tampa Bay Times* (1 Sept. 2011) article on Mike "The Brute" Davis, www.tampabay.com/news/humaninterest/from-pro-wrestler-to-bible-teacher-he-helps-tampa-shelter-residents/1189013. Last accessed 29 Oct. 2016.

Washington State Legislature. Website at leg.wa.gov. The history of 2014 House Bill 2573, with a link to the full text of the bill, is at apps.leg.wa.gov/billinfo/summary.aspx?year= 2014&bill=2573. A report on HB 2573, including a summary of public testimony, is at lawfilesext.leg.wa.gov/biennium/2013–14/Pdf/Bill%20Reports/House/2573%20HBR%20 APH%2014.pdf. The history of 2016 HB 2388, with a link to the full text of the bill, is at apps.leg.wa.gov/billinfo/summary.aspx?bill=2388&year=2016. Last accessed 3 Nov. 2016.

Whiting, Robert. *Tokyo Underworld: The Fast Times and Hard Life of an American Gangster in Japan.* New York: Vintage, 2000.

Wilson, Jim, with Weldon T. Johnson. *Chokehold: Pro Wrestling's Real Mayhem outside the Ring.* N.p.: Xlibris, 2003.

wrestlingclassics.com. Information on the Oct. 5, 1904, Frank Gotch–Dan McLeod American Heavyweight title match in New Westminster, BC, based on research by wrestling historian Mark Hewitt, is posted by Steve Yohe at www.wrestlingclassics.com/cgi-bin/. ubbcgi/ultimatebb.cgi?ubb=print_topic;f=10;t=001311. Matt Farmer's post on wrestling in Washington State in the 1930s (originally posted at www.kayfabememories.com) is at www.wrestlingclassics.com/cgi-bin/.ubbcgi/ultimatebb.cgi?ubb=print_topic;f=10;t= 001815. Information about Fred Kohler is posted by Tiny Roebuck at www.wrestling classics.com/mu/mu-st/mu-st-tragicends.html. Last accessed 5 Nov. 2016.

wrestlingdata.com. Website contains substantial historical data concerning wrestlers and wrestling promotions worldwide, and at least partial career records of nearly all significant wrestlers in the history of Northwest wrestling can be found through this site. Last accessed 31 Oct. 2016.

wrestling-titles.com. A storehouse of searchable information pertaining to pro wrestling history in the Pacific Northwest and around the world. Information about Tex Hager is at www.wrestling-titles.com/us/id/nwa. Last accessed 27 Oct. 2016.

Index